THE BOOKMAN'S GLOSSARY

SIXTH EDITION, REVISED AND ENLARGED

The Bookman's Glossary

SIXTH EDITION
REVISED AND ENLARGED

EDITED BY
JEAN PETERS

R.R. BOWKER COMPANY
NEW YORK & LONDON • 1983

Published by R. R. Bowker Company
1180 Avenue of the Americas, New York, N.Y. 10036
Copyright © 1983 by Xerox Corporation
All rights reserved
Printed and bound in the United States of America

Library of Congress Cataloging in Publication Data
Main entry under title:

The Bookman's glossary.

    Bibliography: p.
    1. Book industries and trade—Dictionaries.
2. Printing—Dictionaries. 3. Bibliography—
Dictionaries. 4. Library science—Dictionaries.
I. Peters, Jean, 1935-   . II. R.R. Bowker
Company.
Z118.B75   1983   070.5'03   83-2775
ISBN 0-8352-1686-1

CONTENTS

PREFACE

The sixth edition of *The Bookman's Glossary* contains definitions of some 1,800 terms used in book publishing, book manufacturing, bookselling, the antiquarian trade, and librarianship. The need for a dictionary of book trade terminology was recognized nearly sixty years ago by the editors of *Publishers Weekly* who, in the July 12, 1924 issue, introduced the first installment of a section entitled "The Bookman's Glossary: Material for a Dictionary of the Booktrade." This first installment explained, "There are numerous technical terms, phrases, words and names used in connection with book-making and bookselling that are not clearly understood by many engaged in the business...," and announced *PW*'s intention to include in forthcoming issues an authoritative glossary of terms used in the "book and allied trades" and subsequently to gather these terms in book form. The section ran under seven subject classifications in installments throughout that year, and in 1925, *The Bookman's Glossary*, in the format we know it today, was first published.

Fifty-eight years later, the sixth edition of *The Bookman's Glossary*, revised and enlarged to reflect an ever changing and expanding book industry, has been compiled. Its objective remains the same as that of its predecessors: to provide a practical guide to the terminology used in the production and distribution of books new and old, not necessarily the technical language of the various sectors of the trade, but rather the words in common use in a publisher's office, in a bookstore, or among book collectors. The fifth edition of the *Glossary* (1975) reflected the emerging use of computerization in the book industry by including for the first time terms used in computerized typesetting. The sixth edition reflects further advances of the computer in the book industry by introducing a selection of terms in electronic publishing.

Limitations in scope have been retained from the earlier editions. The *Glossary* does not include, for example, terminology that would be used by the printer but not by anyone else. Likewise, the library science terminology has been limited to the language that would most likely be encountered in publishing circumstances—the terminology of research, bibliography, indexing, and to some extent, acquisitions. The scope of the biographical sketches remains the same as it was in the fifth edition: men and women of historic importance in bibliography, the graphic arts, and book publishing.

This edition of the *Glossary,* under the direction of a general editor, has been revised by subject specialists in each of the areas covered. Robert Dahlin, Managing Editor of *Publishers Weekly*, revised the publishing and distribution terms and prepared the new terms in electronic publishing. Paul Doebler, Editor-in-Chief, Professional Books, R. R. Bowker Company, revised the printing and computerized typesetting terms. Jerome Frank, Book Design and Manufacturing Editor of *Publishers Weekly*, revised the bookmaking and papermaking terms. The editor revised the terms in the antiquarian and library science fields, as well as the biographical sketches. The subject specialists have thoroughly reviewed and updated the entries from the fifth edition; they have removed terms no longer in use, and have added many new terms that have come into use in the industry since the last edition. Although all areas of coverage have undergone extensive revision, perhaps the most sweeping changes have occurred in the area of book publishing and distribution; also evident is the continued impact of automation on all sectors of the book industry.

This edition of the *Glossary* could not have been possible without the help of many people. Robert Dahlin, Paul Doebler, and Jerome Frank all gave unsparingly of their time, their specialized knowledge, and their advice, for which the editor is deeply grateful. Thanks are due also to Terry Belanger for help and advice, and to Joann Davis, Robert Frase, Donald F. Johnston, Emery Koltay, and G. Thomas Tanselle for their considerable help in sharpening and improving particular definitions.

With this edition, *The Bookman's Glossary* appropriately becomes the first book from the Bowker Book Division to use an electronic text management system in its editing and composition. The new system makes text editing easier and allows more time in which changes can conveniently be made. The new system also creates a database from which future editions of the *Glossary* can be produced.

Many people on the Bowker staff were responsible for the smooth transition to this new composition method. The editor is especially grateful to Paul Doebler, who adapted the software program to meet the *Glossary's* special requirements; to Susan Hostetler, who keyed in most of the text; to Theresa Barry, who supervised the copy editing of the manuscript and the proofreading stages of the printout, as well as the keying in of corrections; to Iris Topel, who supervised the page makeup; and to Julia Raymunt, who supervised the entire editorial production process. Once again the editor is grateful to Alice Koeth for the design of the book and its elegant dust jacket.

Grateful acknowledgment is made to the authors and publishers of the reference works most frequently consulted: *A New Introduction to Bibliography*, by Philip Gaskell (Oxford University Press); *ABC for Book Collectors*, by John Carter, with corrections and additions by Nicolas Barker (Granada); *Glaister's Glossary of the Book*, by Geoffrey Glaister (University of California Press); and other books included in the Selected Reading List.

Jean Peters
January 1983

THE BOOKMAN'S GLOSSARY

AAs Author's alterations (*q.v.*).

AAP Association of American Publishers (*q.v.*).

AAUP Association of American University Presses (*q.v.*).

AB Abbreviation for *Antiquarian Bookman, The Weekly Magazine of the Antiquarian Booktrade.* Started by the R. R. Bowker Company and published by them from January 1948 through June 1953. In July 1953, the serial was bought by Sol M. Malkin, its editor from the start, and published by him until January 1975, when it was bought by its present editor, Jacob L. Chernofsky. It is currently issued as *AB Bookman's Weekly.* Annual numbers (*AB Bookman's Yearbook*) have been issued since 1949.

ABA American Booksellers Association (*q.v.*).

a.c.s.; a.d.s.; a.l.s.; a.ms.s.; a.n.s. Abbreviations for autograph card, signed; autograph document, signed; autograph letter, signed; autograph manuscript, signed; and autograph note, signed. Each piece entirely in the handwriting of the signer. *See also* holograph.

ALA American Library Association (*q.v.*).

ASCII (American Standard Code for Information Interchange) A standard coding scheme accepted throughout the computer field for use in exchanging data between different computer systems.

AV materials *See* audiovisual materials.

abridgment   A work that has been cut or edited to less than its original length. Generally, a work is not abridged by the author but, even so, an effort is usually made to retain the original intent or style of the work.

abstract   Condensed summary of the important parts of a text.

access time   Time taken by a computer to find the place in its memory or storage area at which data is stored or is to be stored. In addition, extra time is required to perform operations once a memory location is reached—*read time* and *write time*. *Read time* is the interval required for the computer to extract data from memory; *write time* is the interval required to enter something into memory.

accession   Addition (of books or other materials) made by a library to its collection.

accordion-pleated fold   A way of folding endpapers so the pleat provides a hinge at the inner joint of the covers to allow the covers to swing open freely and not exert a strain on the first and last leaves of the book.

acid-free paper   *See* paper permanence.

acknowledgment   A notice by the author, generally placed at the beginning of a book and occasionally at the end, in which individuals, groups, or information sources helpful in the research, funding, or moral support required to produce the book are named and their contributions recognized.

acquisition   (1) A work for which a publisher has signed a contract, thereby indicating its intention to publish the book. This may happen quickly if an acceptable manuscript is ready, or it may occur months in the future after the work has been completed. (2) An actual printed book purchased by a library or individual is also called an *acquisition*.

acquisitions editor   A publishing house employee, also called an *acquiring editor*, who is authorized to seek books for publication and to purchase publication rights to literary properties and who subsequently guides the works through the steps of creation, editing, and publication.

added entry   In cataloging, a bibliographic entry in addition to the main entry; also called a *secondary entry*. Cf. main entry. Where author is used as main entry, there may be added entries for joint author, editor, translator, title, series, etc.

addenda (*sing.* **addendum**)   Brief supplemental data added at the conclusion of a book or inserted on a separate sheet. *See also* appendix; errata.

address   An identification for a specific location in computer memory used to retrieve data stored there.

adhesive binding   A high-speed method of fastening loose pages into a solid book block (*q.v.*). with adhesive and gluing the cover to the block to make a completed adhesive-bound book. Only glue, rather than sewing or stitching, holds the book together. Also called *perfect binding* or *unsewn binding*. The technique can be traced back to the 1830s, when William Hancock invented the so-called Caoutchouc binding in England.

Generally, publishers adhesive-bind all mass market paperbacks, many trade paperbacks, and a growing number of hardcover books, primarily because adhesive binding is less expensive and faster than sewing, although, as a binding technique, adhesive binding is considered inferior to sewing.

Adhesive binding converts signatures, or folded sheets, into bound books through a series of consecutive machine operations. First, the gathered signatures are fed into clamps, which convey them through the main binder. There, revolving blades remove the folded backbone edge of all signatures to separate the leaves. The edges of the leaves are then roughed with revolving saws to increase the area of the gluing surface, and a bristle brush removes all paper particles. Next, applicator wheels apply glue to the edges, which bonds the pages together to create the solid backbone. To ensure glue getting between the leaves to create an even stronger bond, manufacturers may use techniques called *notch binding* (*q.v.*) or *burst binding* (*q.v.*).

In paperback and magazine production, paper covers are applied before the adhesive sets and the covered products are then trimmed and are ready for shipment. In hardcover book production, the cover feeder, which applies paper covers for paperbacks and magazines, instead applies two end sheets joined in the center by lining material to cover the spines. The book block is then trimmed and delivered directly to standard case-binding equipment.

Adhesive binding is relatively economical, especially when long runs of the same edition are being bound. The method lends itself well to the mass production of low-priced paperbacks, catalogues, telephone directories, and the like. Also, adhesive binding is finding greater use in libraries for rebinding books that have relatively narrow margins and for rebinding deteriorating books.

Adler, Elmer (1884-1962)   American printer and publisher. Organized Pynson Printers, 1922. One of the founders of *The Colophon, A Book Collectors' Quarterly* and typographical consultant to the *New York Times* and director of its Museum of the Printed Word. Later, research associate in the graphic arts at Princeton University. Founder and director of La Casa del Libro, San Juan, Puerto Rico.

advance   *See* advance orders; author's advance.

advance bound galley   Usually a crude copy of a book reproduced from early galley proofs (*q.v.*) of a newly typeset work. Bound within a plain paper cover that is ordinarily blank except for title, author, publisher, and a brief description, a limited number are created far in advance of publication date expressly for the purpose of sending out copies to acquisitions editors at book clubs or paperback houses, to serializers, to book reviewers, or to personalities apt to give the book a favorable quote. The galleys are generally uncorrected. *See also* advance sheets; f&g's.

advance copies   Copies of a new book sent to reviewers and others before publication date. *See also* review copies.

advance on royalties, advance against royalties   Payment to an author in anticipation of royalties a book will earn. In most cases, the author is not compelled to return the advance, even if it eventually exceeds total royalties earned. *See also* author's advance; royalty.

advance orders   Orders placed by booksellers and others in advance of a book's publication date; generated by the publisher's early sales efforts, the quantity of orders can help determine the number of copies to print, price of the book, and extent of promotion. *Advance* can also be used as a verb; e.g., "The book is advancing well."

advance sheets   The pages of a book, usually unsewn, issued in advance of publication for review or promotion purposes. Because of their frequently inconvenient or unwieldy nature, advance sheets can be cumbersome, and advance bound galleys are more likely to be submitted to book reviewers, etc. *See also* advance bound galley; f&g's.

against the grain The direction across or against the alignment of the majority of fibers in a machine-made sheet of paper. Fibers in machine-made paper tend to lie mostly in one direction, called the *grain direction*. When paper is folded across the fibers (or against the grain), the sheet tends to weaken, and a fold is produced that does not stay closed as well as a fold made with the grain. Also, when the grain runs across the page of a book and into the backbone, it tends to prevent the book from opening easily because the page must bend against the spring tension of the fibers. Against the grain is also called *grain wrong* and with the grain is called *grain right. See also* grain.

agate (1) In hand binding, a piece of agate or bloodstone used in burnishing gold or colored edges of a book. (2) The old way of designating 5½ point type, used in the advertising field to designate the amount of vertical advertising space (14 agate lines to the column inch).

agate line A standard of measurement for depth of columns of advertising space. It is a space one column wide and 1/14 inch deep. Fourteen agate lines make one column inch (*q.v.*).

Aitken, Robert (1734-1802) Philadelphia printer. He printed, among many things, the first complete Bible in the English language in North America. Old Testament finished in 1782, New Testament printed in 1781. *See also* Eliot, John; Sauer, Christopher.

Aldus The shortened form of Aldus Manutius, the Latinized name of Teobaldo Manucci, or Aldo Manuzio (1450-1515), printer, publisher, critic, editor, and scholar and the greatest of Venetian publishers. He organized his printing office in Venice in 1494, and his first publications (both in that year) were the poems of Musaeus and the *Galeomyomachia*. These were followed in 1495 by the Latin grammar of Lascaris. Three kinds of types were designed for and used by him: roman, Greek, italic. The latter, which became known as the *Aldine Italic*, first appeared in the *Virgil* of 1501. The finest of the roman fonts was used by Aldus in the only illustrated work he printed, the magnificent *Hypnerotomachia Poliphili*, which appeared in 1499.

When Aldus died in 1515, his business was continued by his father-in-law, the printer Andreas Torresanus, who died in 1529. Paulus Manutius continued the business when he came of age, and later, his son Aldus Manutius the Second took over, and with his death in 1597 the establishment came to a close.

No printer's device is better known than the device of the dolphin and anchor adapted by Aldus as his mark from a silver coin of Emperor Vespasian. The dolphin stands for speed in execution and the anchor for firmness in deliberation. The device was later taken up by other printers, including William Pickering in the nineteenth century.

The adjective *Aldine*, derived from Aldus, has been applied to certain styles of display types and to various kinds of printers' ornaments of solid face used by Aldus and other early printers. Pickering adopted the name "Aldine Poets" for his fifty-three-volume edition of British poets.

algorithm   A set of rules and procedures for performing computer operations, such as computing the square root of a number or sorting listings from one sequence into another. Computer programs are largely algorithmic in nature.

all firsts   In a book dealer's catalogue, a group of first editions.

all published   A descriptive term for an uncompleted set. For example, if a publication, intended to appear in several volumes, is suspended, the fact is stated as *all published*.

all rights reserved   In a publication, a printed notice that any use of the book or article will not be permitted without the consent of the copyright owner. These rights include dramatic, television, broadcasting, motion picture, serial, republication, etc. This type of notice is not required by U.S. copyright law, but may be needed for international copyright protection in certain Latin American countries that are not members of the Universal Copyright Convention.

allowance   (1) A credit paid by the publisher on the cost of freight. (2) A credit paid by the publisher equal to the value of unsold books returned by a bookseller. (3) A partial or full payment by the publisher for advertising placed by the retailer—hence, the term *cooperative advertising (q.v.)*.

almanac   A publication usually issued annually, containing useful facts and statistical information on a variety of subjects. The information can be both current and retrospective. Originally, a publication containing calendars, weather forecasts, astronomical information, tide tables, etc.

alphabet length   The length of the twenty-six letters of the alphabet in lowercase in any typeface and size, usually stated in points. The relative compactness of different typefaces is determined by comparison of alphabet lengths.

alphanumeric   Contraction for alphabetic-numeric, indicating sets of characters that contain both alphabetical and numerical characters. Such character sets can also contain special symbols and punctuation as well.

alterations   Changes made in proofs.

alternative publisher   *See* small press.

alternative title   Subtitle introduced by "or" or its equivalent; e.g., *Twelfth Night; or, What You Will.*

American Bibliography   *See* Evans, Charles.

American Book Awards   Instituted in 1980 and operated under the aegis of the Association of American Publishers; the successors to the National Book Awards (*q.v.*). For the first time paperbacks were eligible to compete, and, also for the first time, publishers were asked to submit names of books and to pay a specified amount for each nomination to help defray the costs of the award program, which was conceived as a more highly visible media event than the NBA.

American Book Prices Current   *See* auction prices.

American Booksellers Association (ABA)   The national trade association, founded in 1900, for operators of retail bookstores.

American Institute of Graphic Arts (AIGA)   National trade organization of graphic designers, art directors, illustrators, and craftsmen involved in printing and allied graphic arts. The AIGA was organized in 1914 to plan U.S. participation in a Leipzig graphic arts exhibition and has actively stimulated interest in the graphic arts and encouraged those engaged in them ever since. One of its best known events is the annual Book Show (formerly Fifty Books of the Year), although it now has developed programs and exhibitions for all types of graphics, including magazines, television, advertising, and general printed materials.

American Library Association   National professional association of librarians and others interested in the educational, social, and cultural responsibilities of libraries. Founded in 1876.

American point system   The typographic measurement system adopted in 1886 by the United States Type Founders' Association, in which different sizes of type bear a fixed and simple relation to one another. The basic unit of measurement is the *point*, which is .01384 inch, or very nearly 1/72 inch. The *pica* is a secondary unit of measure consisting of 12 points. All type sizes, line measures, spacing, and other typographic dimensions are expressed in these units or in other units based on points, such as *nonpareil* (equal to 6 points), etc. The point system is a modification of the French didot system. There are different systems in some other countries.

Americana   Books, pamphlets, etc., of history, geography, travel, and the like, relating (in its narrower sense) chiefly to the United States. In its broader sense, Americana relates to books concerning not only the United States but also Canada, Mexico, Central America, South America, and the West Indies.

-ana; -iana   A suffix to names of persons or places, denoting a collection of books or other information; e.g., Americana, Johnsoniana, Lincolniana, Shaviana. The *i* is inserted for euphony.

analog computer   A computer that continuously compares variables and indicates quantities directly by such physical means as comparing two opposing voltages and showing the difference on a meter with a moving needle. A digital computer, by contrast, counts discrete units one at a time and displays the final result on a static numerical display after the difference has been calculated.

analytical bibliography   The study of books as physical objects, of the materials of which books are made, and the way in which they are put together, with the ultimate purpose of resolving questions of a book's origins, history, and text. Also known as *critical bibliography*. Analytical bibliography and enumerative bibliography (*q.v.*) are the two major divisions of bibliography.

Anderson, Alexander (1775-1870)   First American wood engraver, notable for his illustrations in the white-line technique of Bewick.

annotation　A note accompanying an entry in a bibliography or catalogue, intended to describe or evaluate the work cited.

annual　(1) A publication issued regularly once a year. (2) Illustrated anthologies of the nineteenth century. Many are now collected because they contain first-edition material by famous authors, often anonymous.

anonymous (anon.)　Authorship unknown or unavowed. The Copyright Office will register an anonymous work, granting the copyright to the publisher or person serving as registrant.

anthology　A collection of writings or passages from the works of one or more authors, usually on one theme, literary type, period, nation, or the like.

antiqua　German typefounding name for roman type. The common German blackface is called *fraktur* (*q.v.*).

Antiquarian Bookman　*See* AB.

antiquarian bookseller　A dealer in old, rare, or secondhand books.

Antiquarian Booksellers Association　The British trade association, founded in 1906. *See also* International League of Antiquarian Booksellers.

Antiquarian Booksellers Association of America, Inc.　The American trade association, founded in 1949, to encourage interest in rare books and manuscripts and to maintain the highest standards in the antiquarian book trade.

antique　(1) Paper whose surface has been neither polished (calendered) nor coated. A smooth antique is called an *eggshell* (*q.v.*). (2) Modern calf bindings made to simulate old bindings.

apocryphal　Of unknown authorship or doubtful authenticity.

appendix (*pl.* appendixes or appendices)　Matter following the text of a book. Usually material that illustrates, enlarges on, or statistically supports the text. A *supplement* is generally more extensive matter, sometimes independent in its argument from the text, or is issued at a later date. Cf. addenda; errata.

approval plan　An agreement between a library and a publisher or wholesaler, under which the latter is given the responsibility of selecting and supplying all current books published in the subject areas, levels, countries, or languages specified by the library. In most approval plans, returns are permitted. Cf. blanket order.

aquatint   An intaglio process of etching (*q.v.*) on copper or steel plates to which acid-resistant granules have first been evenly adhered. Soft, watercolor effects thus become possible, alone or in combination with the line effect that characterizes etchings.

arabesque   Interlaced ornament on book covers in the style of early Arabian designers.

Arabic numerals   *See* numerals, Arabic.

area composition   As used in typesetting, the spatial positioning of type, rules, and other elements that can be set on a phototypesetting machine by means of keyboarding all the required instruction codes at a typesetting keyboard prior to actual setting of type. The photocomposing unit then exposes the type in final position on the film or paper, eliminating the need for hand cutting and pasting of individual elements after typesetting. *See also* copy block.

Armed Services Editions   Expendable paperbound books issued by the Council on Books in Wartime from New York in 1943-1947 and distributed free to members of the U.S. Armed Forces. More than 1,300 different titles were issued. The oblong shape and double-column format of the editions were devised to make possible their printing on presses used by digests and pulp magazines. They were laid out one above the other and cut apart. The use of the books by arrangement with the copyright owners was restricted to overseas distribution and the oblong shape helped to identify them.

armorial binding   A binding decorated with the arms or other device of royalty or nobility.

Arrighi, Ludovico   Early sixteenth-century Roman calligrapher, type designer, and printer whose italic typefaces influenced typography in Italy and elsewhere. He is presumed to have perished in the sack of Rome in 1527.

art, artwork   An overall term used to cover all illustrative material—photographs, drawings, paintings, hand lettering, and the like—prepared to illustrate a book, pamphlet, brochure, advertisement, etc.

art paper Special heavy paper, sometimes colored, used by artists in the preparation of artwork or paper constructions.

artificial language In computer science, a language based on a fixed set of explicitly prescribed rules established before it is used to write anything. Computer programming must be done in artificial languages such as Fortran, Cobol, Basic, etc., because the machine cannot intuitively change its understanding of a natural language such as English, as these languages develop new dimensions. *See also* machine language; natural language.

as issued In the antiquarian trade, "as issued" describes a book in its original condition of publication, and is used most frequently when some feature differs from what is customarily expected; e.g., "without dust jacket, as issued."

as new In the antiquarian book trade, a catalogue description of books approaching the conditions of newness. *See also* mint.

ascender In typography, the part of a lowercase letter that extends above the upper edges of other small letters such as a, c, e, n. Examples of letters with ascenders are b, d, f, h. *See also* descender.

Ashendene Press One of the most distinguished private presses of England, founded in 1894 by C. H. St. John Hornby, partner of the bookselling firm of W. H. Smith & Son. One of the finest products of this press was an edition of Dante's works issued in 1909. The press closed its production in 1935 with *A Descriptive Bibliography*.

association copy A copy of a book that bears an autograph inscription or notes by the author or is in any way intimately connected with the author or with any other prominent person associated with the book. *See Also* presentation copy.

Association of American Publishers (AAP) The national trade association of publishers of general, educational, trade, reference, religious, scientific, technical, and medical books. Formed by a merger in 1970 of the American Book Publishers Council (incorporated 1945) and the American Educational Publishers Institute (an unincorporated association established in 1942 as the American Textbook Publishers Institute).

Association of American University Presses (AAUP) The national trade association, organized in 1937 after an informal beginning, for scholarly publishing divisions of colleges and universities in the United States and Canada.

asterisk   (1) Star-like symbol (*) used in typography to indicate a marginal reference or footnote on the same page. (2) A series of asterisks is sometimes used to indicate an elision. *See also* reference marks.

atlas folio   *See* book sizes.

auction   A selling event entailing competition between parties interested in buying what is being offered simultaneously to all. The highest bidder takes the purchase. The generally unstated purpose of an auction is to invite a rivalry that will drive the purchase price as high as possible. (1) In the book industry, an auction signals the availability of certain publication rights to a work. This type of auction may be engineered by an author's agent selling the rights, or it may be run by a hardcover house selling paperback rights to a property it owns. (2) In the antiquarian trade, an auction involves the sale of old, rare, or otherwise valuable books.

auction galleries   A generic term for auction houses that catalogue and sell private libraries, rare books, autographs, and manuscripts along with the sale of other properties (works of art, furniture, etc.). There have been, and there still are, of course, some auction houses in the United States, Canada, and Great Britain devoted solely to the sale of books and manuscripts. The best lists of firms holding book and manuscript sales are to be found in the various annual volumes of *American Book Prices Current*, in *Book Auction Records*, and in the *American Book Trade Directory* (R. R. Bowker). The best account of American book auctions is to be found in George L. McKay's *American Book Auction Catalogues, 1713-1934: A Union List* (New York Public Library, 1937). This work contains a detailed historical introduction by Clarence S. Brigham, titled *The History of Book Auctions in America*.

auction prices   Book sales and their prices were first regularly reported in Great Britain beginning in 1887. In the United States regular reports began in 1895. In various countries of Western Europe several series of reports were issued, some sporadically, in the twentieth century.

   Book Prices Current began the first regular reports of sales in Great Britain and issued annual records from 1887 to 1948.

Following these annual volumes, *BPC* issued two quadrennial volumes, 1949-1952 and 1952-1956. No further records have appeared in this series.

Book Auction Records began reporting sales in Great Britain in 1902. *BAR* printed the year's records in quarterly parts. Its object was to provide price records as soon as possible after the sales. This quarterly form continued through 1940. Beginning in 1941 the annual form, giving the year's entries in one alphabet, was adopted. The series is currently issued by Dawsons of Pall Mall, Folkestone, Kent, England.

American Book Prices Current, the annual record of book and manuscript sales in the United States, was begun by Luther S. Livingston in 1895, and it has been published continuously since then. In addition to serving as editor and as editorial director of *ABPC* until his death in 1914, Livingston also edited a four-volume compilation (often miscalled a cumulation) published in 1905, titled *Auction Prices of Books... A Representative Record... from the commencement of the English Book Prices Current in 1886 and the American Book Prices Current in 1894, to 1904; and including some thousands of important auction quotations of earlier date.* Since 1956 all major English auctions have been included in *ABPC*. *ABPC* is issued by Bancroft-Parkman, Inc., and since 1980, has been available online through Bancroft-Parkman's bibliographic data base Bookline: UTOPIA.

Book and manuscript sales in the United States from 1941 through 1951 were also reported in *United States Cumulative Book Auction Records*. This publication ceased with the 1951 annual.

Book auction sales in France from October 1918 to July 1931 were reported in *Annuaire des Ventes de Livres*, edited by Leo Delteil, and published in twelve volumes, Paris, 1920-1931. Further French sales were recorded after World War II, when *Le Guide du Bibliophile et du Libraire*, edited by Eric de Grolier, appeared in 1946; this series, in five volumes, covered the sales held in 1944, 1945, 1946-1948, 1949-1951, and 1952-1956. Under different titles and by various publishers, French book auction records have been continued from 1964.

Book auction sales in West Germany, the Netherlands, Austria, and Switzerland have been reported annually since 1950 in *Jahrbuch der Auktionspreise*, published by Dr. Ernst Hauswedell & Co., in Hamburg, West Germany.

audiovisual materials (1) Generally, supplementary teaching materials used in the classroom, library, and the like. Materials usually considered audiovisual include charts, graphs, maps, pictures, slides, filmstrips, videotapes, recordings, motion pictures, television, programmed learning aids, objects, specimens, and models. (2) More specifically, and by extension, nonbook materials, such as tapes, slides, and filmstrips, which require the use of special equipment in order to be seen or heard.

author   (1) In U.S. copyright law, the initial owner of copyright in a work. Under U.S. copyright law, the term "author" can also sometimes include an employer or one who commissions a work, in cases where the work is done for hire. (2) In general parlance, the original writer or composer of a work.

author bibliography   A list of books and articles by and/or about a particular author. It may be a simple checklist or as detailed as a full-dress descriptive bibliography.

author entry   Entry of a work, in a catalog or index, under the name of its author; usually the main entry (*q.v.*).

author-publisher   A writer whose books are self-published. *See also* privately printed.

author-title index   An index that enters each book by title as well as by the author's name, either in two alphabets or combined in one alphabet.

authorized   Something done with the permission of an individual or group holding a proprietary interest. An illustration or quotation may be reprinted if use is authorized by the copyright holder. An authorized biography is one written with the consent of the subject or the subject's heirs. An authorized work may also be sanctioned by a corporation, a government, or a religious body.

author's advance   Payment or payments made by a publisher to an author before sales of the book have properly earned the writer any income. The advance may be the entire sum an author will receive for the book, which makes it work for hire (*q.v.*), or, more commonly, the money may be an advance on royalty (*q.v.*). Traditionally the author's advance, which is determined during negotiation of a contract between author and publisher, was paid half on signing the contract and half on delivery of manuscript. In recent years, the advance is more likely to be paid out over a longer period of time; e.g., a third on signing, a third on delivery of manuscript, and a third on actual publication of the book.

author's agent   *See* literary agent.

author's alterations (AAs)   Changes in typeset matter made by the author, apart from those necessary to correct printer's errors. Alterations are billed as a separate item by the typesetter, and it is customary for the publisher to pass on to the author some part of the charge, usually any amount in excess of 10 percent of the basic composition bill. The costs charged back to the author may otherwise be any amount above a specified fee for AAs that the publisher is willing to absorb. *See also* printer's errors.

author's copies   The complimentary copies, usually six or more, given by the publisher to the author of a book upon its publication.

author's discount   The percent less than list price (*q.v.*) at which an author is able to buy copies of his or her book directly from the publisher. An individual matter set by each author's contract, the discount may range from 20 to 40 percent, and it may apply to books other than the author's own.

author's earn-out   The point at which an author's earned royalties equal the author's advance. *To earn out* is to reach this fiscal equation.

Authors Guild, The   *See* Authors League of America, The.

Authors League of America, The   Established in 1912 by authors wishing to further their professional interests, this national association in turn founded The Authors Guild, Inc. and The Dramatists Guild, Inc., in 1921 to address the needs of its members more specifically. These two components are thus the corporate members of The Authors League of America, and they continue to champion writers in terms of copyright, freedom of expression, book royalty arrangements, terms of contract, etc.

author's proof   The galley proof sent to the author for approval or correction. *See also* galley proofs.

author's rights   Under the U.S. Copyright Act of 1976, the author of a copyrighted work has the right to (1) reproduce the work; (2) prepare derivative works based upon it; (3) distribute the work to the public; (4) perform the work publicly; and (5) display the work publicly. These rights may be assigned under contract separately or together. The term *author* includes the employer in the case of works made for hire. *See also* copyright.

autograph   (1) In the rare book trade, letters, documents, cards, etc., written or signed with a person's own hand. *See also* the abbreviations a.c.s.; a.d.s.; a.l.s.; etc. (2) In the new book trade, an *autographing party* is a publicity device whereby an author signs copies of his or her book for customers in a bookshop.

automatic data processing   The computation, sorting, merging, or otherwise handling of data by means of electronic or electrical machinery that operates with a minimum of human intervention.

automatic distribution   A procedure in which a publisher or wholesaler supplies books to a bookstore according to a determination of appropriate quantities. In trade publishing, quantities are usually subject to the dealer's acceptance. Fully automated distribution is customary in the mass market paperback industry.

autopositive   A type of photographic material that will produce a positive copy of a subject directly without first making a separate negative.

auxiliary storage   Storage or memory capacity outside the main memory in the computer itself. Auxiliary devices include magnetic tape, disk, or drum units and usually hold much larger amounts of data, although access time to the data usually is slower.

avant-garde   French: vanguard. Used as noun and adjective to characterize the expression by individuals and literary groups of experimental or unorthodox forms, ideas, and theories, usually addressed and acceptable to a limited audience. Often applied to little magazines, free verse, experimental fiction, new philosophical, literary, artistic, or political-social ideas, especially in the sixty-odd years from about 1920.

BAL   *See* Bibliography of American Literature.

BAMBAM   Acronym for Bookline Alert: Missing Books and Manuscripts. A nonprofit bibliographic data base that reports missing and stolen books and manuscripts with a value of $50 or more. BAMBAM, used by librarians and antiquarian book dealers, is a part of the Bookline family of data bases, produced and operated by American Book Prices Current.

bds   Abbreviation for boards (*q.v.*).

bf   Abbreviation for boldface (*q.v.*).

BIP   Abbreviation for *Books in Print,* the annual author-title index of books available from publishers in the United States. Published by the R. R. Bowker Company.

BISAC   Acronym for Book Industry Systems Advisory Committee. An ad hoc committee of the Book Industry Study Group (*q.v.*). BISAC is composed of publishers, booksellers, librarians, wholesalers, and representatives of school systems who are working to expand the use of standards in book acquisitions, particularly the use of the International Standard Book Number (*q.v.*) and the Standard Address Number (*q.v.*). The committee has developed a number of standardized formats and systems for better communication between vendors and customers.

BISG   *See* Book Industry Study Group.

BMI   *See* Book Manufacturers' Institute.

b.o.   Abbreviation for back order (*q.v.*).

back margin   *See* margins.

back matter   The leaves following the main text of a book. Back matter can include appendixes, notes, glossary, bibliography, index, etc. Also called *reference matter.*

back order   An unfilled order held for future delivery; generally caused when a book goes out of stock.

back strip   (1) A strip of paper, cloth, or other material pasted to the back of the folded sheets in the binding of a sewn book. (2) In the antiquarian trade the term is also used to mean the outer spine of a bound book.

back to press   The process of reprinting a book when a publisher's stock is exhausted or in danger of becoming so. Going back to press suggests that the book is not out of print (*q.v.*) and that no significant changes other than emendations of minor errors are being made in the book.

back up   (1) To print the reverse side of a sheet already printed on one side. *See also* work and turn. (2) In computer technology, a backup machine accepts the same data and programs as the primary unit in case the first one should break down. Backup units may be in the same plant or office, or they may be available over transmission lines.

backbone   The back of a bound book connecting the front and back covers. Also called *spine, shelfback.*

backed   (1) In bookbinding, a book that has passed through the backing step. (2) Description of a leaf (for example, a frontispiece) that has been repaired by being mounted upon, or being backed by, a new leaf. When highly transparent silk is applied to both sides, the leaf is described as *silked.*

background mode   In computers running more than one program simultaneously, the processing of some work at low priority levels that can be interrupted so that the machine can process higher priority tasks without waiting. Cf. foreground mode.

backing   *See* rounding and backing.

backlining   Extremely durable paper strips glued to the backbone of hardcover books. Also called *backlining paper. See also* lining.

backlist   A publisher's available titles that were printed and released before the current season.

bad break   (1) In page makeup, an illogical or aesthetically displeasing beginning or end of a type column, such as one or two words of a paragraph ending at the top or a subheading occurring on the last line. Always avoided in careful work. (2) In computer typesetting, an improper word division and hyphenation decision made by a computer while following an automatic hyphenation program. *See also* hyphenation.

bands   (1) The horizontal cords running across the spine of a book to which the signatures of the book are sewed. (2) The ridges across the spine of a bound book, under which are the cords.

banned   Prohibited from sale by ecclesiastical or secular authority. *See also* censor, censorship.

basic weight   *See* basis weight.

basis weight   The weight in pounds of a ream (500 sheets) of paper of a specified basic size. All papers are classified into certain categories—such as book papers, bonds, bristols, cover stocks—and each category has a basic size used as a standard in expressing weight. The basis weight is always stated in terms of the basic size, even though the actual sheets may be cut to a different size.

   The basic size for all book papers is 25 × 38 inches. Therefore, a 60 pound book paper would be one for which 500 sheets cut to 25 × 38 inches in size would weigh 60 pounds. The fact that the actual sheets to be used might be a different size would not affect the paper's designation as a 60 pound sheet.

Baskerville, John (1706-1775)   Eighteenth-century English printer and typefounder. In turn stonecutter, writing master, and manufacturer of japanned ware, he turned his attention about 1750 to type designing and printing, and in 1758 was elected printer to the University of Cambridge. His first work was an edition of Virgil (1757). Dedicated to excellence in all elements of book design and production, he did much to raise and influence the standards of his day.

bastard title   The title of a book standing by itself on a page preceding the full title page. Now often also referred to as *half title* (*q.v.*).

batch processing   Processing of computer data in groups and stages, by holding and accumulating large quantities of material serially. *See also* online processing.

battered   In letterpress, type matter or other printing surfaces so worn or injured that they give defective impressions.

battledore   A child's lesson sheet, especially one made of a wooden tablet or varnished cardboard. In use in the late eighteenth century superseding the hornbook (*q.v.*).

Bay Psalm Book   The familiar designation for *The Whole Booke of Psalmes*, the first book of size printed in what is now the United States, and called the *Bay Psalm Book* from its origin in Massachusetts Bay Colony. It was also known at various times as the *New England Psalm Book* and as the *New England Version of the Psalms*. It is the earliest work printed in the United States known to be extant. It was printed in 1640, by Stephen Daye (or Day), at Cambridge, Mass.

bearers   (1) Type-high strips of metal arranged around pages of type when they are locked in forms from which electrotype plates are to be made. (2) In lithographic presses, bearers are rings of steel attached to both ends of printing cylinders; bearers on adjacent cylinders roll against each other, maintaining proper distances and printing pressures between cylinders.

bed   Surface of letterpress printing press upon which type is clamped.

Beirut Agreement   (Agreement for Facilitating the International Circulation of Visual and Auditory Materials of an Educational, Scientific, and Cultural Character) A UNESCO-sponsored international agreement that removes tariffs, discriminatory taxation, quotas, and exchange restrictions for the importation of audiovisual materials certified by the countries of exportation as being of an educational, scientific, or cultural character. Drafted in 1948, the agreement was ratified by the United States in 1967; by 1982 approximately thirty countries were members. A conference was called in Geneva in 1973 to review the Beirut Agreement and the related Florence Agreement (*q.v.*).

Bell, John (1745-1831)   English bookseller, printer, publisher, typefounder, and journalist. Responsible for many innovations in printing—the first to use modern face in England, the first to abolish the long ʃ in printing, and the first to adapt the high standards of Baskerville and Bodoni to the making of low-priced books.

belles lettres   Literature that is purposely sophisticated and elegant; now applied somewhat vaguely to literary works in which imagination and taste are often more important than the ideas they contain.

belt press   A rotary web letterpress for producing a complete book in one pass of the paper through the machine. It is equipped with two endless plastic belts, one for printing each side of the paper. The printing plates, either rubber or plastic, are mounted on these variable-length belts. The press has two printing stations, one for each belt and each side of the paper. After the first side is printed, the paper is turned and put through the second printing station. After printing, the web of paper is slit, folded, cut into page lengths, and finally collated into a complete book. Books are then fed into an adhesive binder, often automatically, as they come out of the press. It is possible to produce a bound book from blank paper with the belt press within approximately two minutes. The machine eliminates the traditional printing of books in sections or signatures, one at a time, and the subsequent folding and gathering operations. This greatly reduces the handling required in the plant and the time needed to produce a printing. The first successful belt press, the Cameron Book Production System, was installed in 1968 by Cameron Machine Co., Dover, N.J., at Kingsport Press, Kingsport, Tenn.

Benday (Ben Day) process (1) The process invented by Benjamin Day, a New York printer (1838-1916), for mechanically producing a great variety of shaded tints and mottled effect on line or halftone printing plates. (2) Mechanical screens and patterns applied by the artist to the original artwork in the form of transparent printed overlays, rather than by the photoengraver or lithographer to the printing plate.

Berne Convention Common name for the agreement establishing the International Union for the Protection of Literary and Artistic Works, to which more than seventy nations are signatory. Begun in Berne, Switzerland, in 1866, and revised five times: Paris, 1896; Berlin, 1908; Rome, 1928; Brussels, 1948; Paris, 1971. Protection under these conventions is extended without formalities to works by nationals of any country on the sole condition that first publication take place in a country that belongs to the Berne Union. The United States is not a member, but, under this proviso, American works can achieve protection in Union countries by simultaneous publication in a member country, such as Great Britain. Also, the United States has agreements such as the Universal Copyright Convention (*q.v.*) with many Berne Union countries.

bestsellers Books achieving the greatest number of current sales. Although usually general in nature, bestseller lists can also be limited to books in particular subject categories; e.g., religious books, science fiction, or other special interests. Numerous publications and organizations compile frequent lists of bestsellers in hardcover or paperback by querying local bookstores or a national cross section of booksellers. The most widely cited lists are those published weekly in the Sunday edition of the *New York Times* and in *Publishers Weekly*.

beveled boards Bookbinder's boards given a slanting or beveled edge before the covering material is put on. A feature of custom-bound leather bindings on extra-heavy volumes.

Bewick, Thomas (1753-1828) *See* woodcut.

biannual A publication issued twice a year. Cf. biennial.

bibelot A small decorative article of virtu that is rare, curious, or beautiful. The word is used by some book cataloguers to describe a small decorative book or literary trinket.

Bible in English (1782, 1781, printed in America)   *See* Aitken, Robert.

Bible in German (1743, printed in America)   *See* Sauer, Christopher.

Bible in Indian (Massachusetts, 1663, 1661, the first Bible printed in America)   *See* Eliot, John.

Bible paper   A thin, opaque book paper possessing strength and durability; suitable for Bibles, encyclopedias, catalogues, etc., where reduction in bulk is desirable. *See also* India paper; Oxford India paper.

Biblia Pauperum (Bible of the poor)   The best known of the block books (*q.v.*), consisting almost entirely of pictures, with text forming an integral part of the picture page. The pictures and the explanatory text (intended to teach biblical truths) were printed from wooden blocks on which the pictures and text were cut by hand. The earlier examples were printed on one side of the leaf only. About ten separate editions in the block book form are known to have been issued, beginning about 1450, some in Latin and some in German. They were not superseded by the invention of printing with movable metal type, but were produced alongside the early printed books until the early sixteenth century. Although printed in large numbers, the block book form of the *Biblia Pauperum* is today extremely rare; only fifteen copies are known to be in existence. An edition printed from metal type was issued about 1462 by Albrecht Pfister of Bamberg.

biblio   A combining form from Greek "biblion," book. Some examples are *biblioclast,* a destroyer or mutilator of books; *biblioklept,* one who steals books; *bibliomancy,* divination by books, especially by passages of Scripture taken at random; *bibliomania,* a mania for acquiring books; *bibliopegy,* the art of binding books; *bibliophile,* a lover of books; *bibliopole,* a bookseller; *bibliotaph,* one who hides books, as in a tomb; *bibliotheca,* a library.

bibliographic information interchange format   A format for the exchange, rather than the local processing, of bibliographic records.

bibliography   (1) The art or science of the description and history of books (their physical makeup, authorship, editions, printing, publication, etc.). (2) A list of works on a given subject or by a given author; the literature of a subject. *See also* analytical bibliography; descriptive bibliography; enumerative bibliography.

Bibliography of American Literature Compiled by Jacob Blanck, published by Yale University Press, 1955.

A definitive bibliography of American literature of the past 150 years. When completed, the work will contain some 35,000 items by nearly 300 selected authors, from the beginning of the Federal period up to and including authors who died before the end of 1930. The emphasis is on authors of belles lettres or work of like character; historians and writers of travel books are included only if of literary interest. Authors primarily of juvenile literature, of scientific and medical works, and of textbooks, sermons, or similar material are excluded. It is planned to have the work completed in eight or nine volumes.

Six volumes have been published to date: (I) Henry Adams to Donn Byrne, 1955; (II) George W. Cable to Timothy Dwight, 1957; (III) Edward Eggleston to Bret Harte, 1959; (IV) Nathaniel Hawthorne to Joseph Holt Ingraham, 1963; (V) Washington Irving to Henry Wadsworth Longfellow, 1969; (VI) Augustus B. Longstreet to Thomas William Parsons, 1973; (VII) James Kirke Paulding to Frank Richard Stockton, 1983.

biennial A publication issued every two years. Cf. biannual.

bimetallic plates For very long runs in offset lithography, bimetallic plates may be used. The printing areas are usually copper; the nonprinting ones are of another metal, such as a nickel or chromium.

binary A situation in which there can be only two possible conditions. The binary number system, which is the basis of digital computers, uses only the digits zero and one. In a computer, the presence of an electrical pulse represents a one, the absence of a pulse represents a zero.

binder (1) One who binds books. (2) A detachable cover for filing magazines, pamphlets, loose-leaf sheets, etc.

binder's board A stiff, high-grade composition paperboard around which the cover cloth on hardcover books is wrapped. Other board types are chipboard and pasted board. Binder's board is the densest and most expensive.

binder's dies Designs or lettering cut or etched in brass or other hard metal and used in stamping or embossing book covers. Sometimes called *binder's stamps* or *book-stamp*.

binder's stamps   *See* binder's dies.

binding   (1) The structural materials, such as thread and glue, that hold a book together, plus the attached cover, which may be cloth, leather, boards, paper, or other material. (2) In book manufacturing, the process of assembling the finished book. For sewn books, this usually includes folding, gathering, collating, sewing, tipping, gluing off, trimming, rounding and backing, lining, casing-in, and jacketing. For adhesive-bound books, the process entails folding, gathering, collating, clamping, edge-cutting, trimming, roughing, gluing, covering, and, when specified, jacketing.

Edition binding is the term used for binding books in hard covers, in commercial quantities; also called *trade binding* or *publisher's binding*. *Hand* or *custom binding* is the binding process carried out as a hand craft. *Library bindings* are specially reinforced for library use. When this is done to sheets before the book has been given a trade binding, it is known as *prebinding*. When it is done after the book has been bound, whether before or after library use, it is known as *rebinding*. *Mechanical binding* uses plastic or metal material to bind the pages; various types of mechanical binding include loose-leaf, plastic comb, and spiral wire binding. *Pamphlet binding* is the binding of self-covered or paper-covered booklets. *Adhesive binding* is a glued binding such as that used on paperback books, large telephone books, directories, etc.; also called *perfect binding*.

Full binding denotes a book bound entirely in leather. In a more general sense, it is a book bound entirely in any one material. *Three-quarter binding* is one in which the leather (or other material, such as vellum), covers the spine and part of each side as well as the corners of the book, and a different material, such as cloth, covers the remainder of the sides. The leather of the sides and corners almost meet. No exact standards exist, since this is a matter of graceful proportion. *Half-binding* is similar to three-quarter binding except that the leather does not extend as deeply into the sides (about one-fourth the width of the boards), and the leather corners are smaller and more in proportion, the three-quarter binding's corners being somewhat oversize. *Quarter-binding* has the spine and only a small part of the sides bound in leather (about one-eighth the width of the boards), and the corners are not leather-covered. *See also* adhesive binding; welded binding.

binding cloth *See* book cloth.

Binny and Ronaldson Archibald Binny and James Ronaldson established, in Philadelphia in 1796, the first typefoundry in the United States to achieve permanency. The firm published in 1812 the earliest known American type specimen book.

biobibliography A list of works by various authors that includes brief biographical information about each author.

bit Abbreviation for binary digit. The word can be used to mean a single unit (one or zero) in a binary number, an electrical pulse, or a unit of data storage capacity in a memory device.

black and white print Any printed image using only blacks or gray tones on a white base sheet. It can refer to photographic prints as well as ink on paper prints.

black letter A term applied to the book-hand and types derived therefrom that developed north of the Alps—boldfaced and angular—from which is descended the modern German fraktur. Black letter, now known to modern printers as Old English, or Elizabethan, was a name invented in the seventeenth century for the types imitated from the handwriting current in England two centuries previously. It was a great contrast to types founded on the Roman or Italian hand revived by scholars of the Renaissance. Also called *gothic*.

blackface *See* boldface.

Blaeu, Willem Janszoon (1571-1638) Founder of the Dutch printing and publishing house of Blaeu, makers of maps, atlases, and globes. He was at one time associated with Tycho Brahe, the famous Danish astronomer. Blaeu is credited with the first significant improvements in the printing press since the days of Gutenberg. The business was carried on and extended by his son John and grandson Willem. Their *Novus Atlas* in six large folio volumes was issued in 1676.

Blake, William (1757-1827) English artist, author, poet, printer, and engraver. Experimented with etched plates on which both text and illustration were printed by a method he devised. He and his wife colored many of the illustrations by hand.

blank An unprinted leaf that is part of a signature (*q.v.*).

blanket order An agreement between a library and a publisher or wholesaler wherein the library will automatically receive one copy of each title of a publisher's output, or one copy of each title in selected subject categories. In most blanket order plans, return privileges are not permitted. Also known as a *gathering plan.* A variation on the blanket order plan is the approval plan (*q.v.*) in which returns are usually permitted.

The blanket order plan, which largely replaces book selection work done within the library, is usually practiced by the larger public and academic libraries; it has all the advantages of (1) getting new publications into the library as close to publication date as possible; (2) reducing paperwork; and (3) cutting acquisitions costs.

Although there are a number of variations on the blanket order plan, one of the oldest and best known is the Greenaway Plan, named for its originator in 1958, Emerson Greenaway, for many years director of the Free Library of Philadelphia. Under the Greenaway Plan, publishers send all their trade books to a library before publication, at the same time review copies are sent out. The plan is used chiefly by public libraries where there is a need to buy multiple copies of books and to get them to readers quickly.

blanking   In binding, the polished impression on cloth covers that is made with a heated brass stamp as a base for lettering or decorative stamping.

bleed   (1) In page layout, extending of a printed image (picture, tint block, etc.) to the very edge of the page, so that no unprinted margin shows. Depending on how many edges a picture or color block touches, pages can bleed one, two, three, or four sides. (2) In lithographic and other chemical printing, a defect due to unwanted dissolving of ink pigment, which results in a stain, or slight change in color, or fuzziness of color image.

blind keyboard   A keyboard-equipped device for encoding data into machine-readable form, but which lacks any device for producing a typescript or hard copy as material is typed. *See also* hard copy.

blind tooling or stamping   Impressions on the cover of a book made by tools or dies without the use of color or metal foil. Also called *blind blocking.*

block   (1) To mount a cut (*q.v.*) on a block of wood or metal to make it type-high. Also British term for a cut. (2) In a computer, a group of computer words stored in successive memory locations or handled in the machine as a unit. *See also* word.

block books (or **xylographica**)   In the early years of the fifteenth century, woodcuts and engravings of religious subjects became well known in northern Europe. As early as 1418 and 1423 woodcuts were made containing dated inscriptions cut on the blocks. As the difference between cutting a few words on a wood block and cutting a text upon it was slight, the next logical steps were to cut upon sets of blocks not only illustrations but also text and to bind the impressions from these blocks into volumes. The books so made are termed *block books* and are looked upon as the intermediate step between the isolated woodcut and books printed from movable type. However, the more popular of the block books continued to be issued for more than half a century after the invention of printing with movable type.

Among the best known block books are the *Biblia Pauperum* (*q.v.*); the *Apocalypse of St. John*; the *Canticum Canticorum*; the *Ars Memorandi* (*How to Remember the Evangelist*); the popular *Ars Moriendi* (*Art of Dying*); and the *Speculum Humanae Salvationis* (*Mirror of Human Salvation*). Despite the large printings of many of the titles, block books today are extremely rare.

block printing   Printing from hand-carved wood or linoleum blocks. *See also* block books.

blocking   Stamping (*q.v.*).

blowup   An enlargement of a photograph, jacket, sample page of a book, review, etc., used for advertising display.

blueprint   A same-size copy made from a translucent original, often used for showing proofs of offset negatives prior to making offset plates. Sensitized blueprint paper is exposed through the original to strong light. The resultant print is blue except where shielded by opaque areas on the original.

The word is used loosely to cover other so-called whiteprint processes (Ozalid, Bruning) which produce same-size copies from translucent originals. These other processes, technically the diazo processes, are more dimensionally stable and produce a positive from a positive in black, brown, or other colors, as well as blue. A vandyke is a brown blueprint. *See also* proofs.

blurb   A sales pitch printed on the jacket or cover of a book or one used in an advertisement of it. Coined by Gelett Burgess in 1907 as a term meaning to hyperbolize or aggrandize one's own wares.

board   *See* paperboard.

board caliper   *See* caliper.

boards   The stiff paperboard used for the covers of books. Made of reclaimed and reprocessed wastepaper, boards may be covered with paper, cloth, leather, or other material. A book is said to be bound in "boards" when the boards are covered with paper only. *See* binder's board.

Bodoni, Giambattista   (1740-1813)   A world famous printer of Parma, who designed the first modern face roman types. His influence has been felt in the printing of all countries. His types, and those that developed from them, became known as *modern*, and the Caslon and Dutch types, which came back to popularity in the middle of the nineteenth century, as *old style*. These terms still persist. His two-volume *Manuale Typografico*, a catalogue of his typefaces, was published in 1818.

body   (1) In metal type, a rectangular piece of metal having a raised type image on one end. The term has been carried over into photographic and struck-image typesetting to express the total vertical dimension within which the type character is located. Thus a 7 point typeface may be set on an 8 point or a 9 point body. This is usually expressed as setting type "7 on 8" or "7 on 9." (2) In bookbinding, the main block of pages that is bound together and then fastened to the covers.

body type   Type used in text matter as opposed to headings and display type.

boldface   Heavy-faced type, also called *blackface*, as opposed to *lightface*.

bolt   The folded or doubled edge of paper at the head, foot, or fore-edge of an untrimmed book.

Boni, Albert   (1892-1981)   Publisher and founder, in 1917, with Horace Liveright (*q.v.*) of the Modern Library series. Boni began his career in the book industry in 1912, when he and his brother, Charles, opened the Washington Square Bookshop in New York City. From their bookshop, the Boni brothers began publishing books and created the Little Leather Library, a series of thirty pocked-sized volumes bound in limp imitation leather, which was the forerunner of the Modern Library. In 1917, Boni formed a partnership with Horace Liveright and issued the first titles in the Modern Library, which quickly became established as the leading American series of inexpensive hardbound reprints of important works of literature and thought. In 1925, the Modern Library was purchased by Bennett Cerf (*q.v.*) and Donald Klopfer. The Boni and Liveright partnership lasted only a year, and in 1918, Boni and his brother established a new publishing company, A. & C. Boni, Inc. In his later career, Boni created the Paper Books Club (1929) and, still later, established the Readex Microprint Corporation (1950). He was active in the latter until his retirement in 1974.

book Various attempts have been made to specify exactly what constitutes a book, as in the 1964 UNESCO recommendation that defines a book as "a non-periodical literary publication containing 49 or more pages, not counting covers," and in ANSI Standard Z-39.8, which similarly defines a book as "a nonperiodical printed publication in hard or soft covers, or in loose-leaf format, of at least 49 pages, exclusive of the cover pages...." The U.S. Postal Service requires that a book be a publication of twenty-four pages, of which twenty-two are printed, with advertising matter limited to incidental announcements of books, in order to qualify for the special fourth class rate (formerly called *book rate*).

Less formally, a book may be any collection of pages or leaves of any material, bound or sometimes unbound, in manuscript or in reproduction, in the form of a scroll (*q.v.*) or codex (*q.v.*); or it may be inscribed in stone or clay or appear in a variety of other forms. In the magazine industry, a specific magazine or issue of a magazine is often referred to as *the book*.

Book Auction Records *See* auction prices.

book block The bound assembly of a book's pages prior to attachment of the cover, or, in a finished book, the pages between the covers. A book block consists of a number of signatures held together either by thread sewn through the paper or by glue. Endpapers are usually pasted to the outside pages of the first and last signatures and are used to fasten the cover to the block. Also called *text block*.

book cloth Specially prepared cloth material used to make covers for books. Cotton *greige goods* (pronounced gray), woven as for any other fabric, are used, without processing, as the base material for book cloth, which falls into three main categories: starch-filled, plastic-impregnated, and plastic-coated (or imitation leather). The same greige goods can be finished in any of the three ways. Greige goods come in several different weights and weaves. The quality of the greige goods is based on the number of threads per square inch and the tensile strength of the threads. Book cloth comes in standard-width rolls of 36, 38, 40, and 42 inches and of varying lengths from 60 to 200 yards. For library binders, smaller rolls are available. Starch-filled cloth was the earliest form of book cloth. Today it is used on all types of books except textbooks. Plastic- (originally pyroxylin, later vinyl) impregnated book cloth may be required by state specifications for textbooks. Coated book cloth is used where the effect of a leather binding is desired.

Book cloth is generally further classified as follows:

Linens—Cloth that is not dyed before the filling and color are put on. This gives a two-tone effect because of the white threads that show through the filling. Both starch-filled and plastic.

Solid or vellum—This means a smooth finish and a solid color. The cloth is dyed first and then coated, and when the cloth is finished, even though the weave of the cloth shows slightly, the color is evenly distributed over the cloth. This finish may be had on starch-filled or plastic-impregnated cloth.

Natural finish—Cloth that is dyed, then filled entirely from the wrong side. In the finishing process the face side remains soft and slightly fuzzy.

Buckrams—There are several different weights of buckram, but all can be identified by the heavy, coarse threads that run through the cloth. Some buckrams are so tightly woven with such heavy threads that they are really canvas. Buckrams can be made in both linen and vellum solid-color finish, and either starch-filled or plastic-impregnated.

Plastic-coated material cannot be made in linen finish because the main idea of this is to hide as completely as possible the fact that there is a cloth base for the material. It is made in two-tone materials, however, one of the most common being the widely used Spanish (antique) finish.

The first commercial use of cloth for bookbinding was made by William Pickering of London about 1820. Before that, publishers issued their books in paper-covered wooden boards, paper-covered paperboards, vellum, wrappers, or leather. John Carter's *Binding Variants in English Publishing, 1820-1900, More Binding Variants,* and *Publisher's Cloth* give interesting historical information.

book club (1) A business that sells books by mail, generally at a lower than retail price, to members only, individuals who contract for its services. When joining, a book club member usually receives a relatively expensive book premium or is allowed to choose a group of books billed at a bargain rate and agrees (although not in all clubs) to purchase some minimum number of books. Selections offered by clubs may be specially and inexpensively reprinted for its members, purchased from publishers' stock, or richly produced as fine original editions.

A publication of some sort is generally mailed monthly or somewhat more frequently to book club members, and the books offered therein are called *selections (q.v.).* A *main selection* is the primary book (or two) of that particular selling period. *Alternate selections* may be additional new books offered. Many book clubs operate on the *negative option* principle. That is, if a member does not wish the main selection that month, a notice must be returned to the club to convey that information. If the notice is not returned, the member will receive the main selection automatically. Usually, when a member purchases a specified number of books through the club, he or she is eligible for a *book dividend,* which may be a free or inexpensive book bonus.

The oldest general-interest book clubs are the Book-of-the-Month Club (1926) and the Literary Guild (1927). Scores of special-interest book clubs offer volumes in the arts, professions, business, recreational areas, and other categories.

(2) A group of readers, sometimes called *reading circle,* who buy books for circulation and possibly discussion among themselves.

book club rights The rights purchased by a book club allowing it to offer a book to its membership. The rights may grant the club permission to print its own edition, or they may involve the club's acquisition of copies of the book printed by the original publisher. Most often the publisher acquires book club rights when it contracts for a book with an author, and when they are sold, the sum realized (which is actually an advance against anticipated royalties) is generally split equally between the publisher and the author. *See also* rights.

book collector   One who puts purpose and system into the acquisition of books. The purpose may be general, as expressing a
desire to have a useful and enjoyable library, or it may be specific
with the intention of covering one or more special areas of interest, or it may be to satisfy the taste of a connoisseur or the research of a scholar.

book-collectors' clubs   In the English-speaking world the oldest
and most exclusive book-collectors' club is the Roxburghe Club,
of London, founded shortly after the sale by auction of the library of the Duke of Roxburghe in 1812. The many other clubs,
most of them in the United States, were founded in the past
ninety years.

The oldest existing American club, the Grolier Club of New
York, was founded in 1884. The objects of all the clubs were
similar to that set forth in the constitution of the Grolier: "...the
literary study and promotion of the arts pertaining to the production of books, including the occasional publication of books
designed to illustrate, promote and encourage those arts..." etc.

The Grolier was followed shortly by Club of Odd Volumes
(Boston, 1886); Rowfant Club (Cleveland, 1892); Philobiblon
Club (Philadelphia, 1893); Caxton Club (Chicago, 1895); and
Dibdin Club (New York, 1897). More followed in the twentieth
century: the Franklin Club of St. Louis; the Carteret Club of
Newark; the Book Club of California; the Zamorano Club of Los
Angeles; etc.

The Hroswitha Club, a group of women book collectors, bibliographers, and others interested in the arts of the book, was
founded in 1944 in New York. The club was named for Hroswitha, the Saxon nun of the tenth century, who was a dramatist
and poet (and probably a book collector), canoness of the Abbey
of Gandersheim, Saxony.

book dividend   A bonus offered by a book club to its members
upon the purchase of a specified number of selections (*q.v.*). The
book dividend may be sent without charge, except for shipping
and handling, or at a price representing a small fraction of its
value, and is thus intended to increase the membership's rate of
purchase. *See also* book club.

book fair   (1) An exhibition of books and related materials, along
with talks by authors and illustrators, and other events. (2) A
trading center for the sale of books and rights and the making of

publishing and copublishing arrangements, or for the presentation of books available for sale or resale. Book trading fairs are now held in several countries of both hemispheres. The fairs began in the early sixteenth century in Frankfurt, Germany, and to this day the major international one is the annual Frankfurt Book Fair. (3) Antiquarian Booksellers Associations of different countries now also hold fairs in various cities of Europe and North America.

Book Industry Study Group (BISG)   An organization of publishers, booksellers, librarians, book manufacturers, and suppliers formed in 1976 for the purpose of promoting and supporting research that will enable the various sectors of the book industry to realize professional and business plans. BISG collects and compiles statistics and issues research reports on the book industry, including the annual publication *Book Industry Trends*.

Book Industry Systems Advisory Committee   *See* BISAC.

book label   *See* bookplate.

book leasing plan   A wholesaler program in which for a set monthly fee libraries can lease and return to the wholesaler high-demand titles in exchange for other titles when demand changes.

Book Manufacturers' Institute (BMI)   National trade association of book manufacturers and book-materials suppliers. Founded in 1920.

Book of Hours; Horae; Livre d'Heures   Book of devotions (hours of the Virgin Mary, passages from the Gospels, private prayers, etc.) intended for the use of clergy and laypersons. In general use in the Catholic Church from the fourteenth to the sixteenth centuries. The manuscript copies, written on vellum, were in many cases brilliantly illustrated and illuminated in colors, and they were costly. The invention of printing made possible the production of inexpensive copies and brought them within the reach of a wider public. The first printed *Livre d'Heures* was issued by Antoine Verard in Paris in 1487. The finest editions were produced in Paris between 1490 and 1505, by Pierre Pigouchet, who printed mainly for the publisher Simon Vostre, and by Thielman Kerver. Various editions were brought out until 1568, after which date publication ceased when Pope Pius V decreed that it need no longer be used by the clergy.

Book of Kells   *See* Kells, Book of.

book packager   Also called a *packager* or a *book producer*, an individual or company who assembles components necessary for book publication—any combination of author, manuscript, book designer, editor, camera-ready copy, printer, or finished book—and sells the property in a specific state of completion to a publisher that will release and market the book as its own or as an acknowledged copublishing project.

book paper   A general term to indicate a class of printing paper used for books, periodicals, catalogues, and other job printing, as distinct from newsprint, for example. Book paper is usually made from all types of virgin and reclaimed pulps (and mixtures of the two), and its basis weight usually ranges from 30 to 100 pounds, but can be lighter or heavier. It is characterized by a wide variety of surface finishes (for example, antique, eggshell, machine, English, supercalendered, dull-coated, matte-coated, etc.), with good formation, printability, and cleanliness. Book paper can be coated to provide such characteristics as brightness, opacity, and printability.

book pocket   Usually stiff paper pasted to the inside of either the front or back cover of a book to form a pocket (or envelope) to hold loose material. For example, a text-fiche (*q.v.*) book includes such a pocket to contain the microfiche sheets.

Book Prices Current   *See* auction prices.

book rate; book post   *See* book.

book scout   *See* scout.

book sizes   There is much confusion about the definition of book sizes and little consistency in usage. The common book trade designation of sizes was based originally on the relation to a sheet of paper measuring approximately 19 × 25 inches. When folded once to make two leaves (four pages), it was a folio; when folded twice, to make four leaves (eight pages), it was a quarto; when folded to eight leaves (sixteen pages), an octavo; when folded to sixteen leaves (thirty-two pages), a sixteenmo, etc. This is the historical background of book sizes and is still used in the rare book trade. In exact bibliographical descriptions, as in describing rare books, the historical definition applies.

However, present trade practice almost invariably refers to a measurement of the height of the binding, not the size of the leaf. Usual library practice calls for the use of centimeters, the measurement again referring to the height of the binding.

With the present variety of paper sizes all dimensions are approximate:

Folio, F°, over 30 centimeters (approximately 15 inches) high

Quarto, 4to, 30 centimeters (approximately 12 inches) high

Octavo, 8vo, 25 centimeters (approximately 9¾ inches) high

Duodecimo, 12mo, 20 centimeters (approximately 7¾ inches) high

Sixteenmo, 16mo, 17½ centimeters (approximately 6¾ inches) high

Twentyfourmo, 24mo, 15 centimeters (approximately 5¾ inches) high

Other sizes include:

Double elephant folio, approximately 50 inches high.

Atlas folio, approximately 25 inches high.

Elephant folio, approximately 23 inches high.

Thirtytwomo, 32mo, approximately 5 inches high.

Fortyeightmo, 48mo, approximately 4 inches high.

Sixtyfourmo, 64mo, approximately 3 inches high.

Any book wider than it is high is designated as oblong and such descriptive note is abbreviated obl. or ob. and precedes such terms as quarto, octavo, etc. If the book is unusually narrow for its height, it is designated narrow and such descriptive note is abbreviated nar.

English usage, even more detailed than American, includes the following:

	Height		*Width*
Pott Octavo	6¼	×	4 inches
Foolscap Octavo	6¾	×	4¼
Crown Octavo	7½	×	5
Large Post Octavo	8¼	×	5¼
Demy Octavo	8¾	×	5⅝
Medium Octavo	9	×	5¾
Royal Octavo	10	×	6¼
Super Royal Octavo	10	×	6¾
Imperial Octavo	11	×	7½
Foolscap Quarto	8½	×	6¾
Crown Quarto	10	×	7½
Large Post Quarto	10½	×	8¼
Demy Quarto	11¼	×	8¾
Medium Quarto	11½	×	9
Royal Quarto	12½	×	10
Foolscap Folio	13½	×	8½

book-stamp   *See* binder's dies.

Book Token   A gift certificate used in the British retail book trade since 1932. *See also* Give-a-Book Certificate.

book trade   (1) Retail bookselling as a whole, considered with its practices, codes, relations with publishers and wholesalers, etc. (2) Loosely, the general, especially trade book, business.

book traveler   A publisher's salesperson. *See* publisher's representative.

Book Week   A week designated by some group or organization for a cooperative promotion of books and reading. It may be dedicated to the promotion of libraries and reading in general as National Library Week, to national book interest, as Canadian Book Week, to local promotion, as Melbourne Book Week, to a special type of book, as Catholic Book Week or National Bible Week, or to enlist wider support for a public library.

In the United States, usually an abbreviated version of Children's Book Week, a special book promotion event held annually since 1919, usually in early November. It is sponsored by the Children's Book Council, which provides posters and other promotional material for the cooperating schools, bookstores, and libraries. Several countries hold simultaneous Book Weeks. In England such Book Weeks are held in the children's rooms of various libraries under the sponsorship of the National Book League.

booklet   A small book or pamphlet, usually paperbound.

Bookline: UTOPIA   *See* auction prices; UTOPIA.

bookmobile   (1) A van or "book truck" arranged for the display and distribution of books sent out by public libraries to city neighborhoods or rural areas not otherwise served by a library.

bookplate   A label pasted to one of the front endpapers of a book for identification of ownership. It is printed with the owner's name, together with a decorative border, an illustration, or an inscription. Often bookplates are inscribed with the term *ex libris* ("from the library of"). A *book label* is usually smaller and simpler than a bookplate, consisting merely of the owner's name.

bookworm   (1) The larva of an insect, probably several species, which injures books by feeding on the paper and binding. Little is known of bookworms and they are rarely seen either dead or alive. In all probability they cannot stand sunlight. They are essentially borers, and their small tunnels often extend through the entire thickness of a book from inner cover to inner cover. Any book suspected of harboring these pests should be promptly isolated and given into the hands of an expert exterminator. (2) A person who is a passionate reader of books.

boolean logic The formal logic structures on which computer programming and sophisticated data-base searching are based. These were first developed as an algebra by George Boole.

bosses Raised brass or other metal pieces on the binding of a book, used for protection and ornamentation.

bound galley *See* advance bound galley.

bowdlerized A word applied to a text altered by the expurgation of words or passages considered offensive or indelicate (by the bowdlerist). The word stems from Dr. Thomas Bowdler (1754-1825), whose name has been associated with various expurgated works, the most famous being *The Family Shakespeare*, which first appeared in the city of Bath, England, in 1807 (twenty plays, in four volumes). No editor's name was given in this edition, but Noel Perrin, in *Dr. Bowdler's Legacy* (New York: Atheneum, 1969), states, convincingly, that the editor was Dr. Bowdler's sister, Henrietta Maria Bowdler (1757-1830), known to her family as Harriet.

When the next edition of *The Family Shakespeare* appeared (thirty-six plays, in ten volumes) in London, in 1818, Thomas Bowdler's name was on the title page as the sole editor, and it remained there until the work finally went out of print well over one hundred years later.

Bowker, Richard Rogers (1848-1933) New York book industry leader, industrial executive, political and civic reformer, news writer, and critic. Bowker began contributing to *Publishers Weekly* from the time of its founding in 1872, and later became its editor and the owner of its publishing firm, which took his name in 1911. He also devoted immense energy to continuing the improvement of bibliographic tools, developing the library movement, and battling for authors' rights and international copyright. In 1876, with PW's founder, Frederick Leypoldt (*q.v.*), and Melvil Dewey (*q.v.*) he founded *Library Journal* and aided in founding the American Library Association.

Bowker Lectures on Book Publishing A series of lectures established in 1935 in memory of Richard Rogers Bowker to provide a forum for the discussion of problems common to authors, publishers, librarians, and readers. The lectures were sponsored jointly by the R. R. Bowker Company and the New York Public Library and were held annually until 1950, then irregularly until 1967, at the New York Public Library. After a lapse of six years, the series was revived in the fall of 1973 under a new title, Bowker Memorial Lectures on Book Publishing, New Series. The School of Library Service, Columbia University, joined with the Bowker Company to cosponsor the new series. The first seventeen lectures were published in book form by the R. R. Bowker Company.

box   On a printed page, featured matter surrounded by rules or white space and placed within or between text columns.

Boydell, John (1719-1804)   The London publisher who, with his nephew, Josiah, published the famous illustrated folio edition of Shakespeare's works, printed mainly by William Bulmer (*q.v.*).

Bradford, William (1663-1752)   First printer in Philadelphia, 1685. Partner with William Rittenhouse, Samuel Carpenter, and others in establishing the first American paper mill in 1690 near Germantown, Pa. Also first printer in New York City, where he settled in 1693. Buried in Trinity Churchyard, New York.

Bradley, Will (1868-1962)   Decorative artist and book and type designer who had a marked effect on American book making in the 1890s, the era of the protest movement against mechanization and commercialism. Founded Wayside Press in 1895, in Springfield, Mass.

braille   A system of characters invented by Louis Braille (1809-1852), used in printing for the blind. These symbols are embossed or raised in relief so that the reading may be done by the sense of touch with the fingertips.

braille paper   A sheet with smooth, level surface and strength suitable for the raised-dot production process used in manufacturing reading material for the blind. *See also* braille.

branching   Programming technique by which a computer is made to choose alternative sequences of instructions for execution. An unconditional branch instruction causes the machine to change the sequence of operations from its normal order in every case in which the instruction is encountered. A conditional branch will cause a change in sequence only if some other condition has been met.

brass widths The widths of characters of type. The term *brass* comes from hot metal typesetting systems that use brass matrices of individual characters to cast type. In computerized typesetting, character width tables are set up in memory, and the machine refers to them to obtain data for computing whether or not a line of type is full. *See also* set size.

brayer Printer's or printmaker's hand inking roller.

break (1) To dispose of a form of metal type that is of no further use by separating material to be remelted from engravings, foundry type, furniture, rules, etc. (2) An interruption in electronic transmission of data.

breakeven point The number of copies of a book that must be sold in order for a publisher to recover its costs for acquiring, producing, and promoting that book. In theory, money earned above this point is profit.

broadband In data transmission, facilities capable of handling frequency ranges greater than those needed for standard high-grade voice communications. Broadband transmission is used for very large amounts of data. *See also* data transmission; narrowband.

broadside A sheet of paper printed on one side only, usually intended to be posted, publicly distributed, or sold. Sometimes called a *broadsheet*.

brochure A printed and stitched book containing only a few leaves; a pamphlet; a treatise or article published in such form. (From the French "brocher," to stitch.)

brownprint *See* blueprint.

Brunet, Jacques Charles (1780-1867) Bibliographer, author of the famous classic in bibliographical literature *Manuel du Libraire et de L'Amateur de Livres,* 6 volumes, Paris, 1860-1865 (5th edition); and *Supplement...*by Pierre Deschamps and G. Brunet, 2 volumes, 1878-1880. The work, generally referred to as *Brunet,* is, despite its age, still an indispensable bibliographical reference book.

brush coated *See* coated paper.

buckles In binding, severe wrinkles that form near the head and back of the folded signatures when the paper is folded at right angles. Also called *gussets*.

buckram   *See* book cloth.

buffer   An auxiliary computer device that stands between other elements in a system, isolating them and permitting them to operate at their own speeds or in their own sequences without affecting other system elements. Used to match units with dissimilar operating characteristics.

bug   A defect that interferes with proper operation of a system. *See also* debugging.

bulk   (1) The thickness of a book without its cover. (2) To *bulk* a book is to give it the appearance of greater size through the use of thick but light paper. Book papers can bulk anywhere from 200 to 2,000 pages to the inch.

Bulmer, William (1758-1830)   Distinguished English printer and bookmaker who printed, under the name of the Shakespeare Press, in partnership with George Nicol and John Boydell the great folio Boydell Shakespeare, issued in nine volumes, 1791-1805.

burin   Engraver's cutting tool.

burnished edges   Colored or gilt edges of a book, which have been made smooth and bright by a polishing tool or agate.

burst binding   In adhesive binding, the term *burst binding* refers to the puncturing of the fold of the signatures that come off a web press. Using male and female dies, cuts or holes are made for deeper penetration of glue (during the later gluing operation) between the pages for greater holding power. On the web press, the perforations remove part, but not all, of the fold and are timed to puncture at rapid intervals. *See also* binding; notch binding.

Bury, Richard de (1287-1345)   English bibliophile, Bishop of Durham, who collected classical manuscripts and founded a library at Oxford. His famous *Philobiblon* was first printed in 1473, in Cologne.

butted   Lines of type or rules set end to end to make a longer line.

buying around   The practice of buying from a foreign supplier or publisher an edition cheaper than the domestic edition, even though the latter, under publishers' contracts, is supposed to be the only edition offered for sale in the domestic market. Thus, an American library or individual may order from an English book wholesaler books at British (presumably lower) prices, rather than from the authorized U.S. publisher or its suppliers.

byte Sequence of eight binary bits, or digits, shorter than a computer word, normally handled as a unit in the machine. *See also* bit; word.

© Abbreviation symbol for the word "copyright," frequently used by itself or together with "copyright" in the copyright notice in publications. The symbol is recognized in the Universal Copyright Convention and, in certain circumstances, can relieve a foreigner from some copyright law requirements in another country.

c. (1) Abbreviation for copyright, used in descriptive notes, although not legally valid in a copyright notice. (2) Often used as abbreviation for circa, although for this ca. is preferred. (3) Invoice symbol for cancelled.

c & lc Proofreaders' marks calling for the use of capitals and lowercase letters. *See also* Proofreaders' Marks at end of book.

c & sc Proofreaders' marks calling for the use of capitals and small capitals. *See also* Proofreaders' Marks at end of book.

ca. Abbreviation for circa (*q.v.*).

C.B.A. (1) Christian Booksellers Association. (2) Canadian Booksellers Association.

CBI Abbreviation for *Cumulative Book Index*, an international bibliography of books in the English language; published by the H. W. Wilson Co.

CCC *See* Copyright Clearance Center.

CIP *See* Cataloging in Publication.

CODEN A unique alphanumeric code assigned as an identifier to serial and monographic publications, developed in 1963 for scientific and technical publications by the American Society for Testing Materials. Chemical Abstracts Service is responsible for assigning CODEN designations.

COM Abbreviation for computer-output microfilm (*q.v.*).

c.o.r. Abbreviation for cash on receipt.

CPU Abbreviation for central processing unit (*q.v.*).

CRT Shorthand for cathode-ray tube (*q.v.*), the screen or television screen on which electronic information can be displayed; a component of a video display terminal (*q.v.*).

c.w.o. Cash with order. Sometimes used in quoting prices to unknown inquirers.

cable television The form of television transmission that relies on some sort of wire or cable connection between sender and receiver. This differs from broadcast television, which sends out its signals over the airwaves. Cable television was originally intended to improve reception of the video aspect of television, but finally grew into a major industry developing its own programming, some of which is derived from book content. *See also* electronic publishing.

Caldecott, Randolph (1846-1886) Noted English illustrator of children's books. In the United States the Caldecott Medal for the best picture book of the year is named for him.

calendar An awareness of the differing calendar systems (those of the past, and those now used) is often important in interpreting dates of books, manuscripts, letters, documents, historical events, etc.

Disorders had arisen in the workings of the old Roman calendar, which differed from the Egyptian and Greek forms, and Julius Caesar ordered a restructuring of the Roman calendar then in use to regulate the civil year entirely by the sun. The calendar that Caesar's decree replaced had been a lunar calendar, with an intercalary month. The first Julian Calendar commenced with the first of January in 46 B.C. Because of an error in intercalations, the Julian year was about eleven minutes longer than the astronomical year, and by A.D. 1582 the date of the vernal equinox became displaced by ten days, a figure that increased in the centuries following. The reformation of the Julian Calendar was commissioned by Pope Gregory XIII, and his decree of March 1582 abolished the use of the Julian and substituted the calendar that has been received in almost all Christian countries and that came to be known as the Gregorian Calendar or New Style. Rome, Spain, Portugal, France, and parts of Italy adopted the new calendar in 1582; the Catholic states in Germany in 1583; the Protestant states Denmark and Sweden did not adopt it until 1700; England and its American colonies not until 1752. Russia used the Julian (Old Style) Calendar until 14 February 1918; the Gregorian (New Style) was then adopted, and thirteen days were dropped to make up the time difference.

England reconciled the eleven-day difference in the two calendars at the time of its change from the Old Style to the New Style by a decree ordering the day following 2 September 1752 to be 14 September 1752. At the same time the commencement of the legal year in England was changed from the twenty-fifth of March to the first of January. (The twenty-fifth of March—the Feast of the Annunciation—in medieval times and later, was the beginning of the new year in England through 1752; in Scotland, January 1 had been adopted for New Year's Day beginning with the year 1600.

The French Revolutionary Calendar of the First French Republic was substituted for the ordinary calendar, dating from the Christian Era, by a decree of the National Convention in 1793. The date of the beginning of the new calendar was set for 22 September 1792, the day from which the existence of the Republic was reckoned. The year, beginning at midnight of the day of the autumnal equinox, was divided into twelve months of thirty days, with five additional days for festivals, and six in every fourth year. Each month was divided into three decades of ten days each, the week being abolished. The calendar years were numbered *An I* (22 September 1792 to 21 September 1793) through *An XIV* (23 September 1805 to 22 December 1805). The calendar was abolished by Napoleon in favor of the ordinary one at the end of the year 1805.

The Hebrew (Jewish) Calendar is a lunisolar calendar, reckoning from the year 3761 B.C., the date traditionally given for the Creation.

The Mohammedan Calendar, a lunar calendar, reckons from the year of the Hegira (flight of Mohammed from Mecca), which took place in A.D. 622.

calendering Process of polishing newly made paper between smooth cylinders under pressure and sometimes heat to make its surface smooth. Paper that receives a minimum of calendering emerges as "antique." With more calendering paper acquires a machine finish, then an English finish, and it finally becomes a supercalendered sheet, which has a glossy finish. *See* book paper.

calf   Calfskin prepared and used for bindings on books.

California job case   *See* case.

caliper   The thickness of paperboard measured in thousandths of an inch, commonly referred to as *board caliper*. Each thousandth of an inch is called a *point of caliper*, or just *point*. Paperboard that is .050 inch thick is said to be 50-point board.

called for   Term used in the antiquarian book trade to describe a book with reference to a criterion laid down by some authority, named or unnamed. For example, a book may be described as being "without the frontispiece called for by Blanck"; or, "with the leaf before the title called for by Storm."

calligraphy   Literally, from the Greek, "beautiful handwriting"; writing as an art. In calligraphy, the letter forms are both inspired and limited by the writing tool—ordinarily the broad-point pen, but occasionally the Spencerian pen, the brush (as in oriental writing), and even the crayon.

calotype   Early photographic process (ca. 1839) invented by William Henry Fox Talbot, also called Talbotype. Paper sensitized with silver iodide was brushed with solution of silver nitrate and acetic and gallic acids and exposed while wet. Translucent paper permitted a positive to be printed and led to the use of the glass plate.

cameo binding   A binding with a cameo-like decoration, usually inset or stamped on the front cover.

camera   In printing, a special large camera used to photograph art, illustrations, photographs, paste-ups, or other copy in preparation for stripping the film negatives or positives into flats. Such graphic arts cameras are used to make both halftone and line shots. *See also* flat; halftone; line drawing; strip in.

camera-ready   Said of artwork, illustrations, paste-ups of type pages, or other materials that are completely ready to be photographed on a graphic arts camera, preparatory to stripping into flats. *See also* camera; flat; strip in.

Cameron Book Production System   Brand name for a commercial model of the belt press (*q.v.*).

cancel, cancellans A new leaf or signature reprinted and inserted because of errors or defects in the leaf or signature replaced. In general, any printed matter substituted for that stricken out.

cancelland, cancellandum The excised portion of a book; usually a single leaf bearing an error.

caps and small caps (c & sc) CAPITALS and SMALL CAPITALS in fonts of type. Directions for the compositor to set in small capitals, with the initial letters in large capitals. *See also* Proofreaders' Marks at end of book.

caption (1) The brief title or description that identifies or explains an illustration. (2) Less frequently, a headline, as of a chapter, table, etc. *See also* legend.

card reader A device for sensing data encoded on a punch card and entering it in the computer. *See also* punch card; read.

carding out Extending a column of metal type by manually inserting strips of card stock or paper between lines of type, when the thinnest metal spacing material would be too thick. Term is sometimes carried over into photographic typesetting, although interline spacing is actually performed mechanically or electronically within the machine.

caret The sign ∧ used to indicate an insertion is to be made. *See also* Proofreaders' Marks at end of book.

Carey, Mathew (1760-1839) A leading publisher and bookseller in the United States in its formative period. He migrated to Philadelphia from Ireland in 1784, published magazines, organized aggressive methods of selling books including subscription and itinerant bookselling (one of his salesmen was Parson Weems). Carey made the first experiments in an American commercial book fair and helped found the first U.S. booksellers' association, 1806. His and his son's firm, Carey & Lea, survives as Lea & Febiger.

cartouche Scroll-like flourish with a pen or brush, used as an ornamental border or frame.

cartridge A container for magnetic tape, similar to a cassette (*q.v.*).

case (1) A preassembled hard cover for a book, which comprises the front and back covers and connecting material across the spine, and wraps around the inside pages. *Casing-in* is the binder's term for inserting the book, when sewed, into its case. Cf. slipcase. (2) A compartmentalized tray in which hand type is kept. Capital letters used to be kept in the upper case, small letters in the lower. The so-called *California job case* accommodates both side by side. *See also* lowercase; uppercase.

case binding (1) A preassembled, one-piece hard cover put around a book block (*q.v.*). (In fine hand binding, the cover is usually not prefabricated, but rather is assembled right on the book.) (2) The process of binding hardcover books in which the cover is made separately and, when put around the book, always projects beyond the edges of the text pages. *See also* binding; case.

casing-in *See* case.

Caslon, William (1692-1766)   English type designer and typefounder. Designed and cast the types that bear his name, the most widely used type designs in English and American printing. Originally famed as an engraver of gunbarrels, he began typefounding in 1720, and in 1734 he issued his famous specimen book of typefaces.

cassette (1) In tape recording, a standard container with two spools that holds magnetic recording tape. First designed for audio recording with tape recorders, such cassettes are now being used in digital data handling systems as a means of storage. (2) In phototypesetting, a portable container for light-sensitive material. The cassette usually attaches directly to the typesetting machine either to feed or receive material.

cast coated *See* coated paper.

casting In metal type production, the process of flowing molten metal against a matrix in a mold and allowing it to cool and harden into individual characters, lines of type, or stereotypes.

Cataloging in Publication (CIP) A prepublication cataloging program established by the Library of Congress (L.C.) in July 1971, wherein participating publishers provide the L.C. with galleys and/or front matter of forthcoming books from which professional cataloging data is prepared by L.C. and returned to the publisher. This CIP data is usually printed on the verso of the title page. In addition, the CIP data is distributed to L.C.'s MARC tape subscribers, so that it can be used in selecting titles for purchase as well as in cataloging procedures. Because CIP helps in acquisitions work, reduces cataloging costs, and speeds the delivery of books to readers, the program benefits the library world and the publishing industry alike. In general, the program's scope includes all U.S. trade monographs as well as other kinds of books collected and cataloged by libraries. As of 1974, publications of selected government agencies are also included in the program.

catalogue (1) A list of books systematically arranged (usually by author or subject), with descriptive information, prepared for a specific purpose; e.g., a publisher's sales catalogue. (2) In a library, a file of bibliographic records that describes the books in the collection.

catchline On proofs, a temporary, identifying headline.

catchword entry The entry of a title in an index, bibliography, or catalogue, by its most important or most easily remembered word.

catchwords (1) The words printed at the head of a column or page to indicate the first and last entries on the page, as in a dictionary. (2) In early books, the word placed at the bottom of each page under the last word in the last line, which was also placed as the first word on the following page. Catchwords originally served as a guide to the printer in imposition and the binder in gathering the signatures.

category publishing *See* genre publishing.

cathode-ray tube An electronic vacuum tube similar to that used in television sets as picture tubes. Images are displayed on the face or screen. In typesetting machines, type characters are displayed at extremely high speeds, and the light thus generated is used to expose photographic materials. In editing and layout terminals, type is displayed for reading by the operator. *See also* character generation; video editing terminal; video layout terminal.

Caxton, William (1422?-1491) The first English printer. He was apprenticed in 1438 to a London silk merchant on his own account at Bruges (1446-1470); governor of English merchants in the Low Countries (1465-1469), with rank and duties similar to those of a British consul or ambassador. After resigning his office as governor in March 1469 he began a translation of Raoul Le Fèvre's *Recueil des Histoires de Troi*, which he finished at the request of Duchess Margaret of Burgundy in 1471. He found it impossible to prepare sufficent manuscript copies to meet the demand, and during a five-month visit to Cologne in 1471-1472, he learned something of the new art of printing. He then established a printing press of his own at Bruges, in partnership with Colard Mansion. His first book was his own translation of the *Recueil*, named in English *The Recuyell of the Historyes of Troye*. The work is undated and bears no place of printing, but most authorities agree that it was printed at Bruges sometime between 1472 and 1474. He printed another translation at Bruges, *The Game and Playe of the Chesse*. He returned to England in the autumn of 1476 and established a press at Westminister, using type and equipment brought over from Bruges. The first known dated book printed by Caxton was issued by him at Westminster on the 18th of November 1477; the work was a translation from the French by Caxton's friend Lord Rivers, titled *Dictes and Sayengis of the Philosophers*.

Between 1476 and his death in 1491 Caxton printed about 100 books. The most notable of these were his folio editions of Chaucer's *Canterbury Tales* (1478), *Chronicles of England* (1480), Higden's *Polychronicon* (1481), Gower's *Confessio Amantis* (1483), Voragine's *Golden Legend* (1484), and Malory's *Morte D'Arthur* (1485). *See also* Worde, Wynkyn de.

censor, censorship   A censor may be a person, persons, or body empowered by law to prohibit the production, distribution, or sale of materials believed to be objectionable for reasons of politics, obscenity, or blasphemy; a censor may also be a self-appointed person or group bringing pressure upon retailers, distributors, exhibitors, educators, librarians, publishers, the press, and public to excise or suppress material the censor finds offensive. Censorship is the act of the censor; e.g., the removal of an offending publication from display, circulation, or sale, barring it from schools, from the mail, or from passage through customs, ordinarily by means of administrative ruling, court order, or community consent. The term *prior censorship* is applied to the excision or suppression of material prior to publication or distribution. Censorship is distinguished from selection, as in the choosing of books for bookstore or library stocks, a process in which the censor's criteria do not or should not apply.

centered dot   A period placed higher than the base line of the typeface. Used to separate syllables (syl · lab · i · ca · tion), to show multiplication ($2 \cdot 2 = 4$), to separate roman capitals in the classic form of tablet inscriptions (M · A · R · C · V · S A · N- · T · O · N · I · V · S). Sometimes called a *space dot.*

central processing unit   The central section or unit of a computer system that actually performs the active data processing procedures. The CPU generally contains the main or core memory, all arithmetic units, and special registers for handling data.

Cerf, Bennett Alfred   (1898-1971) Publisher-publicist, co-founder of Random House (with Donald S. Klopfer). Cerf and Klopfer purchased Modern Library in 1925 and founded Random House in 1927; Cerf was president to 1965, then chairman to 1970. The firm emphasized fine design, developed major U.S. and foreign writers, aggressively merchandised Modern Library, and launched innovative lines for children and young people. The firm's defense of Joyce's *Ulysses* resulted in a landmark anti-censorship decision in 1933. Unique among publishers, Cerf lectured constantly on books and humor, toured bookstores and colleges, wrote gossipy, book-centered columns, and was a star of radio and TV shows.

chain lines   In *laid paper* (*q.v.*), the widely spaced watermark lines that run with the grain. These are visible when one holds the paper up to the light. Caused by the "chain wires" that are twisted around the laid wires to tie them together, the lines are usually about one inch apart. Also known as *chain marks.*

chain printer   A computer-operated device that types out material stored in a computer onto a continuous length of paper. Individual type characters are mounted on an endless chain that rotates past the points of impact. As the proper character passes the position desired, it is struck from behind by a small hammer, impressing the character onto an inked ribbon and then onto the paper. Such machines operate at very high speeds compared to conventional typewriters.

chained books   Books chained to the shelves of university, monastic, and other libraries of the 15th to 17th century to prevent theft.

channel   A path for the transmission of machine-readable data.

In punched paper or magnetic tapes, each row of holes or electrical impulses is considered a channel, and tapes are referred to by the number of channels they hold—six channel, seven channel, etc. *See also* level; track.

chapbook   From the Anglo-Saxon "ceap," meaning cattle (and later Old English, "trade"). Small, cheap book, in a paper binding, popular in England and the American colonies in the seventeenth and eighteenth centuries, containing tales, ballads, lives, tracts, and topical material. Sold by chapmen, i.e., peddlers, hawkers.

chapel   The workers in a printing office, considered a society. As used in the United States, the term applies to the organizational unit of union printers employed in a printing house.

chapter head   A heading printed above the text at the start of a chapter.

character   (1) A letter of the alphabet, numeral, mark of punctuation, or any other symbol used in typesetting. In making a character count, spaces count as one. (2) A defined unit of information stored in and handled by a computer.

character generation   Electronic projection or construction of typographic images in cathrode-ray tube, laser, or other electronic typesetting systems. Such systems permit electronic manipulation of characters, such as the making of an italic out of a roman letter. Also, most electronic systems store characters in digital form by breaking them up into thousands of discrete electronic pulses. This further enables the designs to be changed via computer programming techniques. Character generation typesetting machines can operate at extremely high speeds.

character recognition   Use of a machine to sense and encode into machine language characters that are handwritten, typed, printed, or otherwise indicated graphically. *See also* optical character recognition.

character set   (1) A specific group of characters acceptable to a computer system, which it has been programmed to handle. (2) In typography, a specific group of characters included in a type font or on a typesetting device; or, the lateral width of individual characters. *See also* set size.

character style   Distinguishing design or characterisitics of a typeface (*q.v.*).

chase Steel frame in which metal type in pages is locked up for placing on the press, or for the foundry when plates are to be made.

checklist A list of books, pamphlets, or other material with a minimum of bibliographical description of the works recorded.

chemical pulp The raw material from which better grades of book papers are made. Chemical pulp is made from wood fibers chemically treated to remove the ingredients that cause newsprint (made from groundwood pulp) to become yellow and brittle with age over a relatively short period of time. (Only paper that is acid free, or alkaline, will not yellow or embrittle.) In the pulping process, the wood fibers are chemically digested, or cooked, to liberate the cellulose from the fibrous raw material. Paper made from chemical pulp only is called a *free sheet*, i.e., free of groundwood.

Children's Book Week *See* Book Week.

children's books *See* instructional materials.

China paper A thin, soft paper of a faint yellowish or brownish tint, prepared from the bark of the bamboo. It is much used for fine impressions from wood engravings and occasionally for proofs from steel-plate engravings.

Chinese (or **Japanese**) **style** Said of a book in which each leaf is double thick and uncut, with the interior of the leaf blank.

chipboard A less expensive substitute for binder's board (*q.v.*). It is manufactured from mixed wastepapers to a low density and is used when durability or appearance of a hard cover is not significant. *See also* paperboard.

Chiswick Press Founded in 1811 by Charles Whittingham (1767-1840), at Chiswick, a largely residential district suburban to London. Whittingham was a printer of considerable merit who was famous for a number of small books with brilliantly printed woodcuts and as the printer of attractive popular-priced classics. He was the first to print India paper editions. His nephew, Charles Whittingham the Younger (1795-1876), worked with his uncle from 1824 to 1828, and he took over the Chiswick Press upon the death of his uncle in 1840. He himself was an excellent printer, and he formed an association with William Pickering for whom he did much printing after 1830. After the younger Whittingham's death in 1876, Chiswick Press was taken over by George

Bell. It was at this press that William Morris made his experiments in printing, before setting up his own Kelmscott Press in 1891.

chrestomathy   A collection of choice passages from an author or authors.

circa (ca.)   Latin word for about, around; often used in English with numerals to denote approximate accuracy, e.g., "printed circa 1747."

circuit   A System of electrical components and conductors through which electrical current can flow. In communications, a link between two points.

circuit edges   *See* divinity circuit.

citation   A complete reference to a text that has been quoted or to some source that has been used as an authority.

cities, classical names of   Names used in the colophons or on the title pages of old books may be found, with their modern equivalents, in·the *Dictionnaire de Geographie Ancienne et Moderne*, by P. Deschamps, facsimile edition, 1922, Paris & Berlin; also in *Place Names in Imprints*, by R. A. Peddie, 1932, Grafton, London; and in the *Columbia Lippincott Gazetteer of the World*, edited by Leon E. Seltzer, 1952, Columbia University Press.

claim   A notification sent to a publisher, wholesaler, or other supplier that an order has not been received in the expected period of time.

class "A" library binding   One that meets certain standards set by the Library Binding Institute and the American Library Association.

classified catalog   A catalog arranged by a numeric or alphabetic notation according to subject content. Also classed catalog, or class catalog. Cf. dictionary catalog.

clean tape   A tape containing only the codes required to operate a typesetting machine, with all errors and extraneous codes removed.

clear   To return a computer memory and computation circuits to their original state prior to the start of processing operations.

cleat sewing   *See* sewing.

Cleland, Thomas M. (1880-1964)   Artist, book illustrator, and book decorator, who did much fine work for various presses, including the Merrymount Press.

clipping service, clipping bureau   An organization that makes a business of collecting personal notices, book reviews, etc. from current newspapers and periodicals and furnishing them for a fee to the persons concerned.

close up   To push type closer together by replacing thicker with thinner spaces.

closed-loop system   System in which all operations, once started, take place automatically until the end result is reached, without human intervention. *See* loop; open-loop system.

cloth   The commonest material used for the binding, or casing, of books. A binding described as *cloth* means, unless otherwise indicated, the cover is made of cloth pasted over stiff boards. *See also* book cloth.

coated paper   Paper surfaced with white clay or a similar substance to provide a smooth printing surface. The term covers a wide range of qualities, basis weights, and uses. Coated papers called *enamel* are glossy, but there are also grades of *dull-coated*. The cheaper coated papers have the coating applied right in the papermaking machine and are called *machine coated*. When the coating is applied as a separate and later operation, the process is called *brush coating*. Papers having extra high gloss are called *cast coated*.

Cobden-Sanderson, T. J. (1840-1922)   Founder of the Doves Press (*q.v.*) at Hammersmith, England; he also ranks as one of the great bookbinders of modern times.

cockle   The puckered effect on paper, naturally or artificially produced in the drying process.

code   (1) A system of symbols for representing various other types of data or instructions in a computerized system. (2) To write a computer program or routine.

code set   The coded representation of a given character set.

codex (*pl.* **codices;** *abbr.* **cod.;** *pl.* **codd.**)   A manuscript in book form as distinguished from the papyrus roll, which the codex superseded. The codex owed its existence to the substitution of vellum for papyrus as the common writing material for Greek and Roman literature; vellum was a tough material capable of being inscribed on both sides, and the leaves could be stitched and bound in a form similar to books of modern times. The earliest great vellum Greek codices of the Bible and of Latin classical authors, dating back to the fourth century, are composed of very finely prepared material; some fragments of the codex form of manuscript exist that show the form was already in use in the first centuries of our era. More than 100 Bible manuscripts in codex form, dating from the fourth to the tenth century, written in uncial characters, are known; more than 1,200 dating from the ninth to the sixteenth century written in cursive characters, are also known.

Among the famous Bible codices are the *Alexandrian Codex* and the *Codex Sinaiticus*. The Alexandrian Codex is a fifth-century manuscript of the Scriptures in Greek (containing the New Testament, nearly complete), which had belonged to the library of the patriarchs of Alexandria, in Africa, A.D. 1098, and which, in 1627, was sent as a present to King Charles I. Since 1757 it has been in the British Museum. The *Codex Sinaiticus*, a fourth-century manuscript in Greek (containing the New Testament, twenty-six Books of the Old Testament, and the Apocrypha), was the great discovery of Lobegott Friedrich K. von Tischendorf, the German biblical scholar and critic (1815-1874), in 1844, and a larger portion in 1859, at the monastery at Mount Sinai. The first portion was given to the Leipzig Library, where it still is; the second, and larger portion, was presented to the Russian czar at St. Petersburg (who was patron of the monastery). This portion was acquired by the British Museum in 1933 for £100,000.

coffee table book   Frequently an expensive, large-sized, lavishly illustrated book intended more for perusing than for reading, and therefore likely to be left out on a coffee table rather than placed away on a bookshelf.

cold type   Composition produced on a direct-impression typewriter-like machine; struck-image composition. Preferred usage of this term eliminates both hot metal and photographic composition processes, although photocomposition is sometimes erroneously called cold type. *See also* direct-impression; photocomposition.

Colines, Simon de (1475-1547)   Printer and scholar, who served as foreman in the printing house of Henri Estienne (*q.v.*) and who continued the firm after Estienne's death in 1521. Colines married Estienne's widow and assumed management of the printing plant. His correct texts and fine typography brought fame to the establishment; he printed more than 500 various editions, many of them illustrated, and the house of Estienne was most influential in the French printing renaissance and in the movement to replace gothic types with roman. Colines had recognized the genius of Geoffroy Tory and employed him to design decorations and types for use at the press; he became known for the excellence of his Greek types, and he was the first to use italic types in France.

collate (1) To examine the gathered signatures of a book in order to verify their full count and arrangement. Rare books are collated to verify completeness, including plates, leaves, etc. (2) In binding, to assemble individual sheets or leaves into complete sets, as opposed to gathering, which is the assembly of signatures into complete sets. Collating is done primarily in the binding of smaller booklets, pamphlets, and loose-leaf products. *See also* gathering.

collating mark A short rule or dot that appears on the back fold of each signature of a book, for use in checking the accuracy of gathering. The mark appears on the first signature near the top, on the second a little lower, on the third still lower, etc. When the signatures are gathered for binding, the marks form a diagonal line that would be broken if a signature were duplicated, out of place, or omitted. The older system of marking each signature on the first page with a number, letter, or other symbol is still used in England and to some extent in the United States.

collected author An author whose works have attracted the interest of book collectors.

collected edition The publication of an author's work in a uniform format within one or more volumes. If the books were originally published by several firms, one publisher makes an arrangement with all to publish a uniform edition. A collected edition is not necessarily a complete edition.

college traveler *See* publisher's representative.

collotype *See* photogelatin.

colophon   From the Greek "kolophon," finishing touch. (1) The inscription that the letterer or printer placed at the end of a manuscript or book, with the facts about its production, author, date, title, etc. In late bookmaking the title leaf has largely taken the place of the colophon for recording these details with regard to publication. In modern finely printed books, the use of a colophon has been revived as a place of record for the typographical details. (2) Also frequently but incorrectly used to mean the trade emblem or device of a printer or publisher.

color printing   Generally, (1) use of more than one color in a printed piece, or (2) use of color other than black. However the term *color* is used in a variety of ways. In printing, all inks—even black and white—are considered to be colors because they must be applied individually to the piece. Jobs are described by the number of colors (inks) used on them. A *one-color* job is usually a *black-and-white* job (black ink on white paper), but it can also be another color ink on any color paper.

More esoteric printing jobs may use more colors, although one, two, three, or four are the most common combinations. A job printed in black and red thus becomes a two-color job, and a job printed in red, yellow, blue, and black becomes a four-color job.

The term *four-color* is also used in another sense—as a synonym for process color or full color. *Process color* is the most technically accurate term, referring to the use of four carefully color-balanced inks (yellow, cyan, magenta, black) to print four overlapping halftones; when printed this way, the inks blend to reproduce the full range of colors in the spectrum. *Multicolor* printing must be distinguished from full-color printing. Multicolor printing is any use of more than one ink in a job.

color separation   *See* process color.

colporteur   A traveling book agent, usually of a religious group or society, who sells low-priced tracts.

column inch   A measure of space on a type page, one inch deep and as wide as a column.

combination plate   Plate in which both line and halftone techniques are combined.

command   An instruction or control signal in machine language.

commissioned rep   *See* publisher's representative.

common carrier   Government-regulated company that provides telecommunications services to the general public, such as a telephone or telegraph company.

communications format   *See* bibliographic information interchange format.

compatibility   The ability of one computerized system to accept and handle data from another system. The ability of one set of equipment and programs to be included in a system with other equipment and programs.

compose   To set type to be printed. *Compositor,* a person who sets type; *composition,* the process of setting type or the type set; *composing room,* room where type is set; *composing stick,* a metal tool in which metal type is set.

computer   A device that accepts data, applies programmed sets of processing procedures to it, and produces the results in some usable form. All computers consist, in one form or another, of input and output facilities, arithmetic and logical processing, memory storage, and a control section.

computer graphics   Computer-generated images other than single character symbols, including charts, diagrams, drawings, and other pictorial representations.

computer-output mircrofilm   Microfilm exposed in a special high-speed character generator, called a COM unit, driven directly from computer-generated codes.

computer word   *See* word.

concordance   An alphabetical index of words in a work, or works, of a single author, showing the location in the text where each word may be found.

concurrent processing   Ability of a computer to work on more than one program or task at the same time. Also called *multiprocessing.*

condensed   A narrower and more compact version of a type design.

configuration   A group of machines interconnected and programmed to work as a single integrated system.

conjugate   A leaf comprising either half of a four-page sheet. For example: in a 16-page signature pages 1-2 (leaf 1) would be the conjugate of pages 15-16 (leaf 8) and vice versa.

consignment   *See* on consignment.

console   A control station in a computer system providing various manual controls that may be used to alter the system's operation manually.

contacting   In photography, the process of exposing one piece of photographic material from an image on another piece by placing them physically in tight contact with each other and shining light through the image. Contacting provides duplicate images in a size ratio of one to one only.

contemporary binding   Binding executed in the period of publication of the book.

continuation   A publication issued as part of a series, or as a supplement to an earlier work.

continuation order   *See* standing order.

continuous revision   The practice of revising multivolume reference works, especially encyclopedias, by updating particular articles or sections with each printing rather than by completely revising the entire contents at the time of each new edition.

continuous tape   Synonym for raw tape or idiot tape (*q.v.*).

continuous tone   Photographic image in which density of the gray and black areas varies continuously between the lightest and darkest shades or tone values, as opposed to a line image, in which only two densities—lightest and darkest—are present. The halftone process used to reproduce continuous tone images in printing actually converts the continuous tone areas to line images, which create an optical illusion of continuous tones. *See also* halftone.

control character   A character that initiates a particular action within a computer system.

control unit   Section of a computer that directs all other operations in the system upon instructions received from the program.

conversational mode   Communication between a computer and a terminal in which each entry from the terminal initiates an immediate response from the computer, and vice versa. *See also* interactive mode.

conversion   (1) Changing data from one form to another, such as converting data from one machine language to another, or converting material from magnetic tape storage into phototypeset pages. (2) Changing of a system from one type of equipment or programming to another.

cooperative advertising   In common parlance, coop (pronounced and alternatively spelled co-op) advertising; the practice by which a publisher pays partial or total cost of an advertisement placed by a retailer to promote the publisher's book or books. The advertising, usually requiring a complex contractual arrangement between retailer and publisher, can appear in either the press or the broadcast media. *See also* allowance.

cooperative publishing   *See* vanity publishers.

coordinate digitizing   Method of defining location of elements in a two-dimensional area by use of *x-y* coordinates. Any position on a grid can be defined by two numbers, one for the vertical *x* scale and one for the horizontal *y* scale. Using such data on position, a computer can make up complete typographic arrangements and produce all required instructions for a phototypesetting unit to expose all type in proper position on a page. *See also* grid; grid coordinate system.

copperplate engraving   (1) The process of intaglio engraving on copper for reproduction. (2) The printed image resulting from intaglio printing with such a plate.

copublication   A book resulting from the joint efforts of two or more publishers. The venture may involve companies of more than one nation, although the work may be produced in one language or several in a single country. In either case, there is nearly always a sharing of developmental costs and/or production costs, which otherwise may make publication of a book economically impossible for a single publisher.

copy   (1) A specimen of a given printed piece. (2) Printer's term for manuscript presented for setting in type. (3) Designation for art or illustration material sent to the printer, such as photographs and drawings. (4) A computer operation in which data are taken from memory and transported elsewhere, but the original record of the data is also retained in memory and not erased. *See also* erase.

copy block   Unit of composition that is naturally handled as a cohesive single element, although it may contain a number of type lines and styles. *See also* area composition.

copy edit, copy check   To check a manuscript for house style (*q.v.*) before specifying copy for the printer and to note any necessary corrections in accuracy of fact, spelling, syntax, punctuation, logical construction, possible libel, etc.

copy fitting   Process of adjusting copy to space allotted, before sending to printer. This may be done by changing the space allotment, the length of copy, or the size or arrangement of type.

copy preparation   Act of preparing for the compositor a manuscript that has been copy edited. It includes making the manuscript legible and accurate, indicating style, type, etc. *See also* copy edit.

copyholder   One who reads copy to a proofreader.

copyright   Copyright is literary, dramatic, artistic, and musical property protection as authorized by the U.S. Constitution, "securing for limited Times to Authors ... the exclusive Right to their respective Writings.... " (Article I, Sect. 8). The Copyright Act of 1976 (Public Law 94-553), which came into effect January 1, 1978, is the first major revision of the U.S. copyright law since 1909. Under the 1976 law, a single system of statutory protection exists for all copyrightable works, published or unpublished: copyright protection begins when a created work is set down in tangible form. When a work is published in the United States or elsewhere by authority of the copyright holder, it should contain a notice of copyright consisting of the following three elements: (1) the symbol ©, or the word *copyright*, or the abbreviation *Copr.*; (2) the year of first publication of the work; and (3) the name of the copyright holder. The duration of copyright under the new law varies according to circumstances. For works created after January 1, 1978, the term generally lasts for the author's life, plus fifty years. For copyrighted works published before 1978, the first term of copyright covers a twenty-eight year period but is renewable for an additional forty-seven year term.

For further information, the pamphlet *Copyright Basics Circular R1* is available without charge from the Copyright Office, Library of Congress, Washington, DC 20559; phone (202) 287-8700.

copyright, ad interim   Under the U.S. Copyright Law of 1909, a short-term copyright, lasting for a maximum of five years, for the protection of English-language books and periodicals manufactured and first published outside of the United States. The law permitted the importation of 1,500 copies of works for which ad interim registration had been made. The copyright could be extended to a full copyright term of twenty-eight years if an American edition of the work were manufactured and published with copyright notice during the five-year period of ad interim copyright, and if a claim covering the American edition were registered. Under the 1976 Act, the ad interim rules were eliminated prospectively, but they can still have relevance in determining the copyright status of older works.

copyright, British   Under the United Kingdom Copyright Act of 1956, copyright subsists automatically in every original literary, dramatic, musical, or artistic work if, (a) in the case of an unpublished work, the author was a "qualified " person (e.g., a British subject, or a subject of a country to which the provisions of the act have been applied) at the time the work was made, or (b) in the case of a published work, the first publication took place in the United Kingdom or in another country to which the act has been extended or applied, or the author was a "qualified" person at the time the work was first published. The term of copyright extends for life and fifty years.

copyright, common law   Under the 1909 copyright law, the unpublished works of authors, alien or domestic, if not voluntarily registered in the Copyright Office, were protected under the common law of the various states. This protection was unlimited and free from formalities as long as the work remained unpublished.

Under the Copyright Act of 1976 (Sections 102; 301) a single system of federal statuatory protection was established for all works, published or unpublished, registered or unregistered, that are "fixed in a tangible medium of expression." State common law copyright protection now covers only the narrow area of works of authorship not so fixed.

copyright, international   *See* Berne Convention; Universal Copyright Convention.

Copyright Clearance Center (CCC)   A nonprofit organization established in 1977 in response to the 1976 copyright law that requires that permission of the copyright owner be obtained by anyone doing systematic photocopying or photocopying not permitted under the fair use provision of the law. The Copyright Clearance Center acts as a centralized agency through which permission may be granted to use copyrighted materials and through which fees may be collected. Membership is composed of both the users of photocopied materials (libraries, universities, etc.) and copyright owners (publishers, authors, etc.).

copyright duration   *See* copyright.

copyright fees   *See* copyright registration.

copyright notice   *See* copyright.

copyright registration   As provided by the U.S. copyright statute, a procedure for recording claims to copyright. In order to apply for copyright registration, an applicant must file a completed form and send the required fee, usually $10, together with generally two copies of the work to the Copyright Office. Forms are available from the Copyright Office, Library of Congress, Washington, DC 20559.

core storage   The memory area within a central processing unit (CPU) in a computer system, as opposed to other storage areas on remote devices. So named because CPU memory once was built primarily of tiny doughnut-shaped iron rings that could be magnetized or demagnetized to record presence or absence of data. Today, such newer forms of memory devices as integrated circuits are replacing iron cores in new model computers.

corporate entry   A bibliographic entry in a catalog or index with the name of an organization rather than an individual used as the main heading.

corrigenda   *See* errata.

Coster of Haarlem   *See* movable type.

cottage style   A seventeenth-century style of ornamentation developed by Samuel Mearne, binder to King Charles II. In popular use on Bibles and prayer books. So called because the four corners and lines of parallel-line rectangles used to decorate panels break outward, resembling the gables of cottages.

counter prepack   A display unit, also called a *counter display*, usually constructed of cardboard, large enough to hold a limited quantity of books, but small enough to be placed on a retailer's counter, frequently near the cash register to promote impulse buying. *See also* floor display.

courseware Computer software developed for educational use in the classroom. This instructional material may be designed for use in conjunction with a traditional textbook, or it may be capable of existing alone. It is usually interactive (*q.v.*).

cover price The retail price of a book suggested by its publisher and printed on the dust jacket or cover.

covers bound in The original covers included within a later binding. Occasionally the covers are preserved when the volume is rebound by mounting them as flyleaves or using them as endpapers.

cradle books *See* incunabula.

crash Synonym for super, applied in the lining process. *See also* lining.

creasing Compressing the fibers of paper along a line where a fold is to be made. Done on either a regular printing press, a special cutting and creasing press, or a folding machine by impressing a raised rule or disk against the paper. Creasing not only locates and facilitates the fold but also increases the number of times the paper can be flexed at the crease before breaking. *See also* scoring.

credit line A statement or brief identification providing the name of a photographer, artist, author, agency, or publication responsible for a picture, photograph, article, or quotation that has been reproduced.

critical bibliography *See* analytical bibliography.

crop To trim off. A photograph is cropped when part of the top, bottom, or sides is omitted from its reproduction in order to improve its composition or bring it into proper proportions for the space it is to occupy. A book is said to be *cropped* when the margins have been cut so close that the printing or illustrations have been damaged.

cross-reference In an index or catalog, reference or direction from one specific heading to another.

cross-reference, general Notation under one catalog heading as to where the user may expect to find certain types of entries. For example, a note under the heading "dogs" might read "Here are entered general works on dogs; for information on a particular breed, see name of breed."

crown octavo, crown quarto   *See* book sizes.

crushed levant   Levant morocco, the surface of which has been crushed down and polished. *See also* morocco.

cum licentia   Latin, "with permission." A notice in a book signifying that it is published by leave of the authorities, either secular or ecclesiastical. *See also* cum privilegio; imprimatur; nihil obstat.

cum privilegio   Latin, "with permission." Not in practical use now, but may be found in old books, signifying approval of authority, either secular or ecclesiastical. *See also* cum licentia; imprimatur; nihil obstat.

cumulative index   An index in periodical form, which combines successively the entries of earlier issues or volumes into a single index.

cuneiform writing   Wedge-shaped characters, impressed in clay and baked, used by the ancient Assyrians and Babylonians. Thought to have originated 6,000 years ago, remaining in use until the third century B.C.

curiosa   Term used in classifying books of curious and unusual subject matter. Sometimes used euphemistically as a classification for *erotica* (*q.v.*). *See also* facetiae; pornography.

cursive   (1) Running, flowing, from the Latin meaning coursing. Specifically applied to early writing and lettering on manuscripts. The cursive letters have the strokes joined and letters rounded. (2) American term for certain faces similar to, but more decorative than, italic.

cursor   A spot of light on the face of a video display screen telling the operator where the computer will perform its next operations. The operator can move the cursor to any desired spot on the screen by pressing control keys. An alternative to the cursor is the use of a light pen (*q.v.*).

custom binding   *See* binding.

custom book   A book assembled from a large variety of available materials specifically to the customer's order. Used to some extent now in higher education by a teacher who may choose a set of text materials and then have it manufactured as a textbook in very small quantities for his classes. Under one scheme, the teacher may choose any existing materials so long as permissions to reprint can be obtained by the publisher. In another scheme, the publisher offers a predetermined set of materials from which the teacher may choose.

cut (1) Term sometimes used to mean any printed illustration. (2) Also the engraving or plate from which (in letterpress) an illustration is printed.

cut dummy Complete proofs of the illustrations of a book, arranged in proper sequence and containing the figure and galley numbers.

cut edges One or more edges of a book trimmed by machinery.

cut flush To trim the cover of a book even with its edges. Paperback books are normally flush cut, i.e., cover and pages are the same size after trimming, as distinct from hardcover books, in which the cover overlaps.

cut-in An illustration or other display element set into a type column so that there is type matter on two or more sides.

cycle Time interval required by a computerized system to complete a given set of events and return to a state at which it is ready to start another set of operations.

cylinder press *See* flat-bed cylinder press.

d.s. (*pl.* **ds. s.**) Document signed. A document printed or in the hand of a person other than the signer.

d.w. Dust wrapper. *See* dust jacket.

dagger (†) *See* reference marks.

dandy roll In papermaking, a cylinder of wire gauze that presses upon the drained but still moist pulp just before it starts through the rollers. The weaving, or arrangement, of the wire of the dandy roll leaves its impression on the paper and determines whether it is to be wove paper (with the impression of fine even guaze) or laid paper (with the impression of parallel lines).

When designs or monograms are incorporated into the fine wire of the roll, watermarks are produced.

Presently, plain dandy rolls are used extensively to level the surface or assist in formation; i.e., distributing the solid components of the sheet uniformly. *See also* formation.

data Alphabetic, numeric, and other characters that are processed by a computer.

data bank   *See* data base.

data base   Also called data bank, an accessible collection of information stored within the memory of a computer and sorted there into an organized arrangement of facts that can be quickly manipulated and retrieved. More generally, any compilation of data such as a reference book can be considered a data base, in this case, one that is not automated. *See also* electronic publishing.

data base publishing   The method of capturing facts in a data base to generate publications, or any other product, whether or not in traditional print, that can disseminate the computerized data. *See also* electronic publishing.

data collection   Process of collecting and transmitting data from a number of outlying remote positions to a central point.

data processing   Manipulation of data according to prespecified rules to achieve predetermined results.

data reduction   Transforming large volumes of raw data, via processing, into more useful condensations or simplifications.

data transmission   Sending of coded data over communications links such as telephone lines at high speeds. *See also* broadband.

dating   An extension of the period of credit allowed by a supplier (e.g., a publisher) to a retailer.

Daye, Stephen (1594-1668)   Originally a locksmith by trade. In 1639 he took charge of the first printing press in the English colonies in America at Cambridge, Mass. The press had been obtained for the colony by Rev. Jose Glover, who died in 1638 on his voyage to America from England with the press. The first publication of the press, in January 1639, was a broadside, *The Oath of a Free-Man*, of which no copy is known; the second was *An Almanack, Calculated for New England*, by William Pierce, also in 1639. No copy of this is known. In 1640, Daye produced *The Whole Booke of Psalmes*, commonly known as the *Bay Psalm Book* (*q.v.*), the earliest work printed in the United States known to be extant.

de luxe   A French term meaning, literally, of elegance. Applied to editions finely printed on superior paper—usually limited in number.

deacidification   The reduction or removal of acidity in a material, such as paper, using a mild alkali to neutralize the acid. *See also* paper permanence.

dead matter Previously set type no longer needed for printing. Cf. live matter.

debugging Process of discovering and eliminating errors in computer programs, or detection and correction of malfunctions in equipment. *See also* bug.

decimal classification A classification system for books in a library that uses a notation based on decimal numbers. *See also* Dewey decimal classification.

decision In a computer, the process of comparing two sets of data and choosing among alternative operations to perform based on the results of the comparison.

deck A collection of punched cards containing a set of coded data. *See* storage.

deckle edge The rough edge on a sheet of paper where the pulp flowed under the frame while still liquid. The frame, which forms the border of a hand mold, is called the *deckle*; also the rubber strip that confines the flowing pulp on the screen of a paper machine.

These rough edges are often left untrimmed in the making of books from handmade paper. In machine-made paper, deckle is not obtainable on four sides, but a deckle effect can be imitated.

decoding Interpreting the coded data and instructions in a computer system in order to act upon them. A computer will so interpret instruction codes to trigger subsequent processing routines, for example.

dedication An inscription to honor or compliment someone, usually a patron, relative, or friend. The dedication is usually on the first leaf following the title page of a book. *See also* front matter.

dedication copy A copy of a book inscribed and dated on or near publication date by the author and presented to the person to whom the book is dedicated. Among collectors, the dedication copy ranks as one of the most desirable of the presentation copies of a book.

definitive edition An edition said to be the most authoritative version of a work.

de Graff, Robert Fair (1895-1981)   Publisher who founded the modern American paperback industry. After successfully developing reprint lines for Doubleday (1922-1936) and the Blue Ribbon Books reprints, he founded Pocket Books, Inc., in 1938, believing that pocket-sized, brightly papercovered, twenty-five-cent reprints of good fiction and occasional nonfiction would have wide appeal. Keys to successful operation were mass production printing on rotary presses, combined with distribution through the magazine wholesale system. Simon & Schuster, early backers of the enterprise, bought controlling interest in Pocket Books in 1966.

delete, dele   To remove; omit. A mark used in correcting proof, from the Greek letter delta (δ), drawn in the margin to show that certain characters or words indicated in the line alongside are to be omitted. *See also* Proofreaders' Marks at the end of this book.

delphi method   A forecasting technique based on the judgment of a group of experts whose opinions are solicited through a series of questionnaires that, upon return, are tabulated and analyzed and the results fed back to the experts for further evaluation. The process is repeated a number of times until agreement is reached among the group.

demy octavo, demy quarto   *See* book sizes.

densitometer   Widely used quality control instrument that measures density (opacity) of photographic and printed images. Applicable to the evaluation of most original subjects, photographic intermediates in black-on-white, paper, printing inks, and final printed images of most kinds including process color jobs.

density   (1) In a computer system, the amount of data that can be stored in a given area of memory. (2) In photography, the degree of opacity in a piece of photosensitive material. (3) In typography, the number of type characters fitted into a given area.

dentelle   French word for lace. Used to describe lace-like patterns the binder applies by tool or wheel to the outer or inner borders of a binding.

deposit copies   Free copies of newly published books or other materials sent to the Copyright Office, persuant to U.S. copyright law (Section 407), for the benefit of the Library of Congress.

Derôme   French family in the eighteenth century that added several illustrious names to the art of binding of that period. The most famous was Nicolas Derôme, known as Derôme le jeune (1731-1788).

In hand binding, a style with ornaments of a leafy character, with a rather solid face, though lightly shaded by the graver. It is best exemplified in borders.

descender   That part of a lowercase letter that descends below the small letters such as a, e, o, n, m, etc., as in g, j, p, q, y. *See also* ascender.

descriptive bibliography   (1) The close physical study and description of books; of how a book is put together; of the type, paper, and illustrations that are used; of its physical appearance after it has been printed and bound; of the details of its publishing history. Descriptive bibliography is a division of analytical bibliography (*q.v.*). (2) A book that is the result of such study, that gives full physical description of the books it lists, and distinguishes one printing or edition from another.

desiderata   A list of books wanted.

design   (1) To plan a book's entire graphic format. (2) The specifications for the graphic format of a book.

device   *See* printer's mark; publisher's mark.

De Vinne, Theodore L. (1828-1914)   New York printer of distinguished output. Authority on printing history and practice, printer of the *Century Magazine,* a founder of the Grolier Club, and the author of several books on printing and typography, including *The Invention of Printing* (1876).

Dewey, Melvil (1851-1931)   Originator of the decimal system of classification that bears his name. Founder of the first school for training librarians; co-founder, with Frederick Leypoldt and R. R. Bowker, of the *Library Journal,* and its first editor; one of the founders of the American Library Association, and for many years its secretary and then president. Dewey was an advocate of spelling reform, and used his system in his own writings.

Dewey decimal classification   A system, often referred to as D.C., of dividing knowledge into ten main categories and of classifying books accordingly on a decimal basis, devised by Melvil Dewey in 1876. The main classifications, preceding the decimal point, are:

000 **General Works**	400 **Language**	700 **The Arts**
100 **Philosophy**	500 **Pure Science**	800 **Literature**
200 **Religion**	600 **Technology**	900 **History**
300 **Social Sciences**		

The system is used in many libraries throughout the world as a means of grouping books upon the shelves. *See also* Library of Congress classification.

diaper   In bookbinding, a small diamond-shaped pattern or ornament repeated in a regular all-over design.

diazo   A relatively slow-reacting light-sensitive process in which materials containing azo dyes are exposed to strong blue and ultraviolet light through photographic negatives or positives to form images. Diazo materials are developed by ammonia vapor or alkaline solution and are widely used for photocomposition and lithographic stripping proofs.

Dibdin, Thomas Frognall (1776-1847)   English bibliographer; ordained a clergyman in 1804. The first of his bibliographical works was *Introduction to the Knowledge of Editions of the Classics* (1802), which brought him under the notice of the third Earl Spencer, who opened to him the rich library at Althorp, described by Dibdin in *Bibliotheca Spenceriana* (4 vols., 1814-1815), and three additional volumes issued in 1822-1823. Among the most popular of his discursive works about books were *The Bibliomania, or Book-Madness* (1809); *The Bibliographical Decameron* (3 vols., 1817); and *A Bibliographical, Antiquarian ... Tour in France & Germany* (3 vols., 1821).

Dibdin was the originator and vice-president (Lord Spencer being the president) of the Roxburghe Club, founded in 1812. This was the first of numerous book clubs which have done much service to literature, and to this day it is still the most prestigious.

diced calf or morocco   Binding with cross-lined tooling that creates a pattern resembling dice or small squares.

dictionary (in computerized typesetting)   *See* exception dictionary.

dictionary catalog   A catalog in which all entries (e.g., subject, title, author) are arranged in a single alphabetical sequence (as opposed to a classified catalog).

Didot A family name notable in French printing and publishing. François Didot (1689-1757) founded the firm of Didot, in Paris, in 1713, and many of his descendants were associated with type-founding, printing, or publishing. His grandson, Firmin Didot (1764-1836), continued the firm, which is still in existence today. Firmin Didot was a printer, engraver, and typefounder, whose use of stereotyping revolutionized the making of cheap editions.

die *See* binder's dies.

die-cutting Cutting of odd-shaped areas out of a sheet of paper through use of a specially shaped die. Done on either a regular printing press or a special cutting and creasing press by impressing a raised die into the paper.

digital computer A computer that handles data in discrete, countable units, as opposed to an analog computer, which measures differentials continuously. *See also* analog computer.

digital plotter A computer output device used to draw graphic images on paper under the control of digital signals.

digitizer A device that converts data in non-machine-readable form into discrete, countable digits or bits, such as a unit that breaks up a continuous-tone photograph or a line drawing of a character into an array of electronic bits for storage in a computer system. The array of bits is later used to reconstruct a reproduction of the original image via computer processing.

dime novel A term covering a type of paper-covered fiction, usually priced at ten cents a copy, popular during the latter half of the nineteenth century.

direct-impression A form of composition created by striking the image onto the carrier surface through physical impact of a raised type character against an inked ribbon, which in turn is pressed against a substrate such as paper. Typewriter composition and computer line-printer printouts are the most common forms of direct-impression composition. *See also* cold type.

direct mail Advertising material mailed to prospective purchasers to solicit orders.

discount A percentage deducted from the list (retail) price of a book, thereby determining the cost of the book to the dealer purchasing it from the publisher or wholesaler. Thus, a $10 book sold to a dealer at 40 percent discount costs $6 and from this 40 percent difference, the store's operating costs and profit must be derived. *Trade discounts* (also called *long discounts*), which are established for selling general books to retailers, scale from 30 to 45 percent and upward (depending on the individual publisher and quantities purchased). A trade discount schedule is printed by a publisher to announce the variations in discounts dictated by number of books ordered. Legally, a publisher must offer the same trade discount schedule to all booksellers.

Short discounts are lower discounts, offered on the relatively few retail sales of books ordinarily sold directly to professional persons or institutions. *Library discounts* are special discounts offered to library purchasers. *Professional,* or *courtesy discounts* are those offered to individuals. *Cash discounts* (e.g., 2 percent off the total of a bill if it is paid in thirty days or less) are those offered for prompt payment of an invoice. *See also* markup; net pricing.

discretionary hyphen   A special hyphenation code placed in a word that the computer can use if it needs to break the word at that point to end a line, but which it also can ignore and discard from the final typeset product if the word does not fall at the end of a line.

disk   (1) In photographic typesetting, a circular carrier containing master character images that are used to project characters onto photographic materials. A number of phototypesetting machines use the disk principle. (2) In computers, the predominent form of mass memory currently in use. *See also* disk pack; floppy disk; hard disk.

disk pack   In a computer system, a grouping of magnetic disks, similar in appearance to phonograph records, which are used to store data. Disk packs offer very large storage capacities and random access to the stored data. *See also* magnetic storage; random access storage.

display tube   Synonym for video display tube.

display type   Larger or heavier typefaces or sizes for headings, subheads, blurbs, etc., as distinguished from text type or body type.

divided catalog   A library catalog that has been divided into two alphabetical sequences: main entries, added entries, and title entries in one sequence and subject and form entries in the other.

dividend   *See* book club.

divinity circuit   Flexible binding, usually of soft leather, as seal or levant, with extended edges that bend over the body of the book. Used principally for Bibles and prayer books and sometimes on small secular books for pocket use. Known also as *circuit edges.* Originally in circuit edges the four corners of the overlapping leather were slit. The English name for this binding is *yapp,* named after the London bookseller William Yapp, who invented it about 1860.

divisional title   A page preceding a section or division of a book, bearing the name or number of the section or division. The verso of the page is usually blank. Also called *part title.*

documentation   (1) The systematic collection, classification, recording, storage, and dissemination of specialized information, generally of a technical or scientific nature. (2) Written description of a computerized system's operating programs and facilities. Full and complete documentation is very important to a system's maintenance, and often is the only means of finding out how the system operates when it becomes desirable to do so after its installation.

Dolphin, The   A periodical published irregularly between 1933 and 1941 by the Limited Editions Club of New York. Considered the American successor to the English *Fleuron,* it was planned "for all people who find pleasure in fine books." Number I appeared in 1933, number II in 1935, and number III ("A History of the Printed Book," ed. by Lawrence C. Wroth) in 1938. Number IV appeared in three parts: Fall 1940, Winter 1940-1941, and Spring 1941.

dos-a-dos-binding   Two books bound back to back so that the back cover of one serves as the back cover of the other, with the fore-edges of one next to the spine of the other.

double elephant folio   *See* book sizes.

double numeration   A system of enumeration often used in technical books and textbooks. The number of the chapter is the key number, and illustrations, charts, etc., are numbered on that basis; e.g., Fig. 14.2 indicates the second figure in the fourteenth chapter.

Doubleday, Nelson   Developer of the Doubleday organization as a major, multifaceted enterprise, unprecedented in the book business because of its size and variety. Son of the founder, Frank Nelson Doubleday, Nelson started his own firm in 1910 under the senior firm's wing and developed imaginative techniques for mail-order selling; founded the reprint subsidiary, Garden City Publishing Co., in 1925; took over the Literary Guild and launched numerous other book clubs, making use of the parent firm's Country Life Press; expanded the Doubleday Book Shops; and encouraged an exemplary level of management expertise.

doublure   From the French "doubler," to line. Ornamental lining of a book cover made with tooled leather, silk, or other material.

Doves Press   A private press founded in 1900 at Hammersmith, London, by Thomas James Cobden-Sanderson (1840-1922), and Emery Walker (1851-1933), expert typographer, guide, and inspiration of William Morris's Kelmscott Press. The idea of the Doves Press originated from Cobden-Sanderson, who was not then a printer, but who was a master bookbinder of renown and owner of the Doves Bindery. The two men formed a loose partnership, the money for the press being provided by Mrs. Cobden-Sanderson. Walker designed a special type for the Doves Press, based upon the type used by Nicolas Jenson in his edition of Pliny's *Historia Naturalis* printed at Venice in 1476. Walker's Doves type was the only font used by the Doves Press in the forty-one works issued during its existence, 1900-1916. With the exception of the final *Catalogue Raisonne ... No. III* (1916), none of the works had illustrations, but some, notably *Paradise Lost* (1902) and *The English Bible* (5 vols., 1903-1905), had striking initial letters and opening lines on the first pages printed in red from hand-designed letters drawn by the calligrapher Edward Johnston and carved on wood blocks. *The English Bible* was the most ambitious production of the Doves Press and the only work issued there in folio. Some of the other Doves books were decorated with initial letters and flourishes, in colors, by Edward Johnston, Graily Hewitt, and Ethel Offer.

In 1908 Cobden-Sanderson dissolved his partnership with Walker, and a dispute arose about the Doves type. This dispute was settled, apparently, when both men signed an agreement allowing Cobden-Sanderson the sole use of the type during his lifetime, and that upon the death of either partner the type should revert to the survivor. Despite the agreement, Cobden-Sanderson (who now operated the press alone) decided that no one but himself should ever print with the Doves type. In March 1913 he threw the matrices into the Thames River, and in the autumn of 1916 he threw the type itself into the Thames. It was not until after Cobden-Sanderson's death in 1922 that Walker obtained any form of reparation for the loss of his property. His suit against Cobden-Sanderson's estate was settled privately.

The Dramatists Guild   *See* Authors League of America, The.

dramatization rights   *See* rights.

drop folio   A page number printed at the bottom of a page.

drop initials   Initial letters aligned with the top of the letters on the first text line that follows, but extending below into space provided by indention of the following line or lines.

drop ship   To ship an order to one address (e.g., the customer or a branch store) while billing it to another (e.g., a retailer or the main office).

drum storage   A rotating cylinder with a magnetic surface on which electrical signals can be recorded. *See also* magnetic storage; random access storage.

dry offset   Indirect relief printing; a form of letterpress using shallow-etched plates, rotary presses, and indirect image transfer from the plate by means of a rubber blanket to the paper. The method resembles lithographic offset printing but is known as dry because the plates, being in relief, do not require moistening. Dry offset is used with sheet-fed and roll-fed presses, mainly for various specialties.

dry point   A method of engraving on metal plates with a sharp needle, producing fine lines without acid. *See also* etchings; intaglio printing.

dual pricing   Illegally offering one or more customers in a given category, for example, booksellers, a preferred price on something that should be sold to all buyers in that category at a standard rate. *See also* discount.

dull-coated   A coated paper made without a glossy surface, but smooth enough to take fine halftones. *See also* book paper.

dummy   (1) Unprinted paper, folded, trimmed or untrimmed, bound or unbound, to show size, bulk, and general appearance of a projected publication. Salesmen's dummies usually have the first sixteen or thirty-two pages printed and sometimes repeated, in order to present the appearance of a completely printed book. (2) Galley proofs trimmed and pasted up into layouts of columns and pages for the printer's guidance in making up the pages in type. To make such a dummy is *to dummy up.*

dump   To transfer in bulk the contents of a computer memory to another location, either another section of memory or to some form of output.

dump bin   *See* floor display.

duodecimo (12mo)   *See* book sizes.

duotone   Process for reproducing an illustration in two colors from plates made from one-color original copy.

durable paper   *See* paper permanence.

dust jacket   The paper (or, in some cases, acetate) cover folded over a bound book, not so much to protect the book from dust as to provide printed display and often illustrative material (which sometimes includes biographical information about the author and short critical notices about the book) to enhance the visibility and sale of the book. Hence, the term *dust* used with *jacket* is essentially an archaism, but it has been revived in common usage in the mid-twentieth century. *See also* jacket band.

dust wrapper   *See* dust jacket.

Dwiggins, W. W.   (1880-1956)   Distinguished American calligrapher, designer of books, type, and decorations, whose book jackets, endpapers, hand-drawn lettering for title pages, and original bindings did much to revive interest in good trade book design. Among the types he designed are the Electra and the Caledonia.

EBCDIC   Extended Binary Coded Decimal Interchange Code, a widely used code system for transferring data from one computer system to another.

EDP   Electronic data processing (*q.v.*).

elhi   Abbreviation for textbooks published for the elementary school and high school markets.

e.o.m. Abbreviation for end-of-month.

EX (1) Invoice symbol meaning see explanation herewith. (2) Also an abbreviation for full exchange on returns.

earn-out *See* author's earn-out.

easy book Library term for a children's book for the youngest readers. Primarily illustrative rather than text.

editing (1) Modification of existing text including such functions as adding, deleting, moving, or changing material. (2) In computer terminology, editing operations also are called *file maintenance* and *updating*. *See also* editing terminal; optical character recognition.

editing terminal A computer input/output device that permits the operator to manipulate text within the system by performing basic editing functions. Some terminals also provide formatting functions as well. Terminals are of two general types: hard copy and video display. Both kinds have a standard typewriter keyboard with additional special function and code keys ranged around the standard layout. The hard-copy terminal types out material in the computer, as well as instructions given it and the finished results of editing changes, on a typewriter-style unit. The video display terminal shows the text on a television-like cathode-ray tube screen, and changes made in the text are shown instantly on the video screen. *See also* editing; formatting; hard copy; optical character recognition; video display terminal.

editio princeps Latin for first edition. (1) The first printed edition of a work that existed in manuscript before printing was invented. (2) Sometimes extended to include the first edition of any work newly printed, but for this last meaning the term *first edition* is preferred.

edition (1) One of the differing forms in which a literary work or collection of works is published, e.g., as applied to text, original, revised, enlarged, corrected, etc., either by the author or by a subsequent editor; as applied to format: de luxe, library, paperbound, large-paper, illustrated, etc. (2) All copies of a book printed at any time from a single setting of type. Gaskell, *A New Introduction to Bibliography*, 1972, says, in referring to modern books, "An *edition*, first of all, is all the copies of a book printed at any time (or times) from substantially the same setting of type, and includes all the various impressions, issues, and states which may have been derived from that setting. As to the meaning of 'substantially the same setting of type,' there are bound to be ambiguous cases, but we may take it as a simple rule of thumb that there is a new edition when more than half the type has been reset, but that if less than half the type has been reset we are probably dealing with another impression, issue, or state." *See also* impression; issue; new edition; state.

edition binding   *See* binding.

editor   (1) A person who selects and organizes material to be published. (2) One who prepares for publication a work or collection of works by another or others. The editorial labor may be the revision or elucidation of the text and the addition of introductions, notes, and other critical matter; or it may be limited to the preparation of the matter for the printer and the checking of fact. On the other hand, it may involve seeking out an author to realize an editorial idea; encouraging an author to develop an idea or manuscript he or she has submitted and thereafter offering continuous constructive criticism to help turn it into a publishable book; bargaining with authors' agents; arriving at contract terms; organizing a group of other editors to carry out a complex editorial project; tailoring an editorial plan to meet market and subsidiary possibilities. Editorial departments in major houses are often organized according to these and other functions to be filled. (3) An administrator of an editorial department.

editorial copies   Copies of a book intended for office use or for uses other than distribution and sale. *See also* review copies.

educational materials   *See* book.

Edwards of Halifax   *See* fore-edge painting.

eggshell   A finish on uncoated paper presenting a nonglossy, soft, smooth effect. Most antique paper has an eggshell finish.

electronic character matrix   In all-electronic phototypesetters, the layout of electronic data that describes the image of type characters digitally stored in memory. The data are used to construct characters by drawing lines of light of varying length and spacing on the photosensitive medium.

electronic data processing   Data processing done with electronic systems. *See also* data processing.

electronic publishing   A broad term taking into account the varied forms of publishing or means of disseminating information that have arisen with new technologies. Examples of electronic publishing range from any manner of computerized publishing functions to data base publishing and cable television, videotex and teletext to videodisc and videocassette (*qq.v.*).

electrostatics   The science of static electricity, principles of which are used in xerography and other forms of electrostatic printing. In such printing systems, electrical charges are placed on the sheet to be printed in the image areas, and ink particles are attracted to the image areas by these charges. Then the ink is fused permanently in position. Electrostatics are widely used in photocopying systems and computer printout devices.

electrotype plates, electros   Duplicate plates for letterpress, capable of combining type and pictures in highest quality, suitable for very long production runs. Can be made flat or curved to be used on any kind of letterpress equipment. The making of electros is a complex process requiring, for example, molding of the material, electro-deposition of copper in the mold, casting of metal in the copper shell, finishing, and plating.

Electros were used extensively in book manufacturing, particularly for long runs, but the great advances in web-offset lithography have virtually eliminated their use in the book industry.

elephant folio   *See* book sizes.

Eliot, John (1604-1690)   Colonial clergyman, known as the "Apostle to the Indians." He migrated to Massachusetts in 1631 and settled first in Boston. In the fall of 1632 he became "teacher" to the church at Roxbury, and he served there in that post until his death. From his first sight of the Indians he was inspired with the idea of converting them. He studied the Indian language, and in 1654 he published his *Primer of the Massachusetts Indian Language* (a vanished Cambridge imprint), and in 1664 he completed his *Indian Grammer Begun*. In addition to his various translations of religious works into the Indian language, his literary activities included tracts and reports, and he was, with Richard Mather, one of the editors of the *Bay Psalm Book* (1640).

Eliot's translation of the Bible into the Massachusetts dialect of the Algonquian Indian language was printed at Cambridge, Mass., by Samuel Green and Marmaduke Johnson; the New Testament appeared in 1661 and the Old Testament in 1663. John

Eliot's Bible in the Indian language has the distinction of being the first printing of the Scriptures in the New World.

elite   Elite type is the smaller of the two common styles of typewriter type, having twelve characters per inch as against ten for the larger pica size.

Elzevir   A family of Dutch printers and booksellers. The business was founded in Leyden, in 1583, by Louis Elzevir (1542-1617), and five of his seven sons followed the profession. The firm was best known for its Latin reprints of the classics in pocket-sized editions. Other Elzevirs continued the business until 1791, when the firm closed after having issued over 2,000 works.

em   In America, a unit for measuring area in composition. The size of the em is determined by the particular type font and size being used. The em of a particular font is as wide as the capital letter M and as deep as the point size. The em is often defined to be the square of the type size or body—that is, 10 points wide and 10 points deep for a 10 point type font. While for many faces this is true because the capital M is designed to fit that space, for many other faces the capital Ms are wider or narrower than this, and the ems in those fonts vary accordingly.

It is common to specify paragraph indentations as 1-em, or 2-em, etc. *See also* en.

embossed   Printed or stamped with dies of letters or a design, on paper, cloth, leather, etc., so that the surface of the sheet of material is left with a bas-relief impression of the image.

embroidered binding   Binding ornamented with needlework design in thread or metal.

en   In type measurement, one-half the width of an em (*q.v.*).

enamel   A form of coated paper (*q.v.*).

encode   To translate data into a code, such as the keyboarding of alphanumeric characters and operating instructions into machine-language codes.

end leaves   Synonymous with endpapers (*q.v.*).

end sheets   Synonymous with endpapers (*q.v.*).

endpapers   Strong paper used to fasten the case to the book block during the finding process. The endpapers, white or colored, printed or unprinted, are placed at the beginning and end of a book. One-half is pasted to the inside of the covers, and the fold is usually bound to the outside pages of the first and last signatures. In manufacturing, endpapers are affixed after signatures have been folded. Generally, the choice of endpapers depends on the book's characteristics; i.e., a reference work needs a stock with good folding or flexing strength. Also called *lining papers, end sheets, end leaves,* or *paste-downs.*

English finish   A calendered paper, smooth but without gloss. *See also* book paper; calendering.

engravers' proofs   *See* proofs.

engraving   (1) a halftone or line cut. (2) The printed reproduction from such a cut. (3) The act of making an engraving. (4) An intaglio plate. *See* copperplate engraving.

Properly speaking, an engraving is a plate prepared by incising the design into the surface with a graver or burin. Copper and steel engravings are true engravings. Photoengravings are actually produced by chemical etching, not by engraving.

In the earliest years of printing, illustrations for books were cut in wood. Before the end of the fifteenth century, copper engraved plates came into use and had by the last decade of the sixteenth century essentially changed bookmaking all over Europe. They eventually replaced the woodcut, except for headpieces, tail-pieces, and decorative initials. Copper was followed by steel in the mid-nineteenth century as the popular medium, then by a revival of wood, then by the photographic processes.

Enschedé   Foundry and press established in Haarlem, the Netherlands, in 1703, and still active under the name of Johannes Enschedé en Zonen. The firm has the original matrices from its earliest days and continues to create new types, such as Lutetia, one of the most widely praised of modern fonts, designed by J. Van Krimpen.

enumerative bibliography   The listing of books that bear some relationship to one another, arranged by a system or plan, for example, by author, by subject, or by period. The purpose of enumerative bibliography is to record books rather than to describe them, and therefore entries tend to be brief, usually including only author, title, date and place of publication, and sometimes annotations, rather than providing detailed physical descriptions of the books included. The "Selected Reading List" at the end of this book is an example of enumerative bibliography. Also known as *systematic bibliography*. Cf. analytical bibliography.

ephemera   Material of transitory interest or value; generally pamphlets or clippings.

epigraph   A quotation at the beginning of a book or chapter intended to convey an idea that is developed in the text that follows.

erase   To remove data from memory without leaving a record of it. In a computer, erasing is the equivalent of clearing. In a display device, it is to remove the image from the viewing screen. *See also* clear.

erotica   In cataloguing, amatory books. Technically, erotica are legal; pornographica forbidden; but the distinction is often blurred in the United States. *See also* curiosa; facetiae; pornography.

errata (*sing.* erratum)   Errors discovered in a book after printing. Corrections of these errors are usually printed on a slip or a page and pasted or laid into the volume. In some books errata may be found almost anywhere in the text. Also called *corrigenda*.

error rate   In computer coposition, the ratio of lines with errors in them to total lines, or error words to total words, or error keystrokes to total keystrokes.

escalation clause   A clause in an author's contract with a publisher that entitles the writer to additional or increased payments from the publisher should the book in question achieve certain measures of success. These may include one or more appearances on a bestseller list, a movie sale, or a book club sale. Another escalation clause may enable the author to earn a higher royalty rate as the number of copies sold reach specified plateaus. These clauses are also called *escalators*.

esparto   A coarse wild grass grown in Spain and other Mediterranean countries and used extensively in England for the production of book papers.

Estienne   Name of a distinguished French printing family of the sixteenth century. The firm was founded in 1501 by Henri Estienne, sometimes called Henri I, to distinguish him from his grandson, Henri II (1528-1598). Under the guidance of Simon de Colines (*q.v.*), his successor, and later of his son, Robert Estienne (1503-1559) the second of his three sons, the firm led the French printing renaissance, popularizing roman and italic types and making available inexpensive editions of the classics.

Robert Estienne became printer to Francis I, but later moved to Geneva because of his identification with the Reformation movement. Noted for scholarship as well as for printing, Robert compiled the first modern French-Latin dictionary.

Robert's son, Henri, who succeeded to the business, also edited and printed many editions of the Greek and Latin classics.

The name "Estienne" was Latinized, Stephanus; Anglicized, Stephens—both so listed in some works of reference.

etching　(1) A print from a plate into which the design has been etched (eaten) by acid. (A dry point etching is thus not a true etching.) (2) The process of preparing such a plate.

Evans, Charles (1850-1935)　Librarian and bibliographer, born in Boston in 1850, died in Chicago, 8 February 1935. His fame rests on his monumental historical-bibliographical compilation *American Bibliography, a Chronological Dictionary of All Books, Pamphlets, and Periodical Publications Printed in the United States, from the Genesis of Printing in 1639 down to and including the Year 1820* ... which during his lifetime he completed through the letter M of the year 1799 (Vols. I-XII, printed 1903-1934).

The latter part of the year 1799 and the whole of 1800 were completed by Clifford K. Shipton of the American Antiquarian Society, and his work came out as Volume XIII of Evans, printed in 1955. Volume XIV, an author-title-subject index to Evans, by Roger P. Bristol, was added in 1959. Bristol also compiled an Index of Printers, Publishers, and Booksellers listed in Evans, issued in 1961; and, a preliminary checking edition of a supplement to include titles not found in Evans, issued in 1962.

The period between 1800, when Evans stops, and 1820, when Roorbach starts, is covered by a preliminary checklist "gathered entirely from secondary sources" (admittedly designed as a first step) by Ralph R. Shaw and Richard H. Shoemaker, *American Bibliography; A Preliminary Checklist ... 1801-1819* and addenda volumes. Together 22 volumes, New York, Scarecrow Press, 1958-1966.

Eve　Nicolas and Clovis Eve, both of whom bore the title of binder to the king of France, the first under Henri III and the second under Henri IV and Louis XIII. Clovis was probably son or nephew of Nicolas, and according to an old authority, he invented marbled paper. The name Eve is associated with an elaborate style of hand binding used at the end of the sixteenth and beginning of the seventeenth centuries.

ex-height   *See* x-height.

ex libris   Latin phrase frequently used on bookplates, and coupled with the owner's name, in which case it means "from the library of" that person. Sometimes used as a synonym for the word *bookplate*.

examination copy   A free or on-approval sample of a book given to a prospective buyer (the term suggests an educator) who will, the publisher hopes, study the work, approve of it, and then adopt the book, resulting in multiple orders for institutional use. Also called *inspection copy*.

exception dictionary   In computerized typesetting, a collection of common recurring words that do not hyphenate according to standard rules in the computer's hyphenation program. These exception words are stored in memory with their correct hyphenations, and the computer looks up the proper hyphenations when needed, rather than applying hyphenation program logic.

execute   To perform an instruction or set of instructions on data, both of which were given to the computer prior to the order to execute.

export edition   An edition of a book supplied to a foreign market, in sheets or bound, usually at less than the normal wholesale rate and at a lower rate of royalty.

export representative   An organization handling the promotion and sale of a publisher's books outside the country of origin. The contract usually calls for a commission on sales, and the publisher may share costs of the promotion.

expurgated   An edition of a work from which certain original material considered objectionable has been removed.

external storage   A facility outside of the computer's central processing unit in which additional data can be stored and drawn on as needed. *See also* core storage, disk, disk pack, floppy disk, hard disk.

extra binding   A hand binding of more than usual elegance.

extra-illustrated   Illustrated by extra matter added to and bound into a volume or set. This added material usually consists of engravings, letters, or documents referred to in the text. These are mounted, inlaid, or trimmed to fit the size of the books in which they are inserted.

Sometimes called *grangerized*, because James Granger's *Biographical History of England* was a favorite choice for such treatment.

f&g's   An abbreviation for folded and gathered sheets, which are printed signatures (*q.v.*) loosely collated in sequence to demonstrate the contents of a book. These signatures form the body of the book, assembled but not yet glued, sewn, or bound. F&g's are often used for some prepublication purposes, including advance review by book clubs or reprint houses. F&g's are often employed for illustrated books that are not appropriate for reproduction in advance bound galleys (*q.v.*).

fax   Abbreviation for facsimile.

Fabriano paper   An Italian paper used in fine and special editions, made by an Italian paper mill founded about 1270 and still flourishing.

face   (1) Short for typeface, a design or style of type. (2) The printing surface of a piece of metal or wood type, raised in relief above the body, upon which ink is deposited for transfer to the paper. *See also* typeface.

facetiae   Coarsely witty books; objectionable or indecent works collectively. *See also* curiosa; erotica; pornography.

facsimile edition   An exact reproduction of an original work, often printed by photo-offset lithography.

facsimile transmission   The sending of graphic or pictorial copy over communications links such as telephone lines. A sending unit at one end of the line translates the visual image into a series of electrical signals, which are received at the other end and used to operate a transcription device that reproduces the visual image on paper or photographic material.

faction   A term of recent vintage coined to define a work that liberally adopts people and events from the real world and places them in an imagined context. It is presumably a work of fiction, but the distinction between what is real and what is not is left purposefully vague for the reader. Sometimes called a nonfiction novel. *See also* roman à clef.

fair trade   A legal device no longer in force that was first enacted in the 1930s to prevent price-cutting competition on branded merchandise, such as drugs, appliances, books, etc. The intent was to design fair trade laws permitting manufacturers or publishers, by agreement with retailers, to establish minimum resale prices for specific goods.

fair use   A use of copyrighted material without express authorization by the copyright owner but permitted under law. No specific definition of fair use is given by the law, but the following factors are considered: (1) the purpose and character of the use; (2) the nature of the copyrighted work; (3) the portion used in relation to the copyrighted work as a whole; (4) the effect of the use upon the potential market for or value of the copyrighted work. The application of the fair use doctrine is frequently the subject of litigation.

fantasy   *See* science fiction.

featherweight   A term applied to printing paper that is light in weight, but thick in bulk.

Fell types   Between 1667 and 1672 Dr. John Fell imported from Holland some fine types which he presented to Oxford University. From these were cut fonts that gave a new impulse to English type design. The original fonts are still in use at the Clarendon Press.

festschrift   A collection of essays or biographical, bibliographical, or other contributions by distinguished persons in a profession to honor a colleague, usually on the occasion of an anniversary or other celebration.

field   A group of related characters treated as a unit in computer operations, particularly in setting up storage or file schemes for various purposes.

file maintenance   The activity of keeping a computer file up to date by adding, deleting, moving, or changing data in it. *See also* editing.

fillet   (1) An ornamental line or parallel lines, usually of gold, impressed on the cover of a leather-bound book. (2) The wheeled binder's tool for making the above.

filmsetting Typesetting on film. Sometimes used interchangeably, but incorrectly, with phototypesetting, as phototypesetting also includes material set on light-sensitive paper. *See also* photographic typesetting.

finishing A bookbinder's term for the completion of binding after the book has passed through the forwarding (*q.v.*) operations. In hand binding, finishing includes the polishing of the leather, its ornamentation, and lettering. Finishing is also used (as in *mounting and finishing*) to cover such specialty binding operations as die-cutting, eye-letting, stringing, tin-edging, etc.

firmware Computer program instructions that have been stored permanently or semipermanently in integrated-circuit memory units.

first-choice hyphenation (1) The first choice for hyphenating a word as specified in a dictionary. (2) Computer hyphenation programs often use dictionaries stored in memory to break troublesome words correctly.

first edition (1) The total number of copies first printed from the same type and issued at the same time. (2) The text of a book in its original form as first published. (3) In bibliography, first edition is the same as (1) above with certain refinements pertaining to issue (*q.v.*) and state (*q.v.*).

first printing *See* impression.

first refusal *See* option.

first serial rights The right to reproduce a portion or the entirety of a book in a magazine or periodical in one or more parts before the book's official publication date (*q.v.*). *See also* second serial rights.

firsts First editions.

flag A special code used at the beginning or end of data requiring some type of special treatment, signaling some kind of change in condition.

flat A large sheet of heavy paper or plastic to which offset negatives or positives are taped in the proper printing arrangement, from which an offset printing plate is made.

flat back   A binding on which the back is not rounded. *See also* rounding and backing.

flat-bed cylinder press   Letterpresses having a flat bed containing the type form and a rotating impression cylinder carrying the paper. Such presses are made as single-color, two-color, and perfecting presses that print both sides of the sheet in a single pass.

Flat-bed cylinder presses used to be the workhorses of book printing; they have been superseded by offset lithographic presses. American press builders discontinued making these presses during the 1960s.

flat display   *See* full-cover display.

Fleuron, The   An annual on typography produced in London for seven years (1923-1930) under the editorship of Oliver Simon and Stanley Morison. The distinguished and scholarly character of its contributions had an important effect on the art of printing.

flexible binding   A binding in which the boards are flexible rather than stiff. *See also* limp binding.

floor   In bidding for paperback reprint or other rights to a book or manuscript, a first serious offer, generally a sum of some size that represents the least amount for which rights to the book will be sold, even though the seller will try to better it by interesting other potential buyers in the property. A floor may also be established by a seller as the price under which a book or manuscript will not be sold.

floor display   A sales device used in retail bookstores; also called a *floor dump* or *dump bin*. Frequently it is a self-contained shipping carton holding a quantity of paperbound books that, when assembled, forms an eye-catching and waist-high display unit when placed on the floor. *See also* counter prepack.

floppy disk   Magnetic memory storage disk that is portable and can be easily inserted in and removed from a computer. Especially useful with microcomputers, word processors, and small typesetters, the disks are made of a flexible sheet of Mylar plastic and housed in a paper jacket. Also called *diskettes*.

Florence Agreement   (Agreement on the Importation of Educational, Scientific, and Cultural Materials) A UNESCO-sponsored international agreement that eliminates tariffs, discriminatory taxation, and, to some extent, other trade barriers on a wide range of published materials, art objects, antiques, and scientific apparatus, plus audiovisual materials with an educational, scientific, and cultural character, imported by approved institutions. Drafted in 1950, the agreement was ratified by the United States in 1967; by 1982, ninety countries were members. In November 1976, the UNESCO General Conference, meeting in Nairobi, Kenya, approved a protocol, or supplement, to the original agreement that liberalizes it in several respects, including one optional provision that gives the same duty-free status to microform publications and audio and visual materials as the original agreement gave to printed materials. As of October 1982, the protocol was in force among the first nine ratifying countries. The U.S. Senate approved the protocol as a treaty, but legislation implementing it has not yet passed both houses of the Congress.

floret, flower   An ornament in the shape of a small flower or leaf, used in binding or printing. Sometimes called *printer's flower*.

flowchart   A graphic diagram of functions and sequences involved in the flow of work from start to finish of an operation. It is used in the analysis, planning, and documentation of computer operations and systems.

flush   "Even with." Usually interpreted as meaning even with left margin unless otherwise designated, such as flush right. *See also* cut flush.

fly title   *See* half title.

flyleaf   Binder's blank leaf, following the free front endpaper. Often used, inaccurately, to describe the free front endpaper itself.

foil   Tissue-thin material, faced with metal or pigment, used in book stamping. A heated die impresses the foil onto the cover material, causing the metal or pigment to transfer to the cover.

folding (folded) plate   An illustration that has to be folded to fit into the bound book.

foliation   The numbering of the physical leaves or sheets in a book rather than the pages, which are printed on both sides of the leaves.

folio   A leaf numbered on the recto, or right-hand page; the numeral itself in a book or manuscript in which the leaves are numbered. *See also* book sizes.

follow copy   In typesetting and proofreading, an order to set matter exactly as it appears in copy, making no changes whatever in spelling, punctuation, capitalization, etc. Horace Greeley's famous injunction to his compositors was to "follow copy even if it goes out of the window."

font   From the French "fondre," to cast. Classic definition is complete assortment of types of one face and size. In photographic and electronic composition, a font is used to set many sizes, via enlargement and reduction of the basic character set. A complete font includes capitals, small capitals, lowercase letters, numerals, punctuation marks, ligatures, etc.

foolscap   A sheet of paper about 13 × 16 inches, making, when folded, a page size 13 × 8 inches. The name is derived from the watermark of a fool's cap and bells used by old papermakers. *See also* book sizes.

foolscap folio; foolscap octavo; foolscap quarto   *See* book sizes.

foot   The end or bottom of a page. *See also* head.

footnote   A note at the bottom of a page, usually in smaller type than the text, giving a reference, an authority, or an elucidation of matter in text. *See also* marginalia; reference marks.

fore-edge   The front edge of a book, opposite its spine.

fore-edge painting   A picture painted on the fore-edges of the leaves of a book, over which gold is usually applied. The picture is not visible when the volume is closed, but can be seen by fanning the leaves open obliquely. The *double fore-edge* contains two paintings that can be seen singly by fanning the leaves first one way, then the reverse. A *triple fore-edge* contains two hidden paintings and one visible painting.

The technique of the hidden painting, or paintings, on the fore-edges of the leaves of a book was originated in the mid-seventeenth century in England. It was revived in the latter half of the eighteenth century in England by Edwards of Halifax—the family of bookbinders (William Edwards and his five sons) who operated in the Edwards' hometown of Halifax and in London. William Edwards (1723-1808) is particularly associated with the fore-edge paintings produced by the various Edwards shops; the technique was continued with great success by his son Thomas, who worked in the Halifax shop until 1826. Three other sons,

James, John, and Richard, worked in other Edwards shops in London.

Fore-edge paintings were also produced by other binders of the period, the most notable among them being Kalthoeber, one of five German binders of the late eighteenth century working in London.

foreground mode In computer operations, the processing of high-priority work at the expense of other tasks. Cf. background mode.

foreign rights The right to publish a book, whether in its own language or in translation, outside its country of origin. *See also* rights.

foreword Prefatory or introductory remarks to a book by someone other than the author. *See also* introduction; preface.

form In printing, any assembly of pages that can be printed simultaneously in a single impression of the printing press. In letterpress, the word may refer to the physical metal type or plates as locked up in a chase ready for press or to the planned layout that assigns page positions on the printed sheet. In offset, the word is usually employed only in the latter sense (e.g., "A paper jam occurred toward the end of the run on the third form").

In book printing, a form is likely to consist of 16 or 32 pages, depending on the size of the press, but 24s, 48s, and 64s are not uncommon and 4s, 8s, and 12s do occur.

form entry An entry in an index or catalog that lists books according to (1) the form in which their subject material is organized, such as "Directories" or "Periodicals"; or (2) their literary form, such as "Poetry" or "Addresses, essays, lectures."

form heading A heading used for a form entry (*q.v.*) in an index or catalog.

format The graphic and physical makeup of a book as to size, type page, margins, binding, etc.

format instruction code A special character code used to distinguish between alphanumeric codes and instruction or function codes. Because most keyboards and display devices are limited in the number of different characters they can handle, a special instruction code (such as a $ or #) is inserted just prior to an instruction to tell the machine that what follows is an instruction, not actual text or data. Then standard alphanumeric codes are given a new set of meanings for instruction purposes. When the instruction is completed, a second format instruction code is inserted to tell the computer that what follows is now text or data. *See also* function code; instruction.

format storage   The storage of format specifications in computer memory for withdrawal and use on command from a special code. *See also* macro code.

formation   A property of paper determined by the uniformity of distribution of a sheet's solid components, especially the fibers. This property not only influences the sheet's appearance but also influences the values of almost all other properties. *See also* book paper; paper.

formatting   The insertion of typeface, size, spacing, indention, run-around, or other typographic instructions to direct the typesetting machine to set material in the selected typefaces and in proper position in an area. Formatting can be of two types: *galley formatting* in which type is produced in columnar format, and *page formatting* in which type is positioned within the page area. *See also* editing.

fortyeightmo (48mo)   *See* book sizes.

forwarding   The intermediate steps in binding: rounding and backing or lining. These occur after sewing and prior to the finishing operations. Sometimes included under forwarding are such auxiliary operations as tipping-in, pasting on endpapers, etc. In hand binding, a somewhat different grouping of operations comes under forwarding, including insertion of plates, sewing, tying in of boards and covering. *See also* finishing; sewing.

foundry proofs   *See* proofs.

foundry type   Metal type cast for hand composition, and sold in fonts.

four-color process   *See* process color.

Fourdrinier   Machine for making paper in an endless web, introduced by Henry and Sealy Fourdrinier early in the nineteenth century. Pulp in liquid form is flowed onto a moving wire screen, where most of the water drains out, leaving a layer of solid fibers on the screen. The web then passes through a series of rollers that complete the drying process and impart the desired finish.

Fournier, Pierre Simon (le jeune) (1712-1768)   French engraver and typefounder, who wrote several important works relating to typography. His principal work was the *Manuel Typographique* (2 vols. 1764), the first volume treating of engraving and type founding, the second of printing, with examples of different alphabets. With an older brother, Jean Pierre, he succeeded to the foundry of his father, Jean Claude.

foxing   A brown discoloration of paper; rust. Stains caused by chemical or metallic impurities in the paper.

fraktur   (1) The group name of German blackface type. (2) A type of Pennsylvania Dutch lettering. *See also* antiqua.

Franklin, Benjamin (1706-1790)   Printer and publisher, diplomat, statesman, and scientist. Born in Boston, died in Philadelphia. Apprenticed in 1718 to his brother James (1697-1735), printer; after disagreements with James, left Boston (1723). Settled in Philadelphia, where he obtained employment as printer. He became proprietor of a printing business and publisher of *The Pennsylvania Gazette* (1730-1748). He served as official printer to Pennsylvania, New Jersey, and Delaware. He was the author-printer-publisher of the *Poor Richard* almanacs for the years 1733-1758, issued under the pseudonym Richard Saunders. The annual sale of these almanacs averaged 10,000 copies, far exceeding the sale of any other publication in the colonies. He considered his typographical masterpiece to be *M. T. Cicero's Cato Major, or His Discourse of Old Age*, in the translation of James Logan, chief justice of the Pennsylvania Supreme Court. The work was issued in 1744.

In 1748 Franklin sold his press to his foreman and ostensibly retired from full activity in the printing business. However, in the same year he formed a partnership with David Hall, whom he had engaged five years before, and the firm operated as Franklin & Hall until 1766, under the management of Hall. The output of Franklin's press from 1729 to 1766 as listed in Dr. William J. Campbell's catalogue of *The Collection of Franklin Imprints in the Museum of the Curtis Publishing Company* (1918) comes to 728 entries. This does not include newspapers, paper currency, etc.

After 1748 Franklin devoted most of his time to scientific experiments and to public life. In 1776 he was sent by Congress as one of a committee of three to negotiate a treaty with France; in 1778 he was appointed sole plenipotentiary and remained in France until 1785. During his long stay there he established a little private press for his own amusement at his home in Passy, then a suburb of Paris. The history of the Passy press is told by Luther S. Livingston in *Franklin and His Press at Passy* (New York: Grolier Club 1914). Livingston lists thirty-two entries (often referred to as *bagatelles*, a term meant to include everything printed by Franklin at his Passy press). Will Ransom's *Private Presses and Their Books* (New York: R. R. Bowker, 1929) lists six additional pieces that came to light after 1914.

Franklin established in Philadelphia in 1731 one of the earliest circulating libraries in America (sometimes said to be the earliest), which developed into what is now the Library Company of Philadelphia, and he was one of the founders of the American Philosophical Society (1743). Accounts of his work in public life and his work as a writer, as a scientist, etc., are outside the scope of this entry.

free sheet   Paper made of chemical pulp (*q.v.*) without any admixture of groundwood.

Freedom of Information Act   A federal act passed in 1966 giving citizens access to nonclassified government documents that may otherwise not be released to the public in the course of ordinary activities. The act was strengthened in 1974 over President Ford's veto, but has been weakened by waning federal cooperation since 1980.

freight pass-through   A system designed to help retail booksellers reimburse publishers for shipping costs and to defray the freight charges on books by passing most of these charges on to the public. A publisher's catalogue may indicate a price on which a bookstore can compute its discount according to quantity ordered, but the actual cover price of the book may be raised slightly (3 to 5 percent) to permit the retailer to realize additional money on each sale.

French fold   A sheet printed on one side only and folded into quarters without cutting the fold along the top edge.

French Japon   *See* Japan paper.

French Revolutionary Calendar   *See* calendar.

frisket Originally part of the hand press, consisting of a light metal frame with a paper stencil stretched over it. Windows were cut in the frisket in printing areas where type would contact the paper. The frisket was placed over the inked type form and the paper was laid over it. When the impression was made, the frisket protected the paper from unwanted ink transfer in nonprinting areas. Today, in the commercial art field, special frisket material is used for making protective stencils for artwork.

front matter The pages preceding the text of a book. According to the best usage these should be arranged in the following order: bastard title, or half title; frontispiece; title page (with imprint and date of printing); copyright page (with country where print-ed and number of printings if more than one); dedication; table of contents; list of illustrations; foreword; preface; introduction; half title repeated (optional).

Each should begin on a right-hand or odd-numbered page, except the frontispiece (which faces the title page) and the copy-right page (which appears on the verso of the title page).

If a list of books by the same author, or other books in the same series, is to be inserted, it is printed on the verso of the bastard title, or half title.

frontispiece (front.; frontis.) An illustration facing the title page.

frontlist The group of new books a publisher is offering for sale in the current or upcoming season. Cf. backlist.

fugitive material Printed matter of fleeting interest, produced in limited quantities, such as a program printed for a certain occasion.

fulfillment The procedures entailed in warehousing, shipping, and collection, during which a publisher processes the orders it receives, sends out books, and supplies invoices to its customers.

full binding *See* binding.

full-cover display Also called *flat display* or *face out*; a display of books featuring the front covers rather than the spines.

full measure Extending across the entire width of a type column.

function code A computer code that controls machine opera-tions, as opposed to a code representing an actual typographic or data character. *See also* instruction.

furniture   In letterpress, the wooden or metal spacing material that separates type pages or fills space between type and chase (*q.v.*).

Fust, Johann (d. 1466)   Early German printer. There is no evidence that, as is commonly asserted, Johann Fust was a goldsmith, but he appears to have been a moneylender or banker. Fust became interested in Johann Gutenberg's experiments in printing, and lent him 800 guilders in 1450 and another 800 guilders in 1452, the only security being that of "tools" still to be made. In 1455 Fust brought suit to recover the money he had lent, and on the sixth of November the suit was decided in his favor (*see* Gutenberg, Johann). He then took possession of the printing plant and equipment, and also took into service Peter Schoeffer (1425?-1502), a former scriptor who had been employed by Gutenberg as a typesetter and probably as foreman of the plant. Schoeffer married Fust's daughter Dyna at about this time.

The first known publication of the Fust and Schoeffer office was the *Mainz Psalter* of 1457. The book is the first to give date of printing and the names of its printers. Two separate editions were produced in 1457, one with 143 leaves and another with 175 leaves; ten copies are known today, nine of the former and one of the latter, all printed on vellum. The work is remarkable for the beauty of the very large initial letters, each printed in red and blue. The most ambitious publication of the two printers was the great forty-eight-line Bible, printed in two volumes in 1462. The main text was printed in black with small type; the headings and initial letters in large type were printed in red.

After Fust's death in 1466 the business was continued by Schoeffer, who was recognized always as an excellent printer. He died in 1502, after producing fifty-nine separate works as an independent. In 1470 he issued what is believed to be the first bookseller's advertisement of printed books; it was in poster form, and since it contained a line of type quoted from one of his books, it can also be described as the first type specimen sheet.

g.e.   Gilt edges (*q.v.*).

g.t.   Gilt top. *See* gilt edges.

galley proofs, galleys   Proofs made from type before it has been arranged in page format. Each proof shows the contents of a column of type. The term came originally from hot metal type setting where newly set type was stored in long shallow trays called galleys, which were just wide enough to hold one column of type about 22 inches long. *See also* proofs.

galleys *See* galley proofs.

Garamond, Claude (d. 1561) One of the most distinguished of early French type designers. He was a pupil of Geoffroy Tory (*q.v.*). His famous *Grecs du Roi*, three Greek types based upon the handwriting of the calligrapher Angelos Vergetios, were completed in about 1541, and became models for future designers. His roman and italic types were also great successes, and brought about the decline in the use of the gothic letter. The roman and italic fonts have been revived and put to much use in the present century.

garbage Unwanted or useless data in a computer system, or in the output of a system. The initials GIGO express a maxim in the computer field—garbage in, garbage out—which indicates the importance of putting correct material into a system in the first place.

gatefold A folded illustration or other insert larger than the publication into which it is bound, so that it must be unfolded for proper viewing. A gatefold opens out horizontally to the left or right.

gathering (1) In binding, assembling the signatures of a book in the order in which they are to be bound. (2) In bibliography, used synonymously for signature (*q.v.*).

gathering plan *See* blanket order.

gauffered edges *See* goffered edges.

gelatin print *See* photogelatin.

general-purpose computer A computer designed to be usable for a wide variety of applications, as opposed to a single special purpose. *See also* stored-program computer.

genre publishing Producing books in specific, well-defined, and marketable subject areas. Although the term connotes fiction, the variety of identifiable genres is great, ranging from science fiction to self-help books, from romances to westerns. Also called *category publishing*. *See also* special interest publishing.

Gesamtkatalog der Wiegendrucke　The great catalogue of fif-teenth-century printed books, edited by a committee of German scholars, with assistance from scholars all over the world. Only volumes I-VII and volume VIII, part one (A-Federicis) have been issued, printed at Leipzig (1925-1940). The text is in Ger-man. As far as published, the work is the most comprehensive record of incunabula yet made. The sections published record nearly half again as many editions as Hain's *Repertorium Biblio-graphicum* (Stuttgart, 1826-1838). *See* Hain, Ludwig.

ghost writer　One who writes books or articles for and in the name of another. It may be work for hire (*q.v.*), or the writer may share in any earned royalties. Many books published by celebrities and other nonwriters are actually composed by ghost writers.

gift certificate　*See* Book Token; Give-a-Book Certificate.

Gill, Eric (1882-1940)　Distinguished English artist, illustrator, and designer of types. He made engravings for his own press, St. Dominic, and also for the Golden Cockerel Press (*q.v.*), and type designs such as Perpetua and Gill Sans Serif.

gilt edges　The edges of a book usually trimmed smooth and covered with gold leaf. The abbreviation g.e. means gilt edges; g.t., gilt top; t.e.g., top edge gilt.

gilt extra　Binding with more than the usual gilt ornamentation.

Give-a-Book Certificate　A program introduced in 1947 by the American Booksellers Association to promote books as gifts. The program was discontinued in 1982. *See also* Book Token.

glassine　The transparent paper used as a protective book wrap-per.

glossy print　A photographic print on paper with a shiny finish. Prints intended for reproduction are usually made on such pa-per.

gluing off　Process of applying glue to the spine of a book, either after sewing or instead of sewing.

goffered edges　An indented pattern worked with a heated tool on the gilt edges of the leaves of a book. Also known as *gauffered edges*.

Golden Cockerel Press　English private press founded in 1920 at

Waltham St. Lawrence, Berkshire, by Harold M. Taylor, for the purpose of publishing works of literary merit by young authors. The first book of the press was *Adam & Eve & Pinch Me,* by A. E. Coppard, issued in April 1921. When the original concept failed, the press introduced a new policy of printing fine editions of established classics. Taylor's health failed in 1924, and he sold the press to Robert Gibbings, an artist, who was responsible for the press's important association with the revival of English wood engraving. Every book the press issued between 1924 and 1933 contained wood engravings. Among the well-known artists commissioned to illustrate books from the press was Eric Gill, and some of the best books of the press—*Troilus and Criseyde* (1927), *The Canterbury Tales* (1929), and *The Four Gospels* (1931)—contain wood engravings by Gill. In 1933, the press was taken over by Christopher Sandford, Francis Newbery, and Owen Ritter, and although it no longer printed by hand, the Golden Cockerel typeface, designed by Eric Gill in 1931, continued to be used. In 1959, the press was sold to Thomas Yoseloff, a New York publisher.

Goodhue, Bertram G. (1869-1924)   American architect and designer of type, including the widely popular Cheltenham, and the Merrymount designed for D. B. Updike.

gothic   (1) A style of lettering dating from the twelfth century, the origin of modern black letter (*q.v.*). (2) A term used by bibliographers to describe black-letter type. (3) In the United States, a common bold type style without serifs. *See* sans serif. (4) A romantic novel of suspense with a historical and mysterious setting.

Goudy, Frederic W. (1865-1947)   Notable American type designer. Responsible for more than 100 typefaces, many in general use including the Forum, Kennerley, Goudy, Goudy Open, Hadriano. His wife, Bertha M. Goudy, was a fellow craftsman in their Village Press, Marlborough-on-Hudson, N.Y. His work is described in his own *A Half Century of Type Design and Typography, 1895-1945,* published by The Typophiles.

Grabhorn Press   Founded in 1920 by Edwin and Robert Grabhorn, in San Francisco. In its forty-five-year history, the press produced more than 600 books and became known as the greatest American press of this century. The magnificent Grabhorn *Leaves of Grass,* issued in 1930, is considered the finest production of the press, and ranks as one of the great press books of the century. In 1965, Edwin, the elder brother, retired for reasons of failing health, and the press was disbanded. The following year Robert Grabhorn and Andrew Hoyem, a young San Francisco printer and poet, who had worked at the Grabhorn Press during 1963-1964, formed the Grabhorn-Hoyem Press. Edwin died in 1968. The partnership of Robert Grabhorn and Andrew Hoyem lasted until Robert Grabhorn's death in 1973. Andrew Hoyem continued the direction of the press under his own name until January 1975, when he established the Arion Press.

grain   In a sheet of paper, direction in which most of the fibers lie. In all machine-made paper, the fibers that make up the sheet lie to a large degree in one general direction due to the flow of the pulp on the moving screen that forms the sheet. If the grain of a paper runs parallel to the spine of a book, it opens more flexibly. *See also* against the grain.

grain direction   *See* grain.

grangerizing   The extra-illustrating of one work with matter from other sources. James Granger's *Biographical History of England*, published in 1769, lent itself widely to this practice, having had blank pages bound in to receive any desired illustrations. *See also* extra-illustrated.

Granjon, Robert (fl. 1540-1580)   French printer, type designer, and engraver. Designer of the first italics to be used in the modern manner, that is, complementary to roman; one of the first to introduce the use of round notes in musical notation. Among his many type designs he is known especially for his *caractères de civilité*, a typeface based upon cursive French handwriting. He introduced the *Civilité* types at Lyons about 1557.

graphic arts quality   The print quality obtainable from conventional hot metal or photographic typesetting equipment, as opposed to the quality obtainable from computer printout devices (such as chain prints).

graphics   Broadly used term for any presentation of data in visual form. In contrast to text material, such illustrative material as charts, drawings, art, or any page formatting or area positioning of elements.

graver   *See* burin.

gravure   The major commercial application of the intaglio principle of printing, sometimes used for photographic books and frontispieces. Short-run work is done by sheet-fed gravure; long runs, such as certain national magazines, by rotogravure. The latter is roll-fed and faster. Gravure printing is distinguished by its dense, rich solids, by the unobtrusiveness (almost invisibility) of its screen, and by its ability to print with delicate detail on uncoated paper.

Greenaway Plan   *See* blanket order.

Gregorian Calendar   *See* calendar.

grid   (1) A phototypesetting master carrier of typeface character images from which the machine projects characters onto photographic material. (2) An *x-y* layout of lines over an area for typographic makeup, for location of elements within the area. *See also* coordinate digitizing; grid coordinate system.

grid coordinate system   Synonym for coordinate digitizing system. Also used specifically to indicate a method of making corrections in data in computer memory by specifying the line number, and then word number in which the change is to be made, and then designating the actual characters to be changed. *See also* coordinate digitizing; grid.

Grolier, Jean (1479-1565)   Famous French patron of the arts of the book, born at Lyons, became treasurer-general of France in 1547. He remains traditionally one of the greatest of all patrons of the binder's art, magnificent leather bindings, having been made for him. Many of these bindings were lettered Io. GROLERII ET AMICORUM.

Grolier is the name given to ornamental tooling on hand bindings after his style; i.e., an interlaced framework of geometrical figures—circles, squares, and diamonds—with scrollwork running through it, and ornaments of Moresque character, generally azured in whole or in part, sometimes in outline only.

groove   The depression formed by the rounding and backing process between front and back cover panels and spine of book.

groundwood pulp   The raw material from which newsprint and similar papers are made. Groundwood paper has excellent printing quality and opacity, but lacks the permanence that is obtainable when the wood fibers are broken down more slowly by chemical rather than mechanical means. Paper made from groundwood pulp tends to be brown and embrittle more quickly than paper made from chemical pulp. *See also* chemical pulp.

Grub Street   Described by Dr. Samuel Johnson as "originally the name of a street near Moorfields, much inhabited by writers of small histories, dictionaries, and occasional poems...." The name has been, and continues to be, associated with literary hacks.

guards   (1) Strips of paper or muslin to which text leaves, illustrations, maps, etc., are attached, and by which they are bound into a volume. (2) Strips of strong paper or cloth used to reinforce the first and last signatures of a book. Also called *hinges*.

guillotine cut   A straight cut in paper made by a guillotine-style blade, as opposed to other types of cuts such as die-cutting, slitting, perforating, etc. The edges of most books are trimmed by guillotine cutting.

Guinzburg, Harold K. (1900-1961)   Publisher and book industry leader. He founded in 1925 the Viking Press, which became known for literary and typographic distinction; he helped found the Literary Guild in 1926. He was a strong influence in establishing the National Book Committee and National Library Week (*q.v.*) and was an exponent of publishers' cooperation in reading development. The Book Committee's National Medal for Literature is supported by a fund set up in his memory.

gussets   *See* buckles.

Gutenberg, Johann (1398?-1468)   Printer at Mainz, Germany, long credited with the invention of printing with movable metal types. Son of the general accountant of the city of Mainz, Frilo Gensfleisch, he adopted the surname of his mother, Elsen Gutenberg, because she was the last of her line and the name would otherwise have become extinct.

He moved to Strassburg in about 1430, where he became known as a maker of mirrors. In 1438 he made an agreement with two helpers to give instruction "*in etlicher kunst*" (in a certain art) which various authorities believe was printing. He returned to Mainz in 1448, and in August 1450 he entered into a partnership with Johann Fust (*q.v.*), who lent him 800 guilders, the security being "tools" still to be made. A further 800 guilders was lent by Fust in 1452. Gutenberg is presumed to have begun printing a large folio Latin Bible and to have printed during its progress some smaller books and a broadside Papal *Letter of Indulgence* (1454 and 1455).

In 1455 Fust brought suit to recover the monies he had lent. Evidence given in the records of the lawsuit make it clear that Gutenberg was engaged in printing. The suit was decided in Fust's favor, and as Gutenberg was unable to repay the loan, Fust took over the printing plant. He formed a partnership with Gutenberg's foreman, Peter Schoeffer, and it is most likely that the printing of the Bible begun by Gutenberg was finished by Schoeffer before 1456. The work has been known under several names: the Gutenberg Bible; the Mazarin Bible (so named because the first copy to be given widespread publicity was the copy found in the Mazarin Library at Paris by the bibliographer François Guillaume de Bure in 1763); and, in modern times, as the 42-line Bible, for the number of lines in each printed column. There is no definite proof that the Gutenberg Bible was printed entirely by Gutenberg. The work bears no place of printing, no date, and no printer's name.

Little is known about Gutenberg's activities after his break with Fust. In 1465 the Archbishop of Mainz gave him the post of "salaried courtier for life." His name has been, and still is, associated with the printing of the *Catholicon*, a Latin dictionary written by Joannes Balbus in the thirteenth century and printed at Mainz in 1460. The colophon of the work gives no printer's name, but some experts credit Gutenberg with the printing and say that it was done with equipment lent to him by Dr. Conrad Humery, of Mainz.

gutter   *See* margins.

Hain, Ludwig (1781-1836)   The first bibliographer to make an alphabetical list by author (and where author is unknown, by title) of all incunabula known up to his time. He listed 16,311 books printed before the year 1501 in his *Repertorium Bibliographicum, in quo libri omnes ab arte typographica inventa usque ad annum MD* ... (2 volumes in 4 volumes, Stuttgart, 1826-1838). A *Supplement* ... by Walter Arthur Copinger was issued in London, 1895-1902, 2 volumes in 4 volumes. The *Supplement* contains about 7,000 corrections and gives us a list of about 6,000 volumes not in Hain.

Hain-Copinger lists only about 22,300 editions against the more than 39,000 estimated for the complete *Gesamtkatalog* ..., but Hain will remain a convenient primary reference work until the GKW is completed—if ever it will be. *See* Gesamkatalog der Wiegendrucke.

hair spaces   Very thin spaces, less than five to an em, used for letter spacing and justifying type lines.

half-binding   *See* binding.

half-cloth   A binding with a cloth spine over paper-covered boards.

half title   The title of a book as printed on the recto of the leaf preceding the title page (and frontispiece, if there is one), and occupying a full page. Sometimes used also to refer to the bastard title (*q.v.*). *See also* front matter.

halftone   A technique for reproducing by optical illusion the different tonal shadings in photographs, drawings, or paintings. The continuous shadings in the original are broken up photographically into a series of tiny dots almost invisible to the naked eye. The eye, therefore, does not see the individual dots; rather, it perceives an overall tonal effect created by the dots. To create varying tones, these dots vary in diameter in proportion to the lightness or darkness of the tone being reproduced. Smaller dots when printed will cover less area of the sheet with ink while larger dots will coat a larger proportion of the paper with ink. Therefore, smaller dots will present a lighter overall tonal effect to the eye while larger dots will create darker tonal effects. The dots are made on a printing plate by photographing the original through a ruled screen. A screen with closer rulings achieves better reproduction of fine detail but has to be used on a smoother paper. Lithography can reproduce much finer screens than letterpress.

hand composition   Type set by manually selecting and positioning characters one at a time. In metal-type composition, characters are assembled into lines by placing them in a hand-held three-sided tray called a *stick*, which is adjustable for setting different line lengths. In photographic composition, machines that expose a single character at a time permit the operator to position each character individually, adjusting letter spacing in the process. Photographable camera copy is also created by using transfer characters, symbols, etc., which are preprinted on carrier sheets and coated with a wax-based adhesive; the characters are positioned on the camera copy one at a time and rubbed, or burnished, to make them adhere to the copy.

In a more general sense, hand composition is often used to mean makeup operations when they are performed manually.

handbook   A manual containing concise information on a particular subject, organized for quick reference use, and small enough to be carried in the hand.

handmade paper   Paper made a sheet at a time by dipping up the pulp by hand onto a sieve. The water runs through while the sieve is manipulated in a manner to mix the fibers thoroughly. The pulp is prevented from running over the edge by a thin frame called the deckle. Handmade paper has no grain (i.e., it does not bend or tear more easily in one direction than another), is obtainable only in small sizes, and may have deckled edges on all four sides. All paper was so made until about 1800, when the Fourdriniers perfected a machine with a continuous sieve.

hanging indention   A typesetting format in which the first line of a paragraph is set to the full width of the measure, while the succeeding lines are indented from the left edge. This entry is set as a hanging indention, as are all the entries in this book.

hard copy   (1) A typewritten record of material keyboarded into computer coding. (2) A physically printed (typed or otherwise) output record of a computer's contents.

hard disk   Computer memory storage disks made of rigid material, as opposed to floppy disks that can store larger amounts of material. *See* disk; disk pack; floppy disk.

hard-wired computer   Synonym for wired-program computer.

hardbound   *See* hardcover.

hardcover   A book bound in boards that may be covered in cloth, paper, leather, or plastic, as distinct from a paperback.

hardware   The physical components of a computer system.

head   (1) The top of a page. (2) Word or phrase used to indicate the division of a book into chapters or other subdivisions. The style of type often indicates whether the division is major or minor.

head and tail pieces   Ornamental designs printed at the beginning and end of a chapter or division of a book.

head margin   The blank space above the running head or first line on the page. *See* margins.

headband   (1) A small band of silk or other material attached at the top or bottom (or both) of the spine of a book to add to its appearance. On finely bound books, the headbands are sometimes sewed in by hand.

headline   Display of type set above the text to which it refers. *See also* caption.

hellbox   Box or receptacle in a printing office into which broken or discarded type is thrown.

Heures   *See* Book of Hours.

hieroglyphics   Characters (figures or objects) used in the picture writing of the ancient Egyptians, Thebans, Mexicans, etc.

high-speed printer   Generally any type of computer printout device designed specifically for producing hard copy only, as opposed to an automatic typewriter, which operates at much slower speeds and also has a keyboard for input purposes. Most high-speed printers have been of the chain printer type, but new machines now incorporate electrostatic and ink-jet printing principles. *See also* chain printer; electrostatics; ink-jet printing; line printer.

high-speed reader   Any device that reads data into a computer at speeds compatible with the computer's internal processing speeds. Various types include tape readers and optical page readers. *See also* optical character recognition; tape.

hinges   *See* guards.

Hinman collator   A machine used to compare copies of the texts of the same edition of a printed work in order to identify the slightest differences in the texts by superimposing the image of one page upon another through the use of a series of mirrors. The Hinman collator, invented by Charlton F. Hinman during his work on the First Folio of Shakespeare, replaces the laborious and often inaccurate process of manual collation. *See also* collate.

Hoe, Robert (I, 1784-1833)   Born in Leicestershire, England, emigrated to America in 1803. In 1805 he founded, in New York City, a firm for the construction of large printing presses. In the following century, the firm of Robert Hoe & Co. did more for the improvement of machine printing than any other agency of its time. Hoe's son, **Richard March Hoe** (1812-1886), succeeded to the management of the firm (of which his brother **Robert Hoe II**

was also a member) in 1833. In 1847 Richard M. Hoe developed the Hoe Type Revolving Machine, a great press that revolutionized newspaper printing. Upon his death in 1886, he was succeeded by his nephew **Robert Hoe III** (1839-1909), who himself devised various improvements in printing machinery and developed color presses.

Robert Hoe III was a great book collector and patron of the arts. He brought together the most famous and diversified private library of his time in America. Under the terms of his will the library was sold at auction in New York in 1911-1912. The sale created a tremendous stir, extending to Europe, and the bidding throughout was spirited. The most important event of the sale occurred on its first evening, April 14, 1911, when Hoe's copy of the Gutenberg Bible was acquired by George D. Smith (acting for Henry E. Huntington) for $50,000, the highest price ever paid up to that time for a printed book.

Hoe was active in everything that pertained to books. The Grolier Club of New York, the oldest existing American club devoted to the arts of the book, was founded at his house in 1884 by him and eight of his book-collector friends, and he served as the club's first president.

hollow-back   A book whose cover is not glued to the spine, permitting the cover to bow outward when the book is opened.

hologram   A recording on photographic film of a three-dimensional image that can be reconstructed in three dimensions by passing coherent light through the film. *See also* holography.

holograph   A document wholly in the handwriting of the person from whom it proceeds. *See also* a.c.s.; a.d.s.; a.l.s.

holography   The process of making holograms by lensless photography which employs a laser light source.

Horae   *See* Book of Hours.

hornbook   A thin sheet of paper mounted on a paddle-shaped wooden board, having on it the alphabet and sometimes the Lord's Prayer. The printed material was protected by a sheet of transparent horn. Used in England for learning the elements of reading, from the middle of the fifteenth century and common down to the time of George II. Although the hornbook was used extensively in colonial America in the seventeenth and eighteenth centuries, it is not known that any were locally produced. Genuine examples are now exceedingly rare. *See also* battledore.

Hornby, St. John *See* Ashendene Press.

hot melt In bookbinding, a glue that is applied hot and that sets almost instantly.

hot metal The processes of casting raised type from molten metal. The most common hot metal processes are linecasting (Linotype and Intertype), Monotype, and foundry casting. The latter two cast individual characters, while the former process produces a complete line of type at a time on a single piece of metal.

Hours *See* Book of Hours.

house An industry term for a publishing company; an abbreviation for publishing house.

house style Uniform manner of copy preparation followed by a particular publishing house with regard to grammar, spelling, punctuation, abbreviation, and other points of style.

Hroswitha *See* book-collectors' clubs.

Hunter, Dard (1883-1966) Leading authority on the craft of papermaking, on which subject he published many works. In 1939 he established the Paper Museum of the Massachusetts Institute of Technology.

hurt books Damaged or shopworn books that may be offered at sale prices.

hyphenation In typesetting, the breaking of words at the ends of lines. A computerized typesetting system that does this automatically generally applies a set of hyphenation rules to determine proper breaking points. Because of the many exceptions to such rules in any language, however, such automatic hyphenation programs also usually rely on an exception dictionary of words that do not break according to the rules. Such words are broken according to special instructions for that word in the dictionary. Accuracy of such programs, equipped with exception dictionaries, typically reaches only 97 to 98 percent of all words broken because some words spelled exactly the same are broken differently, depending on the particular definition being used. *See also* exception dictionary; justification.

hyphenation routine   The set of rules and procedures followed by a computer in breaking words at the ends of lines in computerized typesetting.

hyphenless justification   Justification of type lines without using word breaks of any kind. All space in the line is distributed between words and/or between individual characters.

ibid.   Abbreviation for "*ibidem*," the Latin word meaning in the same place. A frequent footnote word referring to the article, chapter, or volume cited in the footnote immediately before.

ID   *See* independent distributor.

ILAB   *See* International League of Antiquarian Booksellers.

illus.   Abbreviation for illustrations or for illustrated.

ISBD(M)   *See* International Standard Bibliographic Description for Monographic Publications.

ISBD(S)   *See* International Standard Bibliographic Description for Serials.

ISBN   *See* International Standard Book Number.

ISR   *See* information storage and retrieval.

ISSN   *See* International Standard Serial Number.

-iana   *See* -ana.

iconography   A detailed list and description of the pictorial or sculptured material connected with a person, place, or thing.

ideal copy   In bibliography, a descriptive term for a perfect copy of a first impression of an edition—complete in all its leaves and considered after examination of many copies to represent the most perfect state of the book—with which all other copies of that impression and later impressions of the edition are compared to determine issues and states.

idem (id.)   Latin word meaning the same or the same as mentioned above.

idiot tape   Encoded tape for input to a computer that contains only codes for type characters. Instruction codes for line justification and hyphenation as well as many typographic format codes are omitted, to be put in later by the computer.

illuminated   Embellished with ornamental letters, scrolls, miniatures, and other designs, usually in gold and color. A feature of many ancient manuscripts and early printed books.

imperfect   A book lacking some leaves or whole signatures, or with leaves or sections either omitted, duplicated, misplaced, or damaged.

imperial octavo   *See* book sizes.

import   A book brought into one country upon or after its publication in another. The importer may act as one of several distributors, or may obtain sole distribution rights within a given area. In the latter case, the importer may stamp or print its own imprint on the title page. Loosely, a book whose publication rights were sold for local manufacture to a country other than that of origin.

imposition   The master plan for arranging pages for presswork so that, when printed and folded, the pages will be numbered consecutively and the margins will be correct. The imposition specifies where each image is to be printed on a large press sheet to create the proper sequence and visual effect after the sheet is processed through various binding steps.

impression   Synonymous with *printing*. The total number of copies of a book printed at one time. There may be a number of impressions (or printings) within an edition.

Some publishers designate the impression or printing of a book with a phrase, such as "First Printing," or a symbol, such as the "A" used by Scribner's for many years, usually placed on the copyright page. Some publishers, however, do not designate impressions at all.

In order to help book collectors recognize first printings, guides have been compiled based on surveys of publisher practices. Perhaps the best known is H. S. Boutell's *First Editions of Today and How to Tell Them* (4th edition, revised by Wanda Underhill, Peacock Press, 1965).

In the early 1970s, some publishers began to identify specific impressions with a horizontal line of numbers—termed the *impression line*—printed on the copyright page usually directly below the country of manufacture. Individual publishers present this impression line in a variety of ways. Some use a simple ascending order of numbers, from 1 to 10; thus:

First Edition
1 2 3 4 5 6 7 8 9 10 (identifying the first printing of the
first edition)

or a descending order of numbers from 10 to 1; or a split line combining year and number, with the last two digits of each of several years on one end of the line and the impression numbers on the other; thus:

82 83 84 85 86 87 88 89 1 2 3 4 5 6 7 8 9 10

Other methods include:

First Edition
1 3 5 7 9 10 8 6 4 2 (identifying the first printing of the
first edition)

First Edition
RRD 0 9 8 7 6 5 4 3 2 1 (a more recent method that
identifies the manufacturer with a letter code)

Printing (last digit): 9 8 7 6 5 4 3 2 1 (perhaps the clearest
method of designating the impression)

When a new impression is printed after the first is exhausted, the manufacturer simply masks out the number "1," leaving the other numbers stand, with "2" identifying those copies as the second printing, thus:

First Edition
2 3 4 5 6 7 8 9 10 (identifying the second printing of the
first edition)

The pre-set line of numbers replaces the earlier, more costly practice of setting type each time a new impression is printed.

impression line   *See* impression.

imprimatur   Latin for "let it be printed." Official approval or license (secular or ecclesiastical) to print or publish a book. Such licenses, usually printed on the verso of the title page, and sometimes on a separate leaf, were common in the sixteenth and seventeenth centuries. The term is still used today by the Roman Catholic Church, which requires that any work—Bible, catechism, theological tract, liturgical book—that purports to represent authentic Catholic teaching have imprimatur. *See also* cum licentia; cum privilegio.

imprint   (1) In a book, the statement that identifies the publisher, usually giving the place and date of issue, printed at the bottom of the title page; occasionally, the name of the publisher's subsidiary or division under which a book is issued. (2) By extension, the printed or published item itself, such as "an early American imprint." (3) The name of a printer on any printed matter. (4) Name and address of a dealer on advertising material.

in print   A book that is available from its publisher.

in quires   The British term for in sheets. *See also* quire.

in sheets   *See* sheets.

incunabula (*sing.* incunabulum)   Latin word for "things in the cradle." The word is used to designate books printed from movable metal type before A.D. 1501, the last half of the fifteenth century being considered "the cradle of printing," during which period over 39,000 separate editions were printed. The Anglicized form *incunable* (pl. *incunables*) came into use in the nineteenth century. *See also* Gesamtkatalog der Wiegendrucke; Hain, Ludwig.

indention   The setting of a line of type to a measure that is narrower than the full width of the type page or column. Quoted matter is often thus set. *See also* hanging indention.

independent distributor   Frequently shortened to ID, a wholesaler who specializes in the distribution of magazines and paperbacks to newsstands, supermarkets, and outlets other than bookstores.

independent store   A single retail outlet, one unaffiliated with any regional or national chain. Although there are more independent stores in the United States than members of chains, independents often charge that chains are sometimes given preferential treatment by publishers because of their enormous volume of orders, which entitles them to a higher discount (*q.v.*) and thus a higher margin of profit.

index   (1) *Index Librorum Prohibitorum*, the list of books that Roman Catholics were prohibited from reading as dangerous to their faith and morals; the latest list was issued in 1948; the publication was terminated in 1966. The list named only those books on which Church authority had been asked to rule. (2) *Index Expurgatorius*, a list of passages to be expunged or altered in works otherwise permitted; out of use today.

index (*pl.* **indexes; indices**)   An alphabetical list usually following the text of a book, which cites page numbers directing the user to names, places, and topics discussed.

India paper   An extremely thin but opaque paper used for thin-paper editions of books. *See also* Bible paper; Oxford India paper.

Indian Bible   *See* Eliot, John.

inferior figures   Small subscript numerals, thus $_2$, used in formulas or to designate a specific leaf in a book.

Information Industry Association   Founded in 1968, a national organization of publishers and other businesses associated with the compilation and dissemination of information either electronically or through print.

information interchange format   *See* bibliographic information interchange format.

information processing   All technical and commercial operations performed by computers. Normally used in a more general sense than the term *data processing*.

information storage and retrieval (ISR)   The process of retrieving documents from a storage place in response to a person's query; this may be a manual operation (e.g., a librarian taking a book off a shelf in the library) or a machine operation involving a computer, a data base, or other automated records.

initial letter   A large capital or decorated letter used to begin a chapter section and sometimes a paragraph.

ink-jet printing   A printing process in which tiny droplets of ink are squirted onto the paper through tiny nozzles. The nozzles can be turned on and off at computer speeds by means of digital signals as the paper passes in front of the nozzles. Characters thus can be formed by selective control of the ink jets. Ink-jet printing is used primarily in computer printout devices today, but experimental full-color prints of high graphic arts quality have been made, and the process may one day find a place in the regular printing industry.

inlaid binding   A leather binding into which other colors or kinds of leather have been inserted for decorative purposes. Also known as *mosaic binding*. *See also* onlay.

input Data or instructions to be placed into a computer system. Input devices, used to input material into a computer, are of several types, including keyboard units, optical character recognition units, tape readers, etc. *See also* high-speed reader; keyboard; optical character recognition; reader.

input-output (I/O) General term for devices used to get data into a computer and bring it out. Often a single device can be used for both functions.

inscribed copy A copy of a book that has been inscribed by the author to the owner at the owner's request, often some time after publication. Cf. presentation copy.

inserts Illustrations, maps, or other material not printed as part of the regular signatures, but in special sections instead. These are inserted in the book during binding. *See also* tipping in.

inspection copy *See* examination copy.

instant book A book inpired by a notable event or issue of great timeliness that is usually produced as a paperback because of the speed of the enterprise. In practical terms, the period from conception to distribution can be less than a week. However, any book that is produced in less time than commonly necessary in the publishing process may be loosely termed an instant book. Bantam Books has been credited with initiating the instant book with the publication of *Report of the Warren Commission on the Assassination of President Kennedy* on September 28, 1964. The book was for sale 80 hours after the document was officially released to the public.

instruction A set of codes that defines something to be done by the computer with the data given it.

instructional materials Any supplementary materials from a general trade or educational publisher used to support educational curricula. Also called *children's books*. The terms formerly used to describe these materials, *juveniles* or *junior books*, are no longer preferred.

intaglio printing From the Italian "intagliare," to cut in. One of the four basic methods of printing, the others being relief, lithographic, and screen process printing. The printing areas on an intaglio printing plate are depressed so that when the entire plate is flooded with ink and then wiped, ink remains in these depressed areas in proportion to their depth. This is the opposite of relief printing where the ink is held by the raised surface, as on type or woodcuts. Intaglio is the method used in etchings, steel and copper engravings, photogravure, and rotogravure.

integrated circuit   A complete electronic device or building block circuit containing various electronic components (often numbering in the thousands), fabricated in a single process on a tiny silicon chip at costs far below those of hand assembly. Today entire central processing units and large blocks of memory are available as integrated circuits, and major advances in this technology are still anticipated. *See* microprocessor.

interactive   In electronic publishing, a program in which an individual enters upon a kind of dialogue with a technologically advanced or computer-assisted device. A two-way cable television system allows interactivity with the viewer responding to material displayed on a screen. A laser-read videodisc (*q.v.*) can also contain an exercise that elicits a response from the person operating the disc player. In most cases, the user's responses determine the course of the program, which can be educational or entertaining or both.

interactive mode   The process of a computer and its terminals responding continuously to each other in conversational mode. *See* conversational mode; online processing.

interface   A point of contact between different parts of a system, different systems, or humans and a machine system.

interleaved   Any special leaves individually inserted between the printed leaves. *See also* interleaving paper.

interleaving paper   Tissue-weight paper placed in front of illustrations in books, or between two or more engravings, etchings, sheets of cellulosic film, etc. Also, a paper inserted between sheets as they come off the printing press to prevent offset (*q.v.*).

internal storage   Storage of data in a memory that is an integral part of the main computer, as opposed to a device that is auxiliary and can be detached.

International League of Antiquarian Booksellers (ILAB)   Ligue Internationale de la Librairie Ancienne (LILA), founded in 1948, is now made up of national associations of antiquarian booksellers of eighteen countries: Australia and New Zealand,

Austria, Belgium, Brazil, Canada, Denmark, Finland, France, Germany, Great Britain, Italy, Japan, Netherlands, Norway, Sweden, Switzerland, and the United States. The league publishes an international directory of member-booksellers and an international glossary of book-collecting terms in eight languages. *See also* Antiquarian Booksellers' Association of America, Inc.

International Standard Bibliographic Description for Monographic Publications [ISBD(M)] An international standard for the communication of bibliographic information for monographic publications, developed under the auspices of the International Federation of Library Associations and Institutions (IFLA). The ISBD(M) specifies the elements that should make up a bibliographic description, the order in which these elements should be presented, and how they should be punctuated. Its objectives are to make records from different sources interchangeable; to facilitate the interpretation of records across language barriers; and to facilitate the conversion of bibliographic records to machine-readable form.

International Standard Bibliographic Description for Serials [ISBD(S)] An international standard for the communication of bibliographic information for serials, developed under the auspices of the International Federation of Library Associations and Institutions (IFLA). The ISBD(S) specifies the requirements for the description and identification of serial publications, the order in which the elements of the description should be presented, and how they should be punctuated. Its objectives are to make records from different sources interchangeable; to facilitate the interpretation of records across language barriers; and to facilitate the conversion of bibliographic records to machine-readable form.

International Standard Book Number (ISBN) An international standard for exclusive identification of books. An International Standard Book Number identifies one title, or edition of a title, from one specific publisher, and is unique to that title or edition. A Standard Book Number was developed by British publishers in 1967, and adopted by the United States the following year. In 1969, the numbering system became an international standard known as the International Standard Book Number. The ISBN is usually printed on the verso of the title page, as well as in some prominent position on the outside of the book, as at the foot of the outside back cover or at the foot of the jacket if the book has one. On some paperback books, the ISBN is printed also on the lower part of the spine to facilitate inventory control. Most U.S. publishers are now participating in the program. When fully implemented, the ISBN system is expected to enable librarians, publishers, wholesalers, and booksellers to handle more effectively the writing, processing, and filling of orders. In the United States, the ISBN Agency is administered by the R. R. Bowker Company. Worldwide implementation of the system is coordinated by the International ISBN agency in Berlin, West Germany. In 1982, forty-two countries were participating in the system.

International Standard Serial Number (ISSN) An internationally accepted code for the identification of serial publications. The ISSN program was developed by the International Organization for Standardization Technical Committee 46, and became operative in the United States in 1971 through the cooperative efforts of the Library of Congress, the American National Standards Institute, and the R. R. Bowker Company. The ISSN appears in a prominent place on each issue of a serial, usually the upper right corner of the front cover. When the program is fully implemented, the ISSN number can be used as a code by indexing and abstracting services; by subscription agents for communications, billing, inventory, claims, etc.; by authors for copyright; by publishers for inventory, ordering, and billing; and by library users for location of the item in the library. In library processing, the ISSN can be used for identification, control on acquisitions (check-in), claiming, accessioning, shelving, cooperative cataloging, etc.; in library reference for retrieval/request identification, interlibrary loan, etc. In machine use, the ISSN will fulfill the need for file update and linkage and retrieval and transmittal of data.

The National Serials Data Program at the Library of Congress is responsible for registering and numbering serials published in the United States. Worldwide implementation of ISSN is coordinated by the International Serials Data System (ISDS), in Paris. In 1982, forty countries were participating in the system.

interpret In computer processing, to translate data in coding of one type into that of another type, or into human-readable form.

interrupt To temporarily stop the normal computer routine, on special signal. Usually the normal routine can be resumed later.

introduction A preliminary portion of a book leading up to the main subject matter. An *introduction* is usually an attempt to define the organization and limits of a work; a *preface*, by contrast, may explain the author's reasons for undertaking the work, his qualifications, his indebtedness to other authorities, etc. *See also* front matter.

inventory   Total stock of materials for sale in the possession of a supplier or seller at a given time; used as a verb, to count these materials.

inverted entry   In an index, an entry made up of several words that have been rearranged to bring the most important words to the front; e.g., title page, engraved.

invoice   The bill for goods or services showing itemized quantities, prices, discounts and terms, and net amount due.

invoice symbols   The following symbols are often used on publishers' invoices:

    C, OC—Order cancelled
    EX—See explanation herewith; or full exchange on returns
    NE, NEP—New edition pending
    NO, NOP—Not our publication, cannot supply
    OP—Out of print
    OPP—Out of print at present
    OS—Out of stock
    NYP—Not yet published
    TOP—Temporarily out of print
    TOS—Temporarily out of stock
    W—Will advise in a few days

issue   A part of an edition printed from substantially the same setting of type as the first printing, but different in some respect, and offered for sale by the publisher as a planned unit. For example, there may be a different title page, new material added in an appendix, an excision in the text, or a new format. Issues are determined by the publisher after a book has been printed. Cf. state.

italic   Sloping types, as distinct from roman types, e.g., *italic*, roman. First used by Aldus Manutius in a Virgil that he printed in 1501. According to tradition, the style was closely copied from Petrarch's handwriting. A distinction is made between true italic characters, with their resemblance to handwriting, and oblique or inclined roman characters. The most obvious difference is between the italic *a* and the inclined roman a. Most electronic typesetting machines now can produce inclined roman type by altering the standard roman designs stored digitally in their memories; true italic, however, requires a separate italic font.

In preparing copy for the printer, or in correcting proof, a single line under a word means *set in italics*.

Ives, Frederic E. (1856-1937)   American inventor who developed the halftone photoengraving process and made many contributions to the technique of color printing.

jacket   *See* dust jacket.

jacket band   A strip wrapped around a book jacket for sales promotion purposes; e.g., to emphasize some late news tie-in. *See also* dust jacket.

Jansen   A French style of binding without line or ornament on the outside cover but elaborately tooled on the inside cover. The name is said to be derived from the Jansenists, an ascetic sect that flourished in the seventeenth century.

Japan paper   An exceedingly strong, long fibered, high-grade paper with irregular formation that is made in Japan and used for printing etchings, photogravures, books, and also for binding. Its irregular formation imitates the old imperial vellum and has a handsome mottled effect. *French Japon* is a good imitation, less expensive, and not as strong; American imitations are sometimes called *Japan vellum.*

Japan vellum   *See* Japan paper.

Japanese style   *See* Chinese style.

Jenson, Nicolas (1420?-1481)   Celebrated printer of the fifteenth century. In 1458 he was sent by Charles VII of France to Mainz to discover the new art of printing. He returned to Paris in 1461, but owing to the death of Charles VII the project of setting up a press was abandoned.

In 1470 he established his own press at Venice. His Roman typefaces influenced printers down to modern times.

job lot   Often a combination of titles forming a singular group, books offered by a publisher or wholesaler at special low prices to close out or cut down stock. *See also* remainder.

job press   A small letterpress, commonly of the platen type, upon which small jobs are printed.

job printer   A printer who handles a miscellany of work such as circulars, forms, stationery, book jackets, etc. A jack-of-all-trades compared to the printer who specializes in books, magazines, labels, or some other line.

jobber   *See* wholesaler.

joint   The hinge joining the front and back panels of a book cover with the spine.

joint author   A person who writes a book in collaboration with one or more associates; generally the participation of all is acknowledged on the title page. Cf. ghost writer.

Julian calendar   *See* calendar.

justification, justify   Process of spacing type lines out to the full line measure to produce columns with even left and right alignments. Lines are usually spaced out either by distributing space evenly between words or by adding thin spaces between characters. Type so handled is sometimes said to be right-justified. This paragraph is an example of right justification.

   In some instances, it is considered preferable, for aesthetic or for technical reasons, not to set type justified, but to give the right-hand edge an irregular appearance, usually known as *ragged right*. This paragraph is set ragged right to show the difference.

   Just as type can be set ragged right, it can be set with the left edge ragged, or with both edges ragged (each line centered in the line measure).

justification routine   The procedure a computer follows in calculating the required spacing to justify a line of type.

juveniles (n.), **juvenile** (adj.)   Children's books or pertaining to them. The terms *instructional materials* (*q.v.*) or *children's books* are preferred.

keep standing   An order to hold onto type, pending the possibility of reprinting.

keepsake   (1) One of the gift books, usually of verse and illustrated, in vogue in the early nineteenth century. (2) Printed mementos issued by clubs or organizations for special occasions. *See also* annual.

Kells, Book of   Illuminated manuscript of the Latin Gospels, found in the ruins of the Abbey of Kells, Ireland, and thought to date from the eighth or early ninth century. It is now in Trinity College, Dublin.

Kelmscott Press (1891-1898)   A private press at Hammersmith, London, founded and directed by William Morris from 1891 to his death in 1896. The books issued from it were exceptional examples of bookmaking, and their beauty of execution and harmony of design were the result of exacting study. The paper and ink were especially made for the books, and three fonts of type were designed—the Golden, the Troye, and the Chaucer—the last used in a folio edition of Chaucer, one of the monuments of modern book printing.

kern   A part of a letter that projects over or under adjacent letters or past the edge of its own body, e.g., many lowercase italic *f*'s. Traditionally, kerned letters are hand designed, but some type designers are now using computers for kerning.

key plate   The plate of maximum detail in a set of color plates to which other plates in the same set are registered.

keyboard   (1) To type out data or instructions on a keyboard device, to encode them for entry into a computer. (2) Typewriter-like device for encoding data for computer processing.

keypunch   A keyboard machine designed for punching punch cards.

keyword   A significant, informative word associated with a document in a computerized information retrieval system for use in searching by subject to recover relevant stored material. Two commonly used search systems are KWIC (keyword in context, such as in a title or text) and KWOC (keyword out of context, standing alone).

kill   Directions to the printer to do away with composed type no longer wanted.

kraft paper   Paper made from wood by the sulfate process. It has excellent strength and durability, but will not bleach as white as the sulfite and soda papers generally used for books. The best wrapping papers are made of brown, unbleached kraft. A binding paper with a kraft base has good folding endurance. Kraft also is used as lining material on the backbone of a book. *See also* lining.

L.C.   Library of Congress.

lc   The abbreviation for lowercase (*q.v.*).

LMP   The abbreviation for *Literary Market Place* (*q.v.*).

l.p.   The abbreviation for large-paper edition (*q.v.*).

l.s. (*pl.* ls. s.)   Letter signed. A letter of which the text is not in the handwriting of the signer.

label   Title of a book printed or stamped on other material and affixed to the book's spine or cover.

lacing in   Method common to hand binding by which cords are carried through holes in the boards of the cover, the ends cut off, hammered down smooth, and firmly glued. The covering material is then pasted over the cover.

laid lines   In laid papers, the light lines made by the laid wires of the mold in handmade paper or dandy roll in machine-made paper. Laid lines usually run across the grain of the paper. *See also* chain lines; laid paper.

laid paper   Paper that, when held up to the light, shows fine parallel lines (wire marks) and thicker crosslines at right angles (chain lines) that are produced by the weave of the dandy roll (*q.v.*) in machine-made paper, or, in handmade paper, by the wires of the mold. Laid paper is handsome in appearance, but has no other advantage over wove paper (*q.v.*).

lambskin   The tanned, smoothly finished skin of a young lamb used as a bookbinding leather during the late nineteenth century. It was used for limp bindings because of its suppleness and absence of blemishes and was valued for its delicate colors. Lambskin is similar to calfskin, but has shorter fibers and is less durable.

laminate   Superimposed layers of material bonded to one another by adhesive or by pressure and/or heat. Book jackets are often laminated to an outer film of clear plastic, primarily to protect the printed surfaces, but also to give the jacket a crisp appearance. *See also* varnishing.

Lane, Sir Allen (1902-1970)   Founder of Penguin Books in 1936 and head of the worldwide paperback publishing house until his death. Apprenticed at seventeen to John Lane at the Bodley

Head, where he learned publishing. In 1936, he resigned to start his own firm. He became recognized as the modern pioneer in the successful paperback publishing of nonfiction, classics, and other serious books, along with quality fiction and children's literature. He was knighted in 1952.

language   A system for defining and assigning meanings to symbols for communicating between people or between people and machines. *See also* artificial language; machine language; natural language.

large-paper edition   A special edition printed from the same type as the standard edition and frequently on better quality paper, but with wider margins on all sides.

large post octavo, large post quarto   *See* book sizes.

laser   Acronym for light amplification by stimulated emission of radiation. A device that projects an extremely narrow, coherent light beam with an intensity that can be used for "drawing" fine images on film or etching vaporizing material from the surface of a printing plate. Use of lasers in typesetting, scanning, platemaking, and photocopy imaging equipment is growing rapidly.

lateral reversal   Change of an image from right to left or from left to right, producing a mirror image of the original. Metal type is laterally reversed from the printed image it makes on paper. Normal emulsion-to-emulsion contact printing with photographic materials produces laterally reversed images. Special reversal films, however, permit the copy to retain the original image direction.

law binding   Originally, a style of plain calf- or sheepskin binding used for law books. Usually with laced-in boards and two or more gold-blocked title labels on the spine (usually red above black). Known also as *law calf* and *law sheep*. In the modern version, light tan buckram has largely replaced sheepskin, which, being short-fibered, has a tendency to dry out and break at the hinges. The case binding of buckram is made to resemble sheepskin and has red and black paper labels blocked in gold.

laydown speed   In phototypesetting, the speed at which characters are exposed onto photographic material.

layout   The working diagram of a page or other spatial area to be made up in type, for the printer to follow. Usually marked to show placement and spacing of text, headings, illustrations, captions, etc., with notes on the sizes and kinds of type to be used.

lead title   The one or more major books on a publisher's seasonal list (*q.v.*). *See also* leaders.

leaded matter   Composition with extra space between the lines in addition to that of the specified type size. In metallic composition, strips of lead material are inserted to create the spaces. Leads are 2 point unless specified thicker or thinner. Most composition systems today, both metallic and photographic, insert this additional space between lines as part of their setting function, thereby eliminating the need for a separate operation.

leaders   (1) Dots or dashes set in succession so as to lead the eye across the page, as in a table of contents. (2) The books of outstanding importance, whether commercially or by virtue of literary accomplishment, in a publisher's list of new publications.

leads   Thin strips of metal, usually two points in thickness (1/36th of an inch) less than type-high, placed between successive lines of type in order to increase the white space between them. Double leads call for two strips. Similar wooden strips are called *reglets*.

leaf   A single sheet containing two pages, one on each side; each of which, in a book, may bear printing, writing, or illustrations. Generally, blank leaves are not numbered.

leaflet   A printed sheet folded once, but not stitched, sewn, or otherwise bound. In a less restricted sense, a small, thin pamphlet.

leased line   Rented telephone line or other communication channel reserved for the exclusive use of the renter.

leasing plan   *See* book leasing plan.

legend   (1) On a map or chart, the key to various signs and symbols used. (2) The brief wording that identifies or explains an illustration. Present usage favors the word *caption* (*q.v.*) for this meaning.

letter spacing   The placing of spaces between the letters of a word. Letter spacing of text is not considered good practice in most cases, but the appearance of words or headlines composed exclusively of uppercase letters can often be improved by letter spacing.

letterpress The process of printing from raised printing surfaces. Also called *relief printing*, letterpress image areas—typefaces, halftones, rules, etc.—are raised, or stand in relief, above the surrounding nonprinting structure supporting them; ink is rolled onto the raised printing surfaces and then transferred to the paper by pressing it onto the raised surfaces.

Relief printing was first used by the Chinese and Europeans for printing from carved blocks containing entire pages of characters or complete illustrations. But it was the invention of movable metal type, generally attributed to Johann Gutenberg (*q.v.*) of Mainz, Germany, about 1445, that opened the way for letterpress to become the foundation of modern printing and publishing over the following 500 years. Letterpress was the dominant printing process for books until about the middle of the twentieth century, when offset lithography superseded it. Flexography, a form of letterpress, is still used extensively for mass market paperbacks.

lettre de forme; lettre de somme; lettre de batarde The three general classifications of gothic type forms as found in the fifteenth century. The first is the pointed and most formal; the second is the round and less formal; the third is a cursive form. They correspond to similar classifications of lettering used in the manuscripts that preceded printing.

level Synonym for channel, usually used to describe the number of rows of code holes across a tape. *See also* channel; track.

Leypoldt, Frederick (1835-1884) German immigrant who became an organizer of the American book trade. After operating his own bookstore in Philadelphia, he invited Henry Holt to join him in a publishing partnership in New York. The house organ of the firm was the *Literary Bulletin*, a compendium of general book news and the precursor of numerous bibliographic tools. Leypoldt and Holt separated, Holt keeping the publishing enterprise, and Leypoldt the bibliographic program. In 1872 Leypoldt became the first editor of *Publishers Weekly*; he originated the scheme of binding up publisher's catalogues, later to be known as the *Publishers Trade List Annual*; and he began or proposed other bibliographic tools that later became standard. Leypoldt, R. R. Bowker, and Melvil Dewey started the *Library Journal* in 1876, and helped found the American Library Association. In 1879 Leypoldt sold the *Publishers Weekly* to Richard Rogers Bowker (*q.v.*), his associate, who, with Mrs. Leypoldt, carried on the business after its founder's death.

libel   Any written statement or pictorial representation that holds a person, organization, or corporation up to contempt and ridicule or pecuniary loss. Slander is verbal (spoken) libel.

library binding   *See* binding.

library edition   An edition, often of a children's book, in an especially strong binding for library use. *See also* binding.

Library Journal   Professional journal of the American library world; founded 1876 by Frederick Leypoldt, R. R. Bowker, and Melvil Dewey (*qq.v*). Published by the R. R. Bowker Company.

Library of Congress catalog card   A printed catalog card issued by the Library of Congress for the use of libraries throughout the United States. As the L.C. Card Division catalogs books for its own collections, it prints extra cards, which are available on a subscription basis or may be ordered by number. A publisher may request a card number from L.C.'s Cataloging in Publication office as soon as a book is in galley form, so that this number can be printed with the copyright information on the verso of the title page. Thus the librarian can order the catalog card by number upon receipt of the book. *See also* Cataloging in Publication.

Library of Congress classification   A system, often referred to as L.C., for classifying and shelving books, developed by the Library of Congress, for its collections.

ligature   Two or more overlapped letters such as fi, ff , fl, ffi, æ , etc., which form a new character in a type font. In metal type, such combined characters must be cast on a single metal body using a single matrix or mold. In photographic or computer-controlled typesetting, such combined characters can often be created by overlapping individual characters but separate ligature designs are often included in fonts despite this capability, in order to permit improved aesthetics.

light pen   A light-detection device shaped like a writing pen, attached to a video display terminal via a wire. When pointed to a particular spot on the display screen, the pen senses light and sends a signal to the computer which is used to tell where on the screen to perform operations. An alternative to the light pen is the use of a cursor on the screen. *See also* cursor.

lightface A term used to distinguish ordinary type, as used in this sentence, from **boldface.**

limited edition An edition of a volume or a set of volumes, of which a stated number of copies is printed. These copies (or sets) are usually numbered consecutively. A special page gives the facts as to the edition limit and the number and often contains also the signature of the author, publisher, or printer.

Limited Editions Club American subscription book club founded in 1929 by George Macy, specializing in finely designed and printed works for its members. Through its policy of engaging the best designers and printers, here and abroad, the club has furthered the arts of the book and brought them home to many who were not previously collectors.

limp binding A binding from which the stiffening board has been omitted. *See also* flexible binding.

line cut, line engraving A photoengraving on metal, usually zinc or copper, of a design in lines, dots, or masses. A *zinc etching* is a line cut on zinc. *See also* engraving; halftone.

line drawing A drawing containing no grays or middle tones; for example, a pen-and-India-ink drawing, a scratchboard drawing, etc. In general, any drawing, including stippled or textured drawings, that can be reproduced without the use of halftone (*q.v.*) techniques.

line editor A person who works closely with an author as a book progresses and then goes over the manuscript, literally line by line, to make certain it is in the best shape it can be for publication.

line printer A computer output device that prints one line of characters at a time across a page. *See also* high-speed printer.

linecasting machine A hot metal typesetting device that casts a complete line of type on one bar of metal. *See also* hot metal.

linen A cloth woven of threads derived from the straw of the flax plant. The straw stems are steeped in water to remove resins and then fermented. The resulting fibers, separated from the woody material, are spun into thread. *See also* book cloth.

linen paper Originally any paper made from linen rags, but the term now is often applied to paper finished with a pattern simulating cloth.

liner   A piece of kraft paper glued to the backbone of a book, not to be confused with super lining.

lines per minute   In typesetting, a basic statement of the speed or throughput of a typesetting machine. Usually expressed in terms of newspaper text lines, which are typically 10½ to 11½ picas wide and contain about thirty characters.

lining   (1) The material pasted down on the spine of a sewn book after gluing off, rounding and backing, and before covering or casing-in. The lining reinforces the glue and helps hold signatures together. The more expensive books are generally lined with a piece of gauze-like fabric called *super* (also called *crash*) and a liner of kraft paper. In less expensive editions, either crash or paper only is used. (2) The process of gluing the crash to the backbone and then applying the kraft as a second layer. (At this point, the headbands are glued to the top and bottom of the liner.) The crash extends beyond the backbone on both sides so it can be glued between endpapers and the front and back covers, giving strength to the hinge areas where the endpapers hold the cover to the book block.

lining figures   *See* numerals, Arabic.

lining papers   Synonymous with endpapers (*q.v.*).

Linotype   A typesetting machine that sets matter in metal slugs or solid lines—hence its name (and pronunciation): line-o'-type. Generally used for all types of typeset products until the advent of photographic and electronic systems. Invented and developed in the United States between 1876 and 1886 by Ottmar Mergenthaler. In 1981, Mergenthaler announced cessation of Linotype manufacture in the United States, although it will continue to produce spare parts. *See also* linecasting machine; Ludlow Typograph; Monotype.

list   All the titles a publisher has available for sale. It includes the entire backlist, the new books of the current season (the frontlist), and forthcoming books. A publisher's *spring list*, on the other hand, is the roster of books scheduled for release during the spring season. *Seasonal lists* are usually the province of hardcover and trade paperbacks and may be issued twice a year (spring and fall) or three times a year (spring, fall, and winter). *Mass market paperback lists* are generally issued on a monthly basis. *See also* backlist; frontlist; midlist.

list price   The price to the retail consumer as suggested by the publisher. It is sometimes printed on the jacket or cover. Occasionally called simply *list*. Cf. net pricing.

literary agent   One who acts on behalf of the author to find a publisher for a written or proposed manuscript and who handles the subsequent subsidiary rights not acquired by the publisher; sometimes called an *author's agent* or *author's representative*. Also one who acts on behalf of publishers to find special types of material or authors to develop that material. The agent is paid on a commission basis by the author. Traditionally the agent's commission has been 10 percent of an author's advance and royalties; in a number of instances today, depending upon the agent, the commission has crept up to 15 percent.

Literary Market Place   An annual directory of the American publishing industry that supplies information on publishers, literary agents, book clubs, trade events, review media, industry-related organizations, and a wide variety of professional services available to the book trade. Published by R. R. Bowker Company.

lithography   The process of printing from image carriers (plates or stones) with both printing and nonprinting areas in the same plane. Also known generically as planographic printing because of this principle. A chemical process is used to separate printing and nonprinting areas; the image carrier is chemically treated to be ink-receptive and water-repellent in the printing areas and water-receptive and ink-repellent in the nonprinting areas. Thus, only the image takes up the ink, which is transferred to the paper. Consequently, each printing cycle requires inking as well as dampening or moistening with a solution consisting mainly of water.

   Lithography was invented about 1796 by Alois Senefelder, in Munich, who originally used smooth porous limestone as an image carrier and transferred the ink by pressing the paper directly onto the stone. Today a variety of thin plates made of metals, plastics, and paper is available, and image transfer is generally indirect, from the plate to a soft blanket and from the blanket to the paper. Indirect printing is widely known as *offset* in contemporary printing parlance. Offset, or offset lithography, has become a most important method for book printing, superseding letterpress in most commercial industry.

Little Blue Book   A series of small, pocket-sized (3½ × 5 inches), low-priced pamphlets (25¢ initially, later 15¢, 10¢, and finally 5¢), so called because of the semistiff blue cover stock in which they were issued. The series, established by E. Haldeman-Julius, in Girard, Kansas, began publication in January 1919, and was sold directly to the public by the publisher through newspaper advertising. The first title was Oscar Wilde's *The Ballad of Reading Gaol*, and it was quickly followed by a wide range of reprints of the classics, both fiction and nonfiction, with the intention of encouraging the general public to read the best books. The series had its heyday in the 1920s and 1930s, and by the time of Haldeman-Julius's death in 1951, had sold more than 300 million copies.

Little Leather Library   *See* Boni, Albert.

live matter   Composed type, plates, or cuts that are being held for future use.

Liveright, Horace B. (1888-1933)   American publisher who in his brief years in the business (1917-1930) brought flair, commercial daring, and new writers into the field and trained brilliant young future publishers (Bennett Cerf, Richard Simon, Julian Messner, and others). In 1917 he formed a partnership with Albert Boni under the firm name of Boni & Liveright, and the firm immediately announced the publication of the first volumes of the Modern Library (later acquired by Cerf and Donald Klopfer). Liveright authors included Dreiser, O'Neill, Edgar Lee Masters, Faulkner, and others.

Livre d'Heures   *See* Book of Hours.

location   A place in computer storage where data may be stored and retrieved from. *See also* address.

locking up   In letterpress, making secure a form of type matter in the metal frame known as a *chase*, preparatory to putting it on the press.

logic system   The set of discrete steps in a computer program followed by the machine to perform various data processing tasks.

logotype, logo (colloquial)   A group of letters cast as a unit. In advertising the term is sometimes used to denote a particular form or style of trade name set in type or drawn. *See also* ligature.

long page   A type page longer than has been specified.

loop (1) Synonym for cycle. (2) Repeated execution of a series of instructions until a terminal condition is met. *See also* closed-loop system; open-loop system.

loose in binding Description of a book, in which sections or the entire block are badly loosened from the case to a more serious degree than shaken (*q.v.*).

loose-leaf binding *See* binding.

loss leader Merchandise advertised and sold at cost or at a loss to attract customers into a store, sometimes to create the impression that the store's other prices are just as low.

lowercase (lc) (1) The small letters of a type font as distinguished from the capitals, or uppercase. So called because in hand-set type they were usually kept in the lower of two cases holding the type assortment. (2) In proofreading, directions to substitute small letters for capitals. *See also* case.

Ludlow Typograph A machine for setting cast metal display type. Brass matrices are set by hand in a special stick. The assembled mats are inserted in a slot over a mold and molten metal is forced up from beneath, thus casting the whole line in a single slug.

MARC (Machine Readable Cataloging) A communications format for the transmission of machine-readable catalog data developed at the Library of Congress and distributed to libraries and other subscribers in the form of magnetic tapes. The numerous applications of MARC include the production of acquisitions list, catalog cards, book catalogs, bibliographies, and book labels.

m.f. Abbreviation for machine finish (*q.v.*).

ms. (*pl.* mss.) Manuscript.

ms. s. (*pl.* mss. s.) Manuscript, signed. A manuscript of which the text is not in the handwriting of the signer.

McCain sewing, stitching *See* sewing.

machine coated *See* coated paper.

machine direction *See* grain.

machine finish (m.f.) Paper that has been made smooth and somewhat glossy by passing through several rolls of the calendering machine. *See also* calendering.

machine language   A language designed to be read by a machine without any translating steps, as opposed to an artificial language or symbolic language, which requires interpretation of its terms into machine language in the computer before its instructions can be executed. *See also* artificial language; natural language; symbolic language.

machine-readable   Encoded in machine language and therefore readable by the machine. *See also* machine language.

machine translation   Automatic translation of one representation to another in the computer. Such translations may include, in addition to the interpretation of programming languages, the translation of natural languages from one to another, such as Russian to English. *See also* artificial language; machine language; natural language; symbolic language.

machining   A term used in England for presswork (*q.v.*).

macro code   A single instruction code given to a computer to represent a complex condition. The computer replaces this macro code with a series of predetermined discrete codes required to produce the final condition. Macro codes are a form of shorthand for reducing the work of putting material into a computer.

made-up copy   An incomplete book whose lack of a leaf, or more, has been made good by the addition of the missing leaf or leaves from another imperfect copy or copies of the same edition. The making-up of a copy of a rare and costly book is not frowned upon, but the makeup must be proclaimed and not concealed.

A modern example of a great made-up copy is the *Pilgrim's Progress* (first edition of Part I), 1678, sold in the Frank J. Hogan sale in New York in April 1946, for $8,000. This volume was made up after 1921 from two (possibly three) imperfect copies, and upon completion it became one of only eleven complete copies known. It is now in the Library of Congress.

magnetic storage   Storage of data by magnetizing or demagnetizing specified memory areas in a computer. Magnetic storage types include core, disk, drum, and tape. *See also* storage.

Mahieu, Thomas   *See* Maioli bindings.

main entry   In a card catalog or index, the bibliographic entry under which full information is given, usually the author entry.

main frame   A large-size central processing unit in a computer system. *See also* microcomputer; minicomputer.

Maioli bindings   Styles of bookbindings by Parisian binders for the sixteenth-century French book collector Tommaso Maiolus (the latinized form of Thomas Mahieu, or Matthieu), secretary to Catherine de Medici. Mahieu, long thought to be an Italian, was a famous collector of about the same time as Jean Grolier (*q.v.*), and many of the bindings in his library used the same form of legend as the Grolier bindings, being lettered on the front cover: THO MAIOLI ET AMICORUM. Most of the bindings were richly gilt with medallion and foliage designs, decorated with flowing interlace strapwork, and with ornaments in outline or azured.

majuscule   From the Latin "majuscula," somewhat greater. Large letters or capitals. In opposition to minuscule, or small letters. Used especially in reference to early roman alphabets. In French *majuscule* is used as a synonym for uppercase.

make-ready   In its broadest meaning, all operations on a press to get a composed form ready for printing. The function of make-ready is essentially the same in all printing processes, but the procedures differ considerably. Modern printing conditions require maximum use of the press equipment, and every effort is made to minimize make-ready time.

makeup   In letterpress printing, the activity of taking type from galleys, putting it into page form, inserting illustrative cuts, dividing the matter into page lengths, and adding running heads, titles of subdivisions, folios, footnotes, etc.

   In photographic and other kinds of nonmetallic composition different makeup techniques are used such as paste-up or stripping. In highly advanced systems of computerized compostition, makeup is a programmed function, often designated as *computerized pagination*.

manila paper   Sturdy paper of a color and finish similar to paper made from manila hemp and used for covers of brochures and similar publications. In current usage, the term has no significance as to fiber composition. Paper made from manila hemp, called *rope manila*, in which the hemp fibers in the paper give it strength, is used for folders, envelopes, and cards. Loosely used to refer to any yellowish paper or bristol board.

manufacturing   In book production, the complete process of composition, printing, and binding.

manufacturing clause   The section of the copyright act that concerns manufacturing requirements and importation of books. Part of U.S. copyright law since 1891, the current manufacturing clause (Section 601 of the Copyright Act of 1976) states that for a U.S. author to obtain maximum U.S. copyright protection on certain nondramatic literary works, the work must be manufactured (printed and bound) in the United States or Canada. The clause was due to be phased out July 1, 1982. However, Congress passed a bill extending the clause for four years. On July 8, 1982, President Ronald Reagan vetoed it, stating it would inhibit free trade. On July 13, 1982, Congress overrode the veto and effectively reinstated the four-year extension of the clause.

manufacturing information   *See* impression.

manuscript (ms)   Literally, handwritten material. (1) A handwritten book, document, or other work. (2) A written or typewritten work of an author, to be used as typesetter's copy.

Manutius, Aldus   *See* Aldus.

marble paper   An end-leaf or cover paper decorated with a marble-like pattern and used in both blank and printed books. *See also* marbling.

marbling, marbled edges   The process of decorating sheets of paper, cloth, or the edges of books with a variety of colors in an irregular pattern like the veins of marble. *See also* marble paper.

marginal head, marginal note   *See* marginalia.

marginalia   Notes or headings written or printed on the margins of a page, including marginal notes, marginal heads, side notes. Usually set in narrow measure in type different from text of page. Footnotes are printed in the bottom margin of the page and shoulder notes at the top and outer corner of the page.

margins   The unprinted space between the main body of the written or illustrative matter and the edge of the page. The traditional ratio is: top margin 2; outside 3; bottom 4; inside 1 1/2. The four margins are also called head, fore-edge, lower, and back, respectively. The space between two facing pages is called the *gutter* or *back margin*.

mark-sensing   A technique of recognizing special marks or nota-
tions on documents, as compared to optical character recognition, which senses alphanumeric characters.

markup   The difference between the cost of a commodity, e.g., a
book, to the dealer and the price at which it is sold to the consumer; usually expressed as a percentage. Literally, the markup is the
percentage by which the cost is increased to reach the retail price.
In common retail practice, however, markup is sometimes used
synonymously with discount (*q.v.*).

mass market paperback   A paperbound book, most often in a size
approximately 4 3/16 inches in width and 6 7/8 inches in height
and with paper covers designed for sales appeal, distributed
chiefly through traditional magazine channels, including newsstands, variety and drugstores, supermarkets, and other mass
outlets. It is also marketed to general bookstores, college stores,
and department stores. A mass market paperback may be either
an original publication that has never appeared in any other
format or a reprint of a previously published hardcover or trade
paperback edition here made available at a significantly lower
price. The paper used in printing the mass market paperback is
frequently inferior to that used in hardcover books or trade paperbacks. Pocket Books is credited with publishing the first mass
market paperbacks in 1939, which explains why books in this
format are sometimes called pocket books. A *mass market trade
paperback* is an informal term for the larger-sized and higher-
priced paperback book of broad commercial potential released
by a mass market publisher and sold through both magazine and
bookstore channels. *See also* trade paperback.

Massee, May (1883-1966)   Children's book publisher and editor
who set standards of literary and artistic excellence that decisively
influenced modern juvenile book publishing. Massee, who had
been a children's librarian, became editor of junior books at
Doubleday in 1923 and founded in 1933 the Viking Press children's book department, which she headed until 1960. A memorial collection of children's books, manuscripts, and working materials, with a research and seminar program, was opened in her
name in 1972 at Kansas State Teachers College.

masthead   A statement of the name, ownership, etc., of a publication. Usually found at the head of the editorial page of a newspa-

per. In a magazine, it is usually on the editorial or contents page. Sometimes called the *flag*.

mat   *See* matrix.

matrix (*pl.* **matrices**)   (1) A metal mold in which type is cast. (2) A papier- mâché, metal, or plastic mold of a page of type from which electrotypes, stereotypes, or plastic plates are made (often called a *mat*, sometimes a *mold*).

matter   Any type, whether standing or in process of being set. It may be live matter or dead matter, open matter (leaded) or solid matter (without leads). The old terms, *fat* and *lean* matter, are still used to indicate the proportion of open spaces or break lines. The fat, of course, gives the compositor far less work to do than the lean.

Matthieu, Thomas   *See* Maioli bindings.

Mazarin Bible   *See* Gutenberg, Johann.

Mearne, Samuel   English binder of the seventeenth century who became in 1660 royal binder to Charles II. He is noted for the so-called cottage style of ornamentation in which rectangles of parallel lines break outward at the corners and/or in the center, resembling the gables of a roof.

measure   The length of a full line of a page or column, normally expressed in picas and points. (*q.v.*).

mechanical   (1) Meticulously prepared layout to guide engraver or printer, showing exact placement of every element, and carrying simulated type and artwork. (2) Camera-ready pasted-up layout containing actual type and art, for use in making photographic negative. *See* camera-ready; paste-up; repro.

mechanical binding   *See* binding.

mechanical pulp   *See* groundwood pulp.

media; medium   Devices used to package and carry informational content, including such printed products as books, magazines, and newspapers; such audio vehicles as tapes and records; such visual products as film and television; such computerized data carriers as tapes, disks, and online transmission; and even such face-to-face communications as meetings and personal presentations. The term *media* is often used incorrectly to refer to one particular information package. However, the correct usage for describing a single information package is *medium*; *media* for more than one.

medium octavo; medium quarto *See* book sizes.

Melcher, Frederic Gershom (1879-1963) Book industry leader, co-founder, in 1919, of Children's Book Week (*see* Book Week), founder and donor of the Newbery and Caldecott Awards for children's books (1922 and 1937, respectively) and, in 1943, the Carey-Thomas Award for excellence in publishing; editor and co-editor (with Mildred C. Smith) of *Publishers Weekly* for forty years. Trained at Lauriat's bookstore, Boston, and Stewart's, Indianapolis, he joined *PW* in 1918. He was a fervent and influential supporter of effective book trade organization; of the development of children's book publishing, bookselling, and library service; of book-focused librarianship; of excellence in book design; of copyright reform; and of freedom from censorship.

memory In the computer field, synonym for storage.

Mergenthaler, Ottmar (1854-1899) *See* Linotype.

merging In computer processing, the combining of two or more separate groups of data into one file. Sometimes referred to as *tape merging* because tapes are often used as the storage medium.

Meynell, Sir Francis *See* Nonesuch Press.

mezzotint An engraving from a copper plate on which the entire surface is slightly roughened. The portions intended to show highlights or middle tones are scraped and burnished while the shadows are strengthened. Very beautiful velvety effects are thus obtained.

microcomputer The smallest class of computer, based on use of a microprocessor and other integrated circuits and housed in desktop units that can be treated as conventional office or home equipment. Also called *personal computers. See* main frame; microprocessor; minicomputer.

microfiche *See* microforms.

microforms A general term embracing both microfilm, with its variations, and also micro-opaque processes.
 All microforms are techniques for greatly reducing size of the

printed page to save both space and copying cost. Reenlargement for reading is normally done by a special projection machine.

Microfilm is usually handled in rolls, either 16mm or 35mm wide. However, it may also be unitized, i.e., cut up and embedded for ease of handling in IBM cards or the like. Microfilms may be either negatives or positives; being transparencies, they may be enlarged by reflection rather than projection.

Microfiche refers to sheet microfilm. The size of the fiche has not been universally standardized, nor has the number of images per sheet, but the standard of approximately 4 × 6 inches adopted by the U.S. government is the most widely used.

Micro-opaques are reduced-size images made on white paper by either photographic or printing processes. They must be enlarged by reflection rather than projection.

Several devices are available that not only enlarge microforms on a screen, but which also make permanent enlarged copies on paper of any desired image at the touch of a button.

microprocessor   A central processing unit built as a single integrated circuit. *see also* central processing unit; integrated circuit; microcomputer.

midlist   The books on a publisher's frontlist (*q.v.*) that appear to have less sales potential than the books considered leaders (*q.v.*). These books are rarely given significant advertising or other budgets (if they have any advertising at all). They also have smaller first printings than leaders, the books from which the publisher anticipates larger revenues.

Mimeograph   A duplicating machine operating on the stencil principle, used for printing forms, letters, price lists, etc. Mimeograph is a trade name for the stencil duplicator made by the A. B. Dick Co. Stencils are usually prepared in the typewriter.

miniature books   Books in small format issued since the middle of the eighteenth century. The dimensions vary from less than an inch square to approximately 2 × 1 1/4 inches. These minature editions are numerous and include the poetry, the Bible, almanacs, gift tokens, etc.

miniatures   Hand paintings used to decorate the text of medieval and Renaissance manuscripts.

minicomputer   A physically small but powerful class of computer that fits between the main frame class and the microcomputer class. Minicomputers started years ago as the smallest type of machine, but have grown in power to rival many smaller main frame models in capability; meanwhile, the newer microcomputers have appeared and have grown up to challenge some smaller minicomputer models. *See also* main frame, microcompter.

mint   A word used by some catalogers in the antiquarian book trade to denote condition "as new."

minuscule   From the Latin "minusculus," rather small. The small roman letters as distinguished from the capitals, or majuscules. In French *minuscule* is still used as a synonym for lowercase.

missal   A book containing the service for the celebration of the mass throughout the year. Sometimes loosely used for any book of devotions.

miter   In both composition and hand binding, to bring materials together at an angle without overlapping; to join lines or rules at angles.

mnemonic   In the computer field, symbolic substitute or abbreviation for a binary numeric code. Used extensively in computer programming to provide more easily read alphabetic representations of the numerical codes required by the machine.

mode   A particular manner or convention of use in which a computer system is operated.

modem   A device that accepts signals from a sending device and modulates them for transmission over a telephone line or other communications channel; also demodulates received signals back into a form a receiving device can accept.

modern   The more recent typeface designs, exemplified by Bodoni, in which the lines are more regular and mechanistic compared to old style (*q.v.*) faces.

This line is set in Bodoni.

Modern Library   *See* Boni, Albert; Cerf, Bennett Alfred.

module   An integrated self-contained unit of a system that can be interchanged readily with other "building-block" units.

mold   *See* matrix.

monitor   To watch over and supervise the correct operation of a system.

monograph   A treatise on one particular subject.

monographic series   A group of monographs usually issued by the same publisher, in succession, numbered or unnumbered, with a series title as well as individual titles, and often in uniform format.

Monotype   A typesetting machine of American origin invented by Tolbert Lanston about 1888. Keyboard action causes holes to be punched in a roll of paper. The punched paper then controls a separate type caster. The lines of type that come from the caster are not solid slugs (like Linotype) but are separate characters, like hand-set type. The Monotype was used for certain books, especially those containing technical signs, tabular matter, etc.

montage   The combination of several pictures or parts of pictures blended into a single photographic display.

Morison, Stanley (1889-1967)   English typographic adviser, designer, and scholar who gave strong impetus to typographic excellence in Western design. For forty years, from 1923, he inspired and guided the Monotype Corporation's program of reviving and modernizing fine classic typefaces; he maintained Cambridge University Press typography at an exemplary level; he modernized the look of the *Times* (London) and designed the Times Roman typeface. Morison wrote numerous scholarly studies including *Type Faces and Type Design, English Liturgical Books, First Principles of Typography, The Typographic book, 1439-1955*, and many more.

morocco   A leather made from goatskin. Morocco is classed as one of the most durable leathers for bookbinding. It is very firm, yet flexible, and is usually finished on the grain side. Said to have been first made by the Moors.
    Levant morocco is a fine, heavy quality with a coarse grain. *Turkey* and *French* morocco are a finer grain, yet heavy in quality. *Niger* morocco is a fine goatskin with a natural finish. Tanned on the banks of the Niger river, it is an acid-free leather used for expensive bindings. *Persian* morocco, having a still finer grain, is made from Persian goatskins. Many imitations are made from sheepskin.
    The history of binding begins with the introduction of this leather and gold tooling at the end of the fifteenth century in Venice and Florence. The goatskins came from the Levant,

where they had long been in use. Gold tooling is said to have been used in Syria at least as early as the thirteenth century, and both this and morocco were first made familiar in Europe through the Italian trade with the East. The earliest European bindings in morocco with gilt decoration so commonly occur upon books printed by Aldus, the great Venetian printer, that many of them are supposed to have been made for him or under his supervision, and the Venetian covers of his time are usually called Aldine bindings.

Throughout the 1800s, morocco was used in the finest bookbinding, and it is still used in the better bindings today, although it is highly expensive and difficult to get.

Morris, William (1834-1896)   English poet, artist, author, and craftsman. Founder of the Kelmscott Press (*q.v.*). In 1888, Morris and a few friends undertook a revival of printing and bookmaking, which had its inspiration in a thorough knowledge of the art of the fifteenth century. No similar movement in modern times has had such a powerful and far-reaching effect. Many fine presses were established as a result of his pioneering.

mosaic binding   *See* inlaid binding.

Mosher, Thomas Bird (1852-1923)   Former sea captain turned publisher and book designer in Portland, Maine. From 1891 he produced a long list of belles lettres, many of them pirated, in formats of delicacy and taste. From 1895 through 1914 he published, in monthly form, *The Bibelot, A Reprint of Poetry and Prose for Book Lovers*, chosen in part from scarce editions and sources not generally known. This publication was later reissued, bound in twenty volumes, and an index volume to the whole was added.

mottled calf   An ornamental treatment of a calfskin binding producing, by ink or acid, a variegated pattern; called *tree calf* when the pattern resembles the grain of gnarled wood.

movable type   Individual characters of type that can be composed into words and lines. The apparatus for casting movable metal type was developed by Johann Gutenberg (*q.v.*) in the middle of the fifteenth century. The actual invention of printing with movable type was probably not made by any one man. There are stories about Coster of Haarlem, there are legal documents relating to Gutenberg at Strasbourg and Mainz as early as 1436, as well as notarial records of experiments by Waldfoghel at Avignon in 1444. But there are in existence no books or pieces of printing that can be definitely proved to have been printed by any of these three men.

The important fact is that printing first became a business at Mainz, after 1445, and spread from there over the world. The first dated piece of type printing is an indulgence of Pope Nicholas V, of 1454.

According to Thomas Francis Carter, a Chinese named Pi Shêng made movable type from clay in the period Ch'ing-li (1041-1049), some 400 years before Gutenberg.

Moxon, Joseph (1627-1691)   London machine maker, printer, and typefounder. Published the first of his *Mechanick Exercises* in 1677, the earliest printers' manual in English.

Multilith   A small offset press used for duplicating forms, form letters, etc.

multiple-access   The principle of providing many access points into a computer for use by more than one person at the same time. *See also* time-sharing.

multiprogramming   A technique of running two or more programs in a computer at the same time.

Mystery Writers of America   A national association of authors founded in 1945 to enhance the prestige of mysteries and the people who write them. Its slogan is "Crime Does Not Pay—Enough." Beginning with the year of its origin, the group bestowed an annual prize for the best mystery writing in a variety of categories called the Edgar Allan Poe Award, which is familiarly known as the Edgar.

NACS   National Association of College Stores (*q.v.*).

n.d.   No date. In cataloging it indicates that no publication date is printed in the book described. If the date of publication is known but is not in the book the date is expressed thus: (n.d., 1850). If the date is in the book but not on the title page it is expressed thus: [1850].

NE, NEP   Invoice symbols meaning new edition pending.

NO, NOP   Invoice symbol meaning not our publication, cannot supply.

n.p.   No place of publication or publisher given.

n.y.   No year given.

NYP   Invoice symbol meaning not yet published.

narrow (nar.)   *See* book sizes.

narrowband   Communication channels which can transmit data at slow speeds, up to 200 bits per second. *See also* broadband; data transmission.

National Association of College Stores   A professional organization that began in 1922 under the name of the College Bookstore Association. Later it became the National Association of College Bookstores; later still, it adopted its present name to indicate the breadth of the merchandise carried by stores catering to college communities.

national bibliography   Commonly, a list of books, current or retrospective, recording the complete or near-complete publishing output of any one country.

National Book Awards   Awards honoring literary excellence, formerly presented annually to authors of books in a variety of categories. Prize money was donated by various book industry organizations. The awards, instituted in 1950, were last presented in 1979 after having been administered successively by the National Book Committee (*q.v.*), the American Academy and Institute of Arts and Letters, and the Association of American Publishers (*q.v.*). They were succeeded by the American Book Awards (*q.v.*).

National Book Committee   A nonprofit society founded in New York in 1954 and discontinued in 1974, devoted to the "wider and wiser use of books." The committee supported the freedom to read, encouraged the wider availability of books, and sponsored National Library Week, the National Book Awards, the National Medal for Literature, and studies related to books and reading. The committee cooperated particularly with the American Library Association and the Association of American Publishers, among other national groups.

National Book Critics Circle   A national organization of book reviewers and writers about books, formed in 1974 to encourage and raise the quality of book criticism. The group instituted the annual National Book Critics Circle Awards in January 1976.

National Library Week   A week-long annual promotional effort, and center of a year-round program for support of libraries, launched in 1958 and sponsored originally by the National Book Committee in cooperation with the American Library Association. When the National Book Committee discontinued operations in 1974, the program was taken over solely by the American Library Association. Specific purposes of the program are to encourage legislation favorable to libraries, expand library use to increasing numbers of people, and defend the freedom to read.

natural language   A language whose rules permit changes in meaning and usage, as opposed to an artificial language which rigidly prescribes every definition prior to use. *See also* artificial language; machine language.

negative   Usually a transparent photographic film on which both the light values and image are reversed—the black of the original subject is white, the light grey is dark grey, left is right, etc. A photostatic negative reverses black for white but, by using a mirror in the process, produces readable rather than mirrored lettering. A negative is the first step in printing by offset and it is usual, after printing, to hold the negatives (or perhaps positives made from the negatives) rather than the plates. A *positive* is the print made from a negative, with light values and image as in the original subject.

negative option   *See* book club.

net   Not subject to discount or reduction. The use of the term in connection with the retail price of new books in the United States began about 1900, when the publishers endeavored to end the then prevalent retail practice of cutting list prices.

The term *net* may also be applied to book prices carrying no discount to retailers, or to indicate that a wholesale price is subject to no further discount. For example an invoice may read "2% 10 days, net E.O.M." meaning that a further 2% cash discount will be allowed for payment within 10 days, after which the full net total is due by "end of month." *See also* net pricing.

net price   What a wholesaler or bookseller pays for a product after all discounts and allowances have been made.

net pricing   A method of determining a wholesale price without reference to a suggested retail price. Under net pricing in the book industry, the publisher sets the price of a book to the bookseller or wholesaler, and each bookselling and wholesaling operation establishes its own resale price to the consumer, thus determining its own margin of profit. No cover price is preprinted on the book or jacket, and the retail price can vary from dealer to dealer. Net pricing, still controversial in book publishing, came into use in the industry in 1979 and began gaining its greatest strength in the college textbook market where, under traditional pricing methods, publishers customarily sell books to booksellers at 20 percent off retail price and there is a low margin of profit. Cf. discount; list price.

new edition An edition of a book containing substantial revisions of existing material and/or new material added; *not* merely a new impression, a reprint, or a reissue from original plates. *See also* edition; revised edition.

nihil obstat Latin for "nothing hinders"; used by a Roman Catholic censor to attest that a book contains nothing damaging to faith or morals. *See also* imprimatur.

noise Random variations in the characteristics of an element that may disturb or interfere with the normal operation of a device or system. Random fluctuations in electrical voltage or current, for example, tend to upset the operation of computer circuits if the fluctuations are too large in magnitude.

nom de plume A pen name; a pseudonym; a writer's assumed name; or a single fabricated byline under which one or more people write.

non-impact printer A type of printout unit that creates characters on paper without the use of impact typing principles. Photographic, electrostatic, or ink-jet techniques usually are used to create images.

nonbook materials Materials that do not meet the definition of a book or periodical (*q.v.*), such as audiovisual materials.

Nonesuch Press Founded in London in 1923 by Francis Meynell, Vera Mendel, and David Garnett to produce worthwhile books in well-designed formats and at a moderate price. Francis Meynell designed the books until 1936, when the Nonesuch, in financial difficulties, was taken over by the Limited Editions Club of New York. After World War II, the Nonesuch again became profitable, and in 1951, the Limited Editions Club returned the titles and style of Nonesuch to Francis Meynell. In 1953, a new company, the Nonesuch Press, Ltd., was formed with Meynell as managing director and Max Reinhardt, who later bought The Bodley Head, a director. Francis Meynell died in 1975. The Nonesuch is now part of The Bodley Head, Ltd., and continues to issue titles under the imprint of The Nonesuch Library.

nonfiction novel *See* faction.

nonpareil The old name for a type size half the size of pica. When a printer inserts a nonpareil of space, he inserts 6 points of space.

nonwoven materials Covering materials other than cloth used in bookbinding. Numerous types are made today including paper and various kinds of plastics. Paper and some plastics are composed of fibers matted into thin sheets, while other types of plastic materials are solid sheets of extruded or otherwise molded material. Many nonwovens combine different papers and plastics in one material, usually by lamination.

notation A system of symbols that represent the divisions of a classification scheme.

notch binding In the adhesive binding of books printed on flat sheets, the term *notch binding* refers to the puncturing of the folds of signatures on the folding machine to make holes for glue to pass through during the later gluing operation and spread between the pages for greater holding power. Unlike conventional adhesive binding, which removes the signatures's fold entirely, notch binding simply punctures the fold along its length with V-shaped (or notch-shaped) holes. *See also* binding; burst binding.

novel A work of fiction of unspecified length, substantial enough to warrant publication by itself in a book of some bulk.

novelization A piece of fiction based on the script of a film, television program, or play, usually published as a paperback original (*q.v.*). Novelizations are most often intended to serve as merchandisers with a blurb such as "Read the Book—See the Movie" promoting the property in both media. *See also* tie-in.

novella A short work of fiction of unspecified length, generally thought to be slighter than a novel. Although two or more novellas may be gathered into a single volume and novellas are often included in a collection of short stories, novellas can be published alone, resulting in a slim book frequently characterized by a generous amount of white space and a larger-than-usual typeface.

numerals, Arabic 1, 2, 3, 4, etc. The numbers 0 to 9 began to appear in European manuscripts in the twelfth century, and their forms, especially the 4, 5, and 7, passed through various stages before reaching approximately the present forms. The Arabs, who gave this system to Europe, probably brought it from India in the eighth century. A legend attributes its introduction into Europe to Pope Sylvester II (999-1003).

Old style Arabic numerals such as 1, 2, 3, 4, 5, 6, 7, 8, 9, 0, have ascenders and descenders. The exigencies of tabular work made it desirable to provide alternate lining figures, modern typefaces that extend from the baseline to the capline, thus, 1, 2, 3, 4, 5, 6, 7, 8, 9, 0.

numerals, Roman   Numerals in the Roman system of notation are still used in the dating of certain books published today; in early bookmaking it was the general custom.

In the Roman system the following are the symbols chiefly used: **I** = 1; **V** = 5; **X** = 10; **L** = 50; **C** = 100; **D** = 500; **M** = 1,000.

Several rules govern the combinations used to express intermediate and higher numbers: (1) Any symbol *following* one of equal or greater value, *adds* its value. Thus II = 2; VI = 6; LI = 51. (2) Any symbol *preceding* one of greater value, *subtracts* its value. Thus IV = 4; XL = 40; CM = 900. (3) When a symbol stands *between* two of greater value, its value is subtracted from the second symbol and the remainder is added to the first. Thus XIV = 14; LIX = 59; MCM = 1,900. The shorter form achieved by subtraction is favored in modern usage: IX rather than VIIII for 9; MCM rather than MDCCCC for 1,900. "Thousands" are sometimes indicated by drawing a line over a numeral: as, $\overline{V}$ = 5,000; $\overline{C}$ = 100,000.

OC   Invoice symbol meaning order canceled.

OCR   Abbreviation for optical character recognition (*q.v.*).

o.k. with corrections   A message on a proof to the printer that the job is approved for further processing when indicated changes are made.

o.p.   Abbreviation for out of print (*q.v.*).

o.p.c.   Abbreviation for out of print, canceled.

o.p.p.   Invoice symbol meaning out of print at present.

o.p.s.   Abbreviation for out of print, searching.

o.s.   Invoice symbol meaning out of stock (*q.v.*).

o.s.c.   Abbreviation for out of stock, canceled.

o.s.f.   Abbreviation for out of stock, to follow.

o.s.i.   Abbreviation for out of stock, indefinitely.

o.s.t.   Abbreviation for out of stock, temporarily.

oblique   *See* italic.

oblong (obl.)   *See* book sizes.

octavo (8vo)   *See* book sizes.

odd sorts   Characters not included in a standard font of type. Also known as *special characters* or *pi characters*. Most composition systems have provisions for adding special characters, the need for which is an important consideration in selection of a composition system.

off its feet   Metallic type is said to be off its feet when it doesn't stand square upon its base, thus creating an unequal impression on the paper.

offline   Part of a computer system not connected directly by wire to the rest of the system. Materials must be hand-carried between the offline part and the main computer. Cf. online.

offprint   A separate printing or reprint of an article or chapter that appeared first in a magazine or some other larger work.

offset (1)   In lithographic printing, a specific press design that transfers the ink twice between printing plate and the final sheet of paper to be printed. The image is first transferred from the plate to an intermediate rubberized blanket, and from this it is "offset" onto the paper. Virtually all lithography except certain special art prints today is produced on offset type presses, and the term *offset* is used almost synonymously with lithographic printing, although it is not truly so (dry offset actually is letterpress printing). Many types of offset presses are used today, including web and sheet-fed equipment as well as single and multicolor presses. The use of the intermediate rubberized blanket permits printing of very fine detail such as fine-screen halftones on papers with rough or uneven surfaces. (2) Synonym for setoff (*q.v.*).

offset paper   Paper that has been treated to give good results in lithographic offset printing.

Old English   An angular type of the black-letter group, abbreviated O.E.

𝕿𝖍𝖎𝖘 𝖑𝖎𝖓𝖊 𝖎𝖘 𝖘𝖊𝖙 𝖎𝖓 𝕺𝖑𝖉 𝕰𝖓𝖌𝖑𝖎𝖘𝖍.

old style   Adaptations of the types of earliest printers, such as Garamond, Elzevir, Caslon. Characterized by their irregular, almost antique lines. *See also* modern.

This line is set in Garamond.

omnibus book   (1) A reprint edition of several works of an author, complete or a selection, in a single volume. (2) A collection of a number of books or stories on a single subject by various authors in one volume.

on approval   A term applied to a transaction allowing the customer the privilege of examining goods before purchase.

on consignment   Merchandise supplied to a dealer on the understanding that it need not be paid for until sold. If not sold, it can be returned to the supplier without penalty. *See also* returns.

on-demand book, on-demand printing   A book manufactured as a single copy at the time a customer wants to buy it. On-demand systems are still not common, being used primarily to produce copies of scholarly works from master files of microfilms. However, new technology for on-demand printing, based on computers and laser imaging, is developing rapidly and should impact certain types of scientific, technical, and business publishing in the next few years. The concept would eliminate major inventory problems.

on press   A job at the stage of being printed.

onlay   A leather binding onto which leather of other colors or kinds has been applied for decorative purposes.

online   Part of a computer system connected to the rest of the system electrically via wires, so that data may be passed back and forth without delays or human handling. *See also* offline.

online processing   Processing of computer data instantly in small units as the data or instructions are received from people operating the machine. Typically, online system users work at video display terminals wired directly to the computer to facilitate instant response by the system. *See also* batch processing.

one shot (1) The reprinting in one issue of a periodical the full text or an abridgment of a book, as opposed to a serialized reprint. (2) A type of hot melt adhesive requiring only one application to bind a book.

ooze leather Calf- or sheepskin with a suede-like finish. Also called *ooze calf*. Ooze leather was originally made by mechanically forcing ooze through the skin to produce a soft, finely grained finish, like velvet or suede. Today, it is generally a tanned calfskin with a soft feel.

opacity In printing papers, the ability to prevent printed images on one side showing through on the other side. Especially important in thin papers.

open-loop system System in which a series of automatic machine operations is interrupted by one or more human operations before the entire cycle is completed. *See also* closed-loop system; loop.

open-to-buy The amount of money available to the manager of a retail store for new purchases in a given period, such as a month. Some book merchandisers consider this a controversial practice, sharply limiting the flexibility of store operation.

operation A defined action that a computer will perform on instructions from its program.

optical center In layout, a visual balance point somewhat above the measured center of a page. When material is thus centered on a page, it is not mathematically but visually centered.

optical character recognition (OCR) An optical-electronic means of reading printed or written data into a computer, converting it into machine-readable code in the process. When printed, typed, or even some kinds of handwritten characters are passed in front of an electric-eye scanning device, it senses light and dark patterns forming the characters. These sensings are converted to electrical impulses representing digital codes, and the computer then translates these codes into machine-language codes. In computerized typesetting, optical character recognition is used primarily to enter data into a computer. However, some editing functions can be performed with certain types of equipment if instructions for making changes are typed out for the scanner in the proper format. *See also* editing.

option   The privilege of first refusal to buy or sell a specific property, such as a manuscript or rights to a book, usually within a given length of time. A clause frequently written into a publishing contract grants the publisher an option on the author's next book with no recompense for that right. It is a clause many authors attempt to evade because it is thought to be overly binding. A movie company may try to finesse its competition by purchasing an option on a literary property, thus taking it off the market while determining the feasibility of adapting the work to the screen. Here, too, the option is usually for a stated amount of time, but it may be renewable with an additional payment.

oral history   Primary source material in the form of tape and/or transcript, resulting from recorded interviews with persons who have recollections of interest to scholars. The first oral history interviews were arranged by Allan Nevins in 1948.

original   Finished camera-ready copy, suitable for reproduction. *See also* camera-ready.

original cloth; original boards; original wrappers   In catalogue description, the covers in which the book was first published.

original parts   A catalogue description of a work first issued in installments at regular intervals, monthly or weekly, in printed and illustrated wrappers. The most popular of these publications in the nineteenth century were the novels of Ainsworth, Dickens, Lever, Surtees, Thackeray, and Trollope.

ornament   Any decorative device, such as a rule, border, initial letter, or design.

out of print (o.p.)   A term used to describe a publication no longer available from its publisher. Traditionally the term is applied when the publisher's stock of a particular edition of a book is exhausted and there are no plans to reprint it. This situation may arise when a book fails to sell in sufficient quantities to warrant the overhead costs of maintaining copies in inventory, when the book is made obsolete by a later edition, or when the publisher has relinquished the rights.

out of stock (o.s.)   A term applied when the publisher's stock is temporarily exhausted, and there are plans, or tentative plans, to reprint additional copies. Cf. out of print.

output   The results of computer processing that are retrieved from the system in some form of display, printout, or storable memory medium.

over the transom   An imagistic description for a manuscript received by a publisher without prior contact with its author or an agent of the author. A literary agent can also be the recipient of such an unexpected and unsolicited work. These manuscripts collectively form a slushpile (*q.v.*).

overlay   (1) In letterpress presswork, the thin sheets of tissue placed under the tympan during the make-ready process to increase or equalize the squeeze or impression on the paper being printed. (2) In artwork, an additional sheet (or multiple sheets) over the basic art, carrying additional art elements that are to be processed separately by the printer and then registered (fitted) accurately to the base art. (3) The protective covering of paper, tissue, cellophane, etc., over the original material.

overprint   (1) To revise printed matter by superimposing new information, sometimes blocking out unwanted images. (2) To print more than ordered. *See also* overrun. (3) In multicolor printing, to obtain different colors by printing various color inks over each other.

overrun   Additional copies above the number ordered to be printed.

oversewn   A method of binding or rebinding a book for extra strength, as for library use, in which each leaf is sewn individually into the book. Oversewing does, however, prevent the book from opening quite flat.

Oxford India paper   Very thin, soft, tough, and opaque paper, used by the Oxford University Press and made at its Wolvercote Mill.

Ozalid   A type of blueprint (*q.v.*).

p. (*pl.* **pp.**)   Abbreviation for page.

PE   The abbreviation for printer's error (*q.v.*).

P.E.N.   An acronym for an international association of people of letters founded in London in 1921. Also spoken as the three initials, the letters stand for poets, playwrights, essayists, editors, and novelists. Established to foster good relations among writers, P.E.N. centers have spread to many countries. The American chapter was formed in 1922.

pH   A chemical term denoting the acidity or alkalinity of a solution. In offset printing pH is a critical measurement for the water, or fountain solution, used in the process. A pH of 7 is neutral. In papermaking, acid-free paper is considered to have a pH of 6.0 or higher. A pH of 7+ is preferred in order to offset any residual acidity in the paper.

port.   Abbreviation for portrait.

p.p.   Abbreviation for postpaid.

PPA   Publishers' Publicity Association (*q.v.*).

prelims.   Abbreviation for preliminary pages, meaning *front matter* (*q.v.*).

prepub   Abbreviation of prepublication. The term is often used to denote a special price or terms offered before the stated publication date of a book.

PTLA   Abbreviation for *Publishers Trade List Annual.*

PW   Abbreviation for *Publishers Weekly* (*q.v.*).

Pablos, Juan   First printer in the New World, an Italian who in 1539 produced in Mexico City a *Breve y Mas Compendiosa Doctrina Christiana* in Spanish and Mexican.

package   An integrated group of components in a computer system, such as a group of programs that operate together or a complementary set of equipment and programs.

packager   *See* book packager.

Padeloup, Antoine Michel (1685-1758)   One of the most famous binders in France in the eighteenth century. Two generations of his family before and two after him were prominent binders. He developed the dentelle, or lace pattern, in decoration, a style that succeeded the pointillé of Gascon.

page   One side of a leaf.

page break   The point in the text of a book where one page ends and the next one begins.

page map　A diagrammatic representation of a page layout on the screen of a cathode-ray tube. Depending on the sophistication of the computer program producing it, a page map is approximately equivalent to an artist's pencil-sketch layout of a page. In computerized page makeup, it is used to position typographic elements on a page area so that the computer can then specify for the typesetting machine where each element should be placed during typesetting. *See also* layout terminal.

page proofs　*See* proofs.

pagination　The numbering of the pages of a book. In electronic composition systems, pagination includes most or all functions of page makeup as well.

painted edges　*See* fore-edge painting.

paleography　(1) An ancient manner of writing; ancient writings, collectively. (2) The study of ancient inscriptions and modes of writing; the art or science of deciphering ancient writings.

palimpsest　Derived from Greek roots meaning "to rub away again." A parchment or other material from which the original writing has been more or less completely erased and new matter written over. A double palimpsest is one that has had two such erasures. Valuable texts have been recovered from such parchments.

pamphlet　In the UNESCO definition, a complete, unbound, nonperiodical publication of not fewer than five nor more than forty-eight pages exclusive of covers. In informal usage, a pamphlet is also considered, ordinarily, to be saddle-bound, with covers of the same paper as the text or of a heavier paper, and may run to many more than forty-eight pages. Cf. book.

pamphlet binding　*See* binding; stitching.

Pannartz, Arnold　*See* Sweynheym, Conrad.

paper　All types of matted or felted sheets or webs produced mostly from cellulosic fibers (but sometimes from mineral, animal, or synthetic fibers), either by a hand-dipping process or on a paper-making (Fourdrinier) machine. Although paper's main ingredient is wood fiber, high grades of writing papers are made with cotton fibers.

Book papers fall into two basic classes: those made from mechanically prepared groundwood, as used in mass market paperbacks, and those made from chemically prepared wood pulp, as used in higher-priced books.

Typically, papers containing acid eventually turn brown, embrittle, and finally crumble. Recently, however, paper mills have begun producing "permanent" acid-free paper (said to last at least 100 years without change) that has a pH of 6.0 or greater, and many publishers are beginning to use this paper to give their books longer life. *See also* paper permanence.

Paper may also be coated or uncoated, sized (for offset printing or pen-and-ink) or unsized, handmade, machine made, laid, wove, etc. It also comes in a variety of surface finishes, from rough to smooth and dull to glossy. *See also* basis weight; bulk; chemical pulp; coated paper; free sheet; grain; groundwood pulp; laid paper; paper permanence; pulp; wove paper.

paper-covered boards   *See* boards.

paper covers   A book covered with a printed or unprinted paper wrapper affixed to the book. Used generally in describing a book not bound in boards, cloth, or leather, such as a paperback book. *See also* paperback; wrappers.

paper permanence   The degree of resistance to deterioration that paper can be expected to possess. The single most important factor affecting the rate of paper deterioration is acid content. Other less important factors are heat, humidity, and atmospheric pollution. A high acid content (pH 5 and under) will increase the tendency of paper to discolor and become brittle. The research of W. J. Barrow has shown that even 100 percent rag content paper will deteriorate rapidly if the acid solutions used in its manufacture have not been neutralized. The reason that Gutenberg's paper has lasted five centuries while the best papers (including 100 percent rag papers) of the early twentieth century have already become brittle has now been determined to be related to acid content.

Although a substantial quantity of paper used in today's printing (especially for newspapers and mass market paperbacks) has a high acid content, and thus a short life expectancy, many paper companies now market acid-free book papers, often called permanent-durable papers, which have a guaranteed life of several hundred years.

Libraries have become increasingly concerned with the physical condition of their collections, especially of books printed after 1800. These books are considered to be in imminent danger of deterioration, due mainly to the destructive materials used in paper production during the nineteenth century. Some of these harmful materials include alum for sizing, chlorine bleach for whitening, and calcium sulfate and barium sulfate for paper loading.

paper weight   *See* basis weight.

paperback   A book, either an original publication or a reprint of another edition, bound with a nonrigid paper cover and usually less expensive than the same title in hardcover. It is said to be paperbound and may even be called a *paperbound*, a word formerly used more frequently than paperback to designate this format. Also called *softcover*. *See also* mass market paperback; trade paperback.

paperback original   A work of either fiction or nonfiction published first in paperback format without having been available previously as a hardcover. It may be a mass market paperback (*q.v.*) or a trade paperback (*q.v.*).

paperback rights   The rights to publish a book in a mass market or trade paperback, as opposed to hardcover, format. The rights may be to a paperback original (*q.v.*) or to a paperback reprint. Rights to mass market and trade paperback editions are usually negotiated separately, but they can be combined in a package deal.

paperboard   A material made of wood pulp or recycled paper stock and generally over .010 inch thick. Thus, all heavyweight paper may be referred to as *paperboard*. However, paperboard is a product with its own characteristics and uses. The grades most commonly used for making cases for books are plain chipboard, pasted chipboard, and specification cover board, which includes both high-quality pasted chipboard and binder's board.

paperbound   *See* paperback.

Paperbound Books in Print   Author-title-subject index of paperback books published and currently available in the United States. Issued twice each year by the R. R. Bowker Company.

papyrus   (1) A writing material used by the ancient Egyptians that was made from the inner bark of a reed of the same name growing on the banks of the Nile. Prepared by laying strips one over another at right angles. Two or three layers were soaked in water and pressed into one sheet. The sheets were joined to produce a roll. (2) A manuscript written on this material.

parameter A specific type of variable in a system that must be defined by someone for the system.

paraph A flourish at the end of an autograph signature. In the Middle Ages this was a sort of rude safeguard against forgery.

parchment A translucent or opaque writing material, also used for bookbinding, made from the inner side of the split skin of a sheep and prepared somewhat like vellum (*q.v.*). It was probably used as early as 1500 B.C. In the second century B.C., Eumenes, king of Pergamum, in Asia Minor, could not obtain sufficient papyrus from Egypt for his large library, so he had his entire library prepared on parchment made from the skins of sheep, goats, and pigs. This parchment became known as *Charta Pergamena*. During the Middle Ages, parchment became the most important writing material, but its importance declined in favor of paper from the twelfth century on. Its present use is restricted largely to state and legal documents, certificates, and the like.

parity check A means of testing the accuracy of data in a computer system through an automatic comparison process. Used extensively to check for errors made in recording or transmitting data.

part title Same as divisional title (*q.v.*).

partial remaindering Selling off at sale or remainder prices an excess portion of a publisher's unsold stock of a book, rather than the entire stock. Thus, some part of the stock remains in print to be sold at the publisher's list price. *See also* remainders.

paste-downs Synonymous with endpapers (*q.v.*).

paste-up (1) Assembly of opaque photographic paper or reproduction proofs containing type and other images into made-up sections or pages by means of pasting them down on a carrier sheet. The result is camera-ready copy (*q.v.*). (2) Assembly of proofs on a layout for guidance of the printer. *See also* camera-ready; dummy; mechanical.

pasted board A stiff material used for the boards of books made by pasting several sheets of paper one upon the other; any kind of paperboard made from thin layers of paper pulp.

pasted chipboard *See* paperboard; pasted board.

pasting in   *See* tipping in.

pattern recognition   Indentification of shapes, forms, or configurations by automatic means. *See also* optical character recognition.

Payne, Roger (1739-1797)   English bookbinder. He was a great craftsman, who is credited with inventing a method of wetting and rolling morocco leather to produce a straight grain; he is also regarded as the creator of a new style of binding decoration. The backs of his books were richly gilt, but the outer sides usually had only corner decorations, his elaborate gilt decorations being reserved for the doublures of his extra special bindings. His favorite designs consisted of crescents, circles, stars, running vines, etc., studded with gold dots. He designed his own tools for his gilt decorative finishing. He bound many of his books in russia leather scented with birch oil; his morocco leathers were mainly of very deep colors of red, blue, olive, and orange. The bills he submitted for his work were as carefully prepared and set forth as his bindings; all the details, even the minutest, are listed, together with all the materials used, and a price is given for each step.

Penrose Annual   Review of the graphic arts, published in London since 1895.

perfect binding   *See* adhesive binding; binding.

perfecting press   A press that prints both sides of a sheet before it leaves the press.

perforated tape   Paper tape on which data have been encoded by punching rows of holes across the tape.

perforating   (1) The cutting of a line of tiny holes or slits in a sheet of paper to facilitate folding or later tearing of the sheet along the line. Done on either a regular printing press, a special cutting and creasing press, or a folding machine by impressing a raised serrated rule or disk into the paper. (2) The punching of paper tape for use in computer systems. *See* perforated tape.

periodical   A serial appearing or intended to appear indefinitely at regular intervals, generally more frequently than annually, each issue of which normally contains separate articles, stories, or other writings. Newspapers and the proceedings or other publications of corporate bodies primarily related to their meetings are not included in this term.

peripheral equipment   Auxiliary devices that may be attached to a computer system to enlarge the machine's basic capacity or to perform special functions.

Perkins, Maxwell Evarts(1884-1947)   Editor whose guidance of numerous important American writers contributed substantially to their development. He joined Charles Scribner's Sons in 1910, was its chief editor (1927-1947), and a company officer. His correspondence with Thomas Wolfe, Ernest Hemingway, F. Scott Fitzgerald, and many others provides fascinating insights into the conduct of author-publisher relations, as shown in *Editor to Author: The Letters of Maxwell E. Perkins*, edited by John Hall Wheelock, and *Dear Scott, Dear Max*, edited by John Kuehl and Jackson Bryer (both Scribner's). A biography, *Max Perkins: Editor of Genius*, by A. Scott Berg, was published by Dutton in 1978.

permanent-durable papers   *See* paper permanence.

permission   Clearance from a copyright owner for another to quote passages or reproduce illustrations from a publication.

photo offset lithography   *See* offset.

photocomposer   A machine used in lithographic and gravure platemaking to exactly position and expose multiple copies of the same image with extreme precision on large plates or cylinders. (Not to be confused with photographic typesetting equipment.)

photocomposition   (1) The process and product of photographic typesetting. (2) The making of multiple exposures of the same or varying subjects on a single photographic negative. (3) The making of precisely positioned multiple exposures of the same image on press plates. *See also* photocomposer.

photoengraving   *See* engraving.

photogelatin   A printing process, (also called *collotype*, in which a plate with a gelatinous surface absorbs and transfers ink in proportion to the amount of light exposure it is given during platemaking. Often used for frontispieces, facsimile reproductions, and fine illustration work in general. Unlike the more common printing processes, photogelatin uses no screen. Delicate tones and fine details are reproduced without being broken up into halftone dots.

photographic typesetting   Used generally as a synonym for photocomposition, although the term *photocomposition* actually encompasses several other processes, as well as more steps within the type composition field. In type composition, photocomposition can include film stripping or paper paste-up procedures for makeup operations, while photographic typesetting is limited to actual setting of type. *See also* photocomposition.

photogravure   *See* gravure.

photolettering   Use of a wide variety of devices for hand-positioning images to be set photographically on film or paper. Generally used for display and special typefaces. *See also* photographic typesetting; phototypography.

photomechanics   Devices or manual operations that employ both photographic and mechanical principles.

photomontage   *See* montage.

Photostat   A photographic copy of a document, drawing, printed page, etc. The resulting image may be made the same size as the original or enlarged or reduced. The first Photostat copy is a negative, reproducing white for black, and is reversed or "wrong-reading." If "right-reading" black for black is desired, a positive Photostat is made from the negative Photostat. The name *Photostat* is applied both to the machine and the resulting copies.

phototypesetting   Synonym for photographic typsetting.

phototypography   Synonym for photocomposition, but with emphasis on typographic considerations.

pi character   A miscellaneous character not part of a standard complement on a typesetting machine, but nevertheless required to produce certain types of work. The term *pi* comes from the printer's word for spilled or unsorted types. *See* pie; *see also* odd sorts.

pica   (1) A unit of the printer's standard measurement system. A pica is equal to 12 point, or approximately one-sixth inch. (2) The old name for a type size measuring about six lines to the inch, equivalent to 12 point. (3) The larger of the two most used kinds of typewriter type having ten characters per linear inch. (The other kind, *elite*, has twelve characters per linear inch.) *See also* American point system.

Pickering, William (1796-1854)   English publisher and bookseller whose fine taste in book production made his imprint famous. He set up his own bookshop in 1820 and began publishing in 1821. Among his first publications were the early volumes of a series that became famous: the Diamond Classics, well-printed little books in 32mo and 48mo sizes, that included the works of Shakespeare, Homer, Virgil, and Dante. Several of the volumes were bound in what is believed to be the earliest form of publisher's cloth.

In 1829 Pickering formed an active association in the production of fine books with Charles Whittingham the Younger, an association that lasted until Pickering's death in 1854. In 1830 Pickering began to issue the Aldine Edition of the *British Poets*, Fifty-three volumes, completed in 1845. The publication marked the adoption by Pickering of the dolphin-and-anchor device of Aldus (*q.v.*), to which he added the inscription "Aldi Discipulus Anglus." Among the many fine books published by Pickering mention must be made of his splendid reprints of the Book of Common Prayer of 1549, 1552, 1559, 1604, 1637, 1662, and 1837. The seven volumes were issued in 1844.

picking A defect in a printed image resulting when paper particles are pulled off the sheet by ink that is too tacky.

pickup Composed type matter that has been kept standing since its first use and is being *picked up* for further use.

pie; pi Type accidentally mixed up, or "knocked into pie."

pigskin The tough, strong skin of a pig, used in binding. The graining can be easily distinguished from the graining of morocco by the little hair punctures that show on the surface.

pin seal *See* seal.

piracy, pirate *Piracy* is the production or publishing of a book without permission of and without recompense to the copyright owner; a *pirate* is the offending party; *to pirate* is to commit piracy. In recent times, book pirates have been numerous, primarily in Asia, where, in several countries, local proprietors of small offset lithography shops have copied Western books for sale at prices lower than those charged for imported editions. Authorization of reprints at low or merely token royalties has grown as one answer to this practice; development and enforcement of national copyright laws is another answer. *See also* Universal Copyright Convention.

plagiarism   The use of another's concepts or words without permission, without acknowledgment, and without noting that the
new work into which they have been incorporated is not all one's
own. This literary theft is a crime.

planography   One of the four basic principles of printing, the
others being relief, intaglio, and screen process. Lithography
(*q.v.*) or lithographic offset is a planographic process. In planography the printing areas and the nonprinting areas are in the
same plane, neither raised nor depressed. Inking is possible because the printing areas are made chemically ink-receptive and
the nonprinting areas are made ink-repellent.

plant   A publisher's designation for a printer's establishment.

plant costs   Although the components will vary from publisher to
publisher according to accounting procedures, these generally
comprise the one-time costs in manufacuring a book, such as
those involved in preparation of artwork and illustrations, composition, plates, etc. Cf. running costs.

Plantin, Christophe (1520?-1589)   The greatest of all printers at
Antwerp. He was a Frenchman, born near Tours. After serving
an apprenticeship as a printer, he set up a shop in Paris in 1546.
Two years later he gave it up and moved to Antwerp, where he
opened a shop and sold books, prints, and tooled leather. In 1555
he began a publishing business that flourished, and by 1570 his
establishment became one of the most celebrated of the time. He
was appointed court printer to Philip II of Spain, and his large
plant employed over 150 workmen.

The most noted of all his fine publications is the great Polyglot
Bible, *Biblia Sacra: Hebraice, Chaldice, Graece & Latine* (8 vols.,
1568-1573). Eminent French type designers, notably Granjon
and Garamond, prepared special types for this work, which is
unrivaled in printers' achievement.

Upon Plantin's death in 1589 the business passed to his son-in-
law Jean Moretus, and it was carried on by the Moretus family in
the original Plantin house until 1876, when the city of Antwerp
and the Belgian government united to purchase it as a public
museum. All of the records of the business, the fonts of type, the
cases with wood blocks and metal cuts, etc., are here preserved,
making this museum the most significant and instructive of printing meccas.

plastic comb binding   *See* binding.

platen press   A style of printing press in which the paper rests on a flat surface known as the *platen* and is forced against the printing image carrier, which is positioned on another flat surface known as the *bed*. Cf. flat-bed cylinder press; rotary press.

plates   (1) Illustrations printed separately and inserted in a book when bound. (2) The master surfaces from which printing is done, such as electrotype plates, stereotype plates, engraved plates, offset lithographic plates, rubber plates, plastic plates, photogelatin plates, gravure plates, etc.

plug   (1) To mention, praise, or publicize a book. An author will appear on a television or radio talk show to plug a new book. (2) Plug was once used more commonly than today as a term for an unsalable book.

pochoir   The French word for stencil. A stencil process similar to silk screen, except that paper stencils are often used and the color is daubed through rather than drawn across the open areas of the stencil. Pochoir cannot reproduce such letters as the O and A in one operation without the use of disfiguring bridges to hold the stencil together. The process permits the use of watercolor inks with an unpolished finish not obtained by colors printed under pressure. Extensively used in France. *See also* screen printing.

pocket part   A supplement intended to update an already published book, especially a law book. Its name is derived from the pocket provided at the back of the book for insertion of the parts.

point   (1) In the antiquarian trade, a peculiarity, typographical or other, that distinguishes a particular copy of a book from other copies of the same edition or impression and by which priority of issue is often determined. (2) In type, *see* American point system. (3) In bookmaking, the term used to denote each thousandth of an inch of paperboard thickness, or caliper (*q.v.*).

point system   *See* American point system.

pointillé   A form of gilt decoration on bookbindings in which scrolls and other ornaments consist of dotted instead of solid lines. This style was used with great effect by the seventeenth century binder Le Gascon (*q.v.*).

polyglot   (1) One who speaks or writes several languages. (2) A book containing versions of the same text in several languages—especially the Scriptures in several languages.

Three famous polyglot bibles are the Complutensian Polyglot (also called the Ximenes Polyglot, after Cardinal Ximenes, its patron), printed 1513-1517 at Complutum (now Alcalá de Henares); the Antwerp Polyglot, or Biblia Regia, published by Christophe Plantin, at Antwerp, 1568-1573; and the London, or Walton's Polyglot Bible, edited by Brian Walton, Bishop of Chester, and issued in 1654-1657.

pornography　From the Greek, meaning "writing about harlots" originally applied only to treatises on prostitutes and prostitution, but is now used to describe writings of an obscene or licentious character. Sometimes catalogues of books include such items under the terms *erotica, curiosa,* or *facetiae (qq.v.).*

positive　*See* negative.

Pott octavo　*See* book sizes.

prebinding　*See* binding.

preface　A short explanatory note by the author preceding the text of a book and usually touching on the purpose of the book, its sources, extent, etc. Foreword *(q.v.)* often has the same scope as preface but is written by someone other than the author. An introduction, however, forms part of the work itself.

The preface affords the author an opportunity to speak to the reader in a comparatively direct and personal manner, and to acquaint the reader with the considerations that impelled the author to write the book. At the end of a preface it is customary for the author to acknowledge the services of those who assisted in writing the book, or who helped in reading the proofs, or who contributed information, etc. *See also* front matter.

preprint　Copy of a book or section of a book or periodical usually issued in a limited paperbound quantity for some special purpose before publication date.

presentation copy　A copy of a book that bears a presentation inscription by the author. A presentation copy must be a gift from the author, and the inscription is usually dated on or near publication date. A book merely signed or inscribed by the author at the owner's request is an *inscribed copy (q.v.). See also* association copy.

press proofs　*See* proofs.

press queries (or **printer's queries**)   Queries to the author marked on proofs by the printer's proofreader.

press run   Number of copies to be printed, usually larger (to allow for spoilage) than the binding order.

presswork   The process of preparing a printing press to run a job, plus the running of the paper through the press. The three major steps in printing a book are composition, presswork, and binding.

printer   In computers, an output device for producing the results of computer processing on paper.

printer's error (PE)   In typeset material, an error made by the typesetter; in proofreading, such an error is marked *PE*. The typesetter assumes the costs for printer's errors. *See also* author's alterations.

printer's flower   *See* floret.

printer's mark   Decorative device of a printer for the identification of his or her product. *See also* colophon.

printing-image carrier   A generic term for the wide variety of intermediate masters used on printing presses to print images on the paper or other substrates. Print-image carriers are the result of the image conversion process beginning with original art and copy. Among them are type forms, various kinds of offset plates, rotogravure cylinders, screen process screens, curved stereotype and electrotype plates, flexographic rubber and plastic plates, and many others.

printing presses   Machines equipped for producing the final printed images by inking the printing-image carrier (*q.v.*) and transferring the ink image, directly or indirectly, onto the paper or other printing stock. In sheet-fed presses the printed sheets are piled prior to removal from the press; in roll-fed presses, the web may be sheeted, folded, or otherwise processed.

printout   A record on paper of the results of a computer's computations and processing. *See also* printer.

private book clubs   *See* book-collectors' clubs.

private press   A printing establishment that undertakes only works of interest to the owner. The books issued from a private press are generally hand set and hand printed in limited editions, and although they may be offered for sale to the public, it is usually directly through subscription rather than through regular book trade channels. As John T. Winterich defined it, "A private press is ... an enterprise conceived, and masterfully and thoroughly carried out, by a creative artist who (whether or not he likes to cover some of his expenses by sale) does his work from a sincere conviction that he is so expressing his own personality." (From *Private Presses and Their Books*, by Will Ransom, published 1929 by the R. R. Bowker Company.)

privately printed   In the antiquarian book trade, a cataloguer's term for a work not published for sale. Also applied, loosely, to books issued from a private press, or books printed for private distribution only.

prizes   For complete information about literary prizes, refer to *Literary and Library Prizes* (R. R. Bowker, 1980).

process color   The technique used by printers to reproduce an infinite range of colors with a limited number of inks, sometimes called *four-color printing,* since yellow, cyan, magenta, and black are the colors normally used. Successful results are often achieved with only three colors, the black being omitted. More than four colors may also be used on occasion. *See also* color printing. The term *color separation* is given to the procedures by which a full-color original is photographed or scanned through color filters that sort out all the yellows for one plate, all the cyan components for another, etc.

processing section   The part of a computer that does the actual work on data. *See also* central processing unit.

program   (1) The complete set of instructions in machine language that directs the computer to perform each operation at the right time in proper sequence. (2) The act of writing a program.

programmer   One who writes a computer program.

programming   The process of writing a computer program.

progressive proofs   Proofs of plates for process color printing, showing each color separately and also the combined colors in the order they are to print (second on first; third on second and first; and fourth on third, second, and first).

proofreader   Person who reads printer's proof against the copy from which it was set, in search of errors.

proofreaders' marks   *See* table at end of book.

proofs, proof sheets   Trial prints from type, plates, or cylinders, etc. Proofs required of matter set in type for publication in book form are, successively: (1) galley proofs (*q.v.*); (2) page proofs, with galley corrections made and the type set up in page form; (3) foundry proofs, if duplicate plates are to be made; (4) stone proofs, made after a letterpress form has been locked up but before it is put on the press; (5) press proofs, made on the printing press just prior to starting the run. When engravings are made, engravers' proofs are supplied and used for checking the quality of the work and for dummying up in pages. For offset, gravure, and photogelatin, page proofs of type are followed by reproduction proofs (perfect proofs intended to be pasted up into mechanicals and photographed) and blueprint or vandyke prints are made of forms prior to making the final plate.

prospectus   A descriptive circular used in soliciting orders, sometimes including a sample page or illustration, and generally distributed before publication of a book.

protection   A once current term for what is now called a publisher's returns policy. *See also* returns.

provenance   A record of ownership of a book or manuscript.

pseudonym   An assumed name or nom de plume.

public domain (in the)   Not protected by copyright.

publication date   The date, more and more theoretical, when a book is made available to the public. The theory holds that a book will be released on publication date in retail outlets across the country; this is the day on which the publisher hopes to orchestrate the appearances of book reviews, advertisements, publicity, and perhaps an author tour. To achieve simultaneous introduction of a book throughout the country, publishers must send out review copies and start the promotion and distribution processes well in advance of publication date. However, the designated day has become increasingly meaningless. Today more than a few publishers ship books to dealers up to several months ahead of publication date (sometimes now called *release date*), and they are placed on sale correspondingly early. In some respects, this is in response to economic worries that a book withheld may lose sales for the publisher or for the bookstore. The practice also gives rise to the growing number of second, third, or even fourth printings before publication, because if its stock of a popular book is in danger of being exhausted, the publisher will probably go back to press for a new printing even before the designated publication date. Early reprintings can also occur when swelling numbers of advance orders (*q.v.*) indicate that the initial printing decided upon was too small to satisfy the immediate demand for a book. Publication date is frequently shortened to *pub date*.

publisher   An individual, company, organization, or group that issues or causes to be issued books, periodicals, music, maps, or the like. Publishing as a business apart from bookselling developed about the middle of the nineteenth century.

The publisher's functions consist of selecting the manuscript; acquiring publishing rights; editing the manuscript; having the type set; ordering, puchasing, or leasing the plates; designing the format; arranging for the purchase of paper and other materials and for printing and binding the book; promoting and advertising the book; devising an imprint to identify the publisher on the title page, spine, and jacket of the book; distributing the book; arranging for sales of subsidiary rights; paying royalties to the author; generally undertaking the ultimate risk of the venture as entrepreneur.

Publishers' Ad Club   An industry association established in the early 1930s for the purpose of gathering professionals together to hold informal discussions centering on problems relating to advertising, promotion, and publicity. Originally called Publishers' Adclub.

publishers' binding   The ordinary trade binding of a book as distinguished from bindings made to special order. *See also* binding.

publisher's device   *See* publisher's mark.

publisher's mark   A symbol used by a publishing house to identify its product. Also known as a *publisher's device* or *logo*; sometimes incorrectly referred to as a *colophon* (*q.v.*).

Publishers' Publicity Association   An industry association spun off from the Publishers' Ad Club in 1963 to reflect the growing importance of publicity, as well as to acknowledge the new professional separation between advertising and publicity departments.

publisher's representative, sales representative A salesperson who visits prospective customers of a publisher (booksellers, librarians, university department heads, school authorities, wholesalers, purchasing agents) to show samples of or literature about the firm's forthcoming titles, to obtain orders for them as well as for backlist books. Sometimes called a *sales rep*, this person also transmits complaints and assists in promotional activities and other areas. A sales representative may cover a broad geographical expanse or a limited one, may be on a publisher's staff or may be self-employed and selling the lists of a number of publishers. The former are called *house representatives* and the latter are called *commissioned sales representatives,* or *reps,* because they earn a commission on the books they sell. The sales representative is also known as a *traveler* or *book traveler.* A person selling books for adoption in universities and other places of higher learning is called a *college traveler.*

Publishers Weekly Journal of the American book industry, founded in 1872. Provides current news and reports on trends, companies, persons, and business activities and methods in all areas of the business and profession of books; features extensive listings and reviews of forthcoming books. Published by the R. R. Bowker Company. *See also* Richard Rogers Bowker; Frederick Leypoldt; Frederic G. Melcher.

publishing In a theoretical sense, the dissemination of information. In customary industry usage, all that is entailed in the act of committing words or symbols to paper and distributing them in the configuration of a newspaper, magazine, or book. *See also* electronic publishing; publisher.

pull-case A protective box for books, pamphlets, etc., that often consists of two separate parts: the lower, in which the book is placed, and the top, which fits over the lower. The pull-case provides nearly airtight protection. Also called *pull-off box, pull-off case,* or *pull-off cover.* It is also referred to sometimes, although incorrectly, as a *solander* (*q.v.*).

pulls An English term for proofs (*q.v.*).

pulp (1) The mixture of water and fiber from which paper is made. Fiber is usually taken from wood or rags or a mixture of both, but may be from straw, bark, or any fibrous material. *See also* chemical pulp; groundwood pulp; rag paper. (2) A magazine printed on paper made of groundwood pulp (newsprint). *See also* slick.

punch card   A standard-size card in which holes are punched to encode data for entry into a computer.

punch tape   Synonym for perforated tape (*q.v.*).

pyroxylin   Plastic material (cellulose nitrate) used for impregnating or coating book cloth.

quad   Metal blank used for filling spaces in metal typesetting; abbreviated from *quadrat*, a square. The em quad (so called because it occupies about the same space as a capital M) is a common unit of measurement and spacing. An en quad is half the width of an em quad. Quads are also cast in two-em and three-em lengths. Although photographic and electronic typesetting employ other processes for inserting blank space in typeset lines, the terms and concepts of quads and quadding have been carried over to define spacing units and functions in the newer processes. *See also* quadding.

quadding   Positioning of type lines horizontally either flush to the left margin, centered, or flush to the right margin.

quality paperback   *See* trade paperback.

quarter-binding   *See* binding.

quarto (4to)   *See* book sizes.

query   A marginal note in copy or on proofs, to call attention to some matter in doubt.

quire   (1) A little-used paper term, a printer's quire is twenty-four sheets. The term is uncommon in the book industry but is still used by stationers. (2) A signature (*q.v.*). *See also* in quires.

quoins   Wedges used to lock up metal type pages in the chase.

r.p.n.d.   Abbreviation for reprinting, no date.

rack   A unit commonly made of wire designed to display magazines or books. A rack may be massive and permanent, but it is usually light enough to be portable, and it may even revolve. Also called a *book rack* or a *fixture*.

rag-content paper   *See* linen paper.

rag paper   Paper made from cotton or linen rags. Many fine writing or book papers are sold as 25, 50, 75, or 100 percent rag. Rag paper can withstand many folds before tearing, but proof is lacking that it has any more permanence than paper made from wood by the chemical pulp process. *See* chemical pulp.

random access storage   A storage technique that enables data stored at any location in the memory to be retrieved about as quickly as data stored at any other location, as opposed to sequential storage (*q.v.*), which often requires searching through a long string of data to find that desired.

rarity   The degrees of rarity are as infinite as the needs of antiquarian bookmen. John Carter's chapters on "rarity" and "condition" in *Taste and Technique in Book-Collecting* should be required reading for every bookman. The following terms were proposed as basic by the trade journal *Antiquarian Bookman* (now called *AB: Bookman's Weekly*):

Unique: characterization of an item when no other copy is known or recorded.

Extremely rare: examples turn up in a specialist's hands but once in a lifetime.

Rare: examples turn up in a specialist's hands but once in a decade.

Scarce: examples turn up in a specialist's hands but once in a year.

Ratdolt, Erhard (1442?-1528)   German printer and typecutter, born at Augsburg. Printed at Venice between 1476 and 1486; returned to Augsburg in 1487 and was printer there until his death.

At Venice, Ratdolt was in partnership with Peter Loeslein and Bernhard Maler. They produced decorated books by typographical methods, and were among the first to print in several colors on one page. Their printing of Johann Mueller's *Kalendarium* of 1476 is the earliest book to contain a complete decorative title page.

raw data   Data that have not been acted upon by the computer.

raw tape   Synonym for idiot tape (*q.v.*).

read   In computer processing, the function of sensing and extracting data within a computer or section of a computer.

read-out   (1) The process of sensing data within a computer or section of a computer and transmitting it out to another location, such as external memory or a printout device. (2) A visual display (usually lights on a control panel) of conditions inside a computer.

reader   One who reads manuscripts for a publisher, literary agent, or book club and reports on the advisability of publishing them. A *first reader* first screens the manuscripts coming into the publishing house, selecting those that may deserve at least one more scanning.

real time   Performance of computer operations well within the time span required to perform related physical processes, so that the computer operations appear instantaneous or nearly so, and do not limit or slow down a person working with the system.

ream   A standard parcel of paper, formerly twenty quires, or 480 sheets, now usually 500 sheets. Handmade and drawing papers may contain 472, 480, or 500 sheets.

The standard quantity now adopted by many American paper dealers is 1,000 sheets, thus doing away with the ream as a basis of count. In England the standard basis is also 1,000 sheets. Basis weight, however, is still expressed in terms of a 500-sheet ream. *See also* basis weight.

rebacked   A volume repaired by replacing the old spine with a new one.

rebinding   *See* binding.

recased   The sheets of a book rebound in its original covers, in the covers of another copy of the same title, or in a new case.

recto   A right-hand page of a book; also the front of a separate printed sheet. The left-hand page and the reverse of a printed sheet is called the *verso*.

red under gold   A method of treating the edges of book leaves by staining them red and gilding over the stain. The treatment is largely restricted to the top edge. Frequently used on Bibles, prayer books, dictionaries, etc. Occasionally used in printing illustrations, as in the Greek medallions in the original Lawrence *Odyssey*, designed by Bruce Rogers.

reference marks   Printer's marks used to indicate references to other books or passages or to footnotes on the page. When more than one reference is given on a page, the order of the marks is as follows: * (asterisk), † (dagger), ‡ (double dagger), § (section), ‖ (parallel), ¶ (paragraph). If necessary, the series is repeated, using two of each mark in the same order. Superior figures (*q.v.*) are more often used for the same purpose.

register (1) Correct positioning of pages on the sheet for printing. In book work, accurate register means keeping to the specified margins, a good test being to see whether the work on an even-numbered (left) page exactly backs the preceding type page. In color work involving more than one plate, accurate register is essential. When there is a faulty adjustment the printing is said to be *off register* or *out of register*. (2) The register (in its use in incunabula) is a list of the signatures often given at the end of early books, especially those printed in Italy. Its purpose is to indicate to the binder the order and number of the gatherings.

reglet A thin wooden strip used for spacing between units of type matter. *See also* leads.

reissue A new impression of a published work from the type, plates, or film of the original edition. In the mass market paperback trade, a reissue is a new printing from a previous edition, often with a new cover design.

rejection slip A printed slip sent out by a publisher with a returned manuscript informing the author that the manuscript is not acceptable or will not be taken for publication.

release date *See* publication date.

relief printing A generic term for all kinds of printing, letterpress in particular, in which the printing area is in relief, above the supporting material. Other examples of relief printing are flexography, which uses rubber plates, and, in a sense, rubber stamping.

remainder A publisher's overstock of a title whose sale has slackened, offered at greatly reduced price through jobbers and booksellers. A remainder may sell so well—perhaps because the original trade offering was overpriced—that a publisher or wholesaler will be induced to reprint an inexpensive hardcover edition of the remainder and advertise it accordingly; e.g., "Originally published at $14.95. Now only $3.95." These are also called *sale books* or *promotional books*. An author's royalty is not earned when overstock is remaindered. *To remainder* is to sell overstock as noted above. *See also* partial remaindering.

remainder dealers   Specialists in purchasing remainders (*q.v.*) from publishers.

remake   To repage a book, completely or partly; to rearrange typographic elements in a page or publication.

remote station   Input-output device located some distance from a computer, usually connected to the system by wire in an online mode, but not necessarily.

rental library   A collection of books, in a bookstore or a library, usually current fiction, for lending at a rental fee for a stated period. Aso known as *lending library*.

reprint   A term used in the publishing industry to indicate a new printing of a text; however, it is a term that should be avoided in bibliographical description because it is not precise enough to take into consideration the technical distinctions between *edition, impression, issue*, or *state* (*q.v.*).

repro   Type and/or artwork set on photosensitive paper for pasting onto mechanicals to be photographed. A repro, short for reproduction proof, is camera-ready copy. Also, a clean, sharp proof of a page, made on coated paper, which can be photographed for reproduction. The resulting image on film negative is transferred to a plate by a photosensitive process.

reproduction proofs   *See* proofs.

reprography   A group of printing and reproduction processes used mainly internally in companies and other organizations for quick-service duplicating needs. Processes include diazo, xerography, offset lithography, and microfilming.

reps   *See* publisher's representative.

resetting   Setting type again, because of corrections, additions, etc.

residual rights   The publishing rights that rest with the copyright holder, or the publishing rights purchased by others (for a particular purpose or a specified length of time) that will revert to the copyright holder when the period has elapsed or when the purpose, e.g., publishing and keeping a book in print, has been discharged.

resolution   The ability to render or retain fine detail in an image that has been processed photographically. A measure of such an image's quality.

retouching   Modifying or improving artwork, film positives or negatives, or a printing plate by hand.

retrospective bibliography   A bibliography that includes publications issued in previous years as distinct from a current bibliography, which includes only recent publications.

returns   Unsold books returned for cash or credit to the publisher. The publisher's stated terms under which he does this constitutes his returns policy. One of the more troublesome aspects of trade publishing, returns are financially burdensome for both bookseller and publisher as overhead, i.e., inventory costs, transportation charges, bookkeeping, and other expenditures of personnel time. In the early 1980s, a number of publishers attempted to limit or refuse returns and increase dealer discounts; the experiments have met with varying success.

reversal processing   In photography, the production of a positive from a positive copy or a negative from a negative copy, through a special chemical process.

review copies   Copies of a newly published work dispatched by its publisher without charge to obtain a review, notice, or record in trade, consumer, or professional publications. *See also* advance copies; examination copy.

revise   Any proof made after an earlier proof has been read and corrections made. *See* proof.

revised edition   A new edition of a book with changes from the original or previous edition. The changes may include new or revised material within the text or added as a supplement, and may be made by someone other than the original author. Also called *new edition* (*q.v.*).

right-reading   A film image in which the type reads from left to right and top to bottom when the emulsion side faces the viewer. *See also* wrong-reading.

rights   Rights to a literary property include the following: prepublication serial (first serial rights); book publication, including book club; postpublication serial (second serial rights); book reprint; dramatization; musical comedy; amateur leasing; motion picture (commercial and noncommercial); radio; television; mechanical, electronic, or xerographic reproduction or other kinds covered in the inclusive term *reprographic reproduction*; condensation and abridgment; anthology; translation; quotation; merchandising and other commercial exploitation rights. Most of these are also commonly referred to as *subsidiary rights* and are governed by the prevailing copyright law. The author and literary agent may retain some or all of the rights or may sell them to a publisher or other firm.

Rittenhouse, William (1644-1708)   Mennonite clergyman and industrialist. Born in Muelheim, Prussia; immigrated to America in 1688 and settled in Germantown, Pa.; chosen first pastor of the Mennonite group there; elected bishop (1703) of the first Mennonite church in America.

In 1690 he organized a paper-manufacturing company, and in partnership with Samuel Carpenter, William Bradford, and others, he built the first paper mill in America.

river   A streak of white space in printed matter resulting from the fact that the spaces between words in several lines happen to occur almost one below the other.

roan   An inexpensive binding leather made of sheepskin, colored and finished in imitation of Morocco.

Rogers, Bruce (1870-1957)   Distinguished American book designer, printer, and designer of fine typography. He first gained attention with his designs of the limited editions issued at the Riverside Press between 1900 and 1911. A year's association with Carl Purington Rollins at Rollins's private press, in Montague, Mass., produced, among other works, the famous edition of Maurice de Guerin's *The Centaur*, 1915, in the translation by George B. Ives, set in Rogers's new Centaur type. There followed work in London with Sir Emery Walker and at the Cambridge University Press; then at Harvard University Press, the Rudge Press, and Oxford University Press. His Homer, *The Odyssey*, 1932, in the translation by T. E. Shaw [Lawrence]; his Oxford Lectern Bible, 1935; and the Bible designed in 1949 for the World Publishing Company rank among his most notable books.

Rollins, Carl Purington (1880-1960)   One of America's eminent book designers. In 1909 he established the Montague Press (at Montague, Mass.), a small private press which became known for the quality of its output. In 1918 he joined the Yale Press, and from 1920 to 1948 he was Printer to Yale University. *See also* Rogers, Bruce.

roman à clef   French for "novel with a key." Used to describe a work of fiction in which actual persons or events are disguised to a lesser or greater degree.

Roman numerals   *See* numerals, Roman.

Rosenbach, Abraham S. W. (1876-1952)   Bibliophile and antiquarian bookseller who served as counselor and book buyer for famous American book collectors of his time.

rotary press   A style of press that prints from the curved plates held on a cylinder; the most efficient style of press for fast and long-run presswork. The printing units consist of two, three, or more cylinders. In direct printing these are the plate cylinder and the impression cylinder; in indirect, or offset printing, a blanket cylinder is added.

The image carriers for rotary presses vary according to many considerations. High-quality letterpress uses mainly curved electrotypes; rubber and plastic plates are used in flexography and on the belt press; newspaper relief printing employs curved-cast stereotype plates or plastic plates. Offset lithography uses a range of thin plates, from paper for short runs to steel for very long ones. Rotogravure uses etched cylinders instead of plates.

Rotary presses, in many sizes and styles, are made for printing of sheets and rolls, printing in one or more colors in one pass through the press, and printing the sheet or web on one or on both sides in various color combinations. Some web presses are equipped to fold and cut the printed paper into units of different sizes; some are connected to fabricating equipment.

rotogravure   *See* gravure.

rounding   *See* rounding and backing.

rounding and backing   The shaping of the book block after trimming and before lining. Rounding imparts the characteristic concave shape to the front edge of an edition-bound book and the convex shape to the backbone. The shaping keeps the pages within the area of the cover, protecting them from damage. During rounding, rollers and formers roll the outside pages away from the backbone toward the front of the book, while the center pages are pushed in toward the backbone. Then the entire backbone is hit and rubbed from side to side by a curved backing iron.

This causes the sewn edges of the signatures to fan out, or flare. The flared areas act as hinges, or joints, when the cover is attached. The backing process makes the spine of the book wider than the rest by the thickness of the covers, thus providing a shoulder against which the boards of the front and back covers fit.

routine In a computer, a set of procedures to be performed in proper sequence. *See also* program; subroutine.

routing Cutting away nonprinting areas of a letterpress printing block that would be likely to catch ink and thus leave a blemish on the sheet.

royal octavo, royal quarto *See* book sizes.

royalty A compensation to the author or owner of a copyright paid by the publisher, usually on the basis of a percentage of the list price of the book on each copy sold, but sometimes paid on a percentage of the wholesale price or on the publisher's total receipts. No royalty is paid on review copies or on copies sold as remainders. A lower rate is paid on reprints, book club editions, and many scholarly works and on copies sold by mail order or exported.

roxburghe A style of binding with a plain roan back, cloth or board sides, gilt top, and other edges untrimmed. The style was used for the publications of the Roxburghe Club, a private book-collector's club, founded in London in 1812, and named for the Third Duke of Roxburghe.

rub-out code A code used to cancel out previously encoded data in a perforated paper tape.

rubbed A cataloguing term in the antiquarian book trade, indicating that the binding of the item listed shows signs of chafing.

rubric The heading of a chapter or other division of a book, printed in red ink, with the rest of the text printed in black.

rules Strips of brass or type metal used to print lines and borders.

run (1) A single processing of data by a computer under control of a program. (2) A single printing session on a press; multicolor jobs require more than one press run to apply different colors if the machine cannot print all of the colors at one time.

run-around A blank area in a type column less than full column

width, created when some of the lines in the column are shortened to allow a cut or other featured material to appear within
the text area.

run in   A direction to set composed matter without a paragraph or
break; to make one paragraph of two or more.

run on   The extra quantity of printed pieces produced when the
printing press is allowed to continue after the specified quantity
is completed. The extra cost of these copies is usually figured as
paper, presstime, and binding only and the pieces are said to be
produced at *run on cost.*

running costs   The variable costs, such as paper, printing, and
binding, in manufacturing a book. These costs are determined by
the size of the print run. Cf. plant costs.

running head   The line that appears across the top of a printed
page. Usually the title of the book appears on the left-hand page
and the chapter title on the right-hand page. Running heads are
discretionary and may be omitted.

russia leather   A high-grade binding leather, now made from various skins although originally made in Russia from the hides of
young cattle. Besides the tanning, it is treated with birch oil,
which gives it its characteristic odor and protects it from insects.
It is usually colored red with brazilwood.

SAN   *See* Standard Address Number.

SBN   *See* International Standard Book Number.

sc   (1) Abbreviation for small caps (2) Abbreviation for supercalendered paper.

SCOP   Abbreviation for Single Copy Order Plan, now replaced by
Single Title Order Plan (STOP) (*q.v.*).

ser.   In cataloging, abbreviation for series (*q.v.*).

SLA   *See* Special Libraries Association.

sq.   A catalogue abbreviation describing the book as approximately square in shape.

STC   *See* Short-Title Catalogue.

STOP   Single Title Order Plan (*q.v.*).

Sabin, Joseph (1821-1881)   Bibliographer, bookseller, cataloguer, and auctioneer of books, was born in Branston, England, in 1821. He came to the United States in 1848 and engaged in bookselling and bibliographical work in Philadelphia and New York. He opened his Nassau Street bookshop in New York in 1864, and he became one of the leading booksellers in the city. He compiled the catalogues of many important book auction sales and served as book auctioneer at the house of George A. Leavitt & Co.

After his death in 1881 Sabin became better known as a bibliographer and distinguished expert of American books than as a rare book dealer. His great work, and that which gives him undying fame, was his *Dictionary of Books Relating to America, from Its Discovery to the Present Time* (also known by its original half-title, *Bibliotheca Americana*), which during his lifetime he finished to the letter O. After Sabin's death the work was continued by Wilberforce Eames and completed by Robert W. G. Vail.

Of the total 172 parts (twenty-nine volumes), Sabin completed the first eighty-two parts (vols. 1-14, printed 1868-1884); parts 83 to 116 were done by Wilberforce Eames (vols. 15-20, printed 1885-1892). The work was dormant from 1893 to 1924. In 1925 Elizabeth G. Greene and in 1927 Marjorie Watkins joined Eames as his assistants, and the work was resumed with part 117, printed in 1927. R. W. G. Vail headed an enlarged staff in 1927-1929; in 1930 he became joint editor, and the printing of the *Bibliotheca Americana* was completed with part 172 of the twenty-ninth and last volume of the work, issued in 1936. The title page of volume 29 carries the statement "Begun by Joseph Sabin, continued by Wilberforce Eames, and completed by R. W. G. Vail for the Bibliographical Society of America."

Sabin is the most comprehensive reference work relating to Americana; 106,413 numbered entries are given, but the actual number of titles recorded is much greater as that total does not count the added editions and titles mentioned in the various notes.

In 1973, the Whitston Publishing Co., Troy, N.Y., began publication of *The New Sabin; Books Described by Joseph Sabin and His Successors, Now Described Again, on the Basis of Examination of Originals, and Fully Indexed by Title, Subject, Joint Authors ...*, edited by Lawrence S. Thompson, professor of Classics, University of Kentucky. By 1982, eight volumes had been published.

saddle sewing　*See* sewing.

saddle stitching　*See* stitching.

saddle-wire stitching *See* stitching.

sales representative *See* publisher's representative.

sample pages Experimental pages of a prospective book, set during the planning stage and used as a model for setting the entire book.

sans serif A style of typeface distinguished by the absence of serifs, or ticks, on the ends of strokes; originally known as gothic. Two modern examples of sans serif are Futura and Gill. *See also* gothic; serif.

Sauer [Sower], Christopher (1693-1758) Born near Marburg, Hesse; immigrated to Philadelphia in 1724; set up as a farmer in Lancaster; established himself in Germantown in 1731, where he dealt in imported German theological treatises. Took up printing on his own account and in 1735 he issued the first German almanac to be published in the colonies. In 1743 he printed an edition of the Bible in German (Martin Luther's translation), the first Bible in a European language printed in the colonies.

Christopher Sauer the Younger (1721-1784) continued the business, but in 1778 he was arrested on suspicion of treason and all of his property was confiscated; the sheets that were on hand of the German Bible he had printed in 1776 were converted into gun-wadding by the American troops, and that edition came to be known as the Gun-Wad Bible.

scaling The process of calculating and indicating how an illustration is to be cropped and how much it must be enlarged or reduced to fit into the layout.

scanner (1) A device for sensing the presence or absence of data on various surfaces presented to it, such as magnetic tapes, disks, or printed sheets. (2) A color separation machine that generates process-color film negatives or positives by photo-optically breaking a full-color master into the four process colors and electronically correcting for color-balance errors. *See also* optical character recognition.

Schoeffer, Peter (1425?-1502) *See* Fust, Johann.

Schuster, Max Lincoln (1898-1971) Editor and publisher of books of quality, designed for large sale. With Robert L. Simon he founded Simon and Schuster in 1924. Schuster's flood of ideas for books of lively educational value combined with popular appeal and tasteful typography was a key to the firm's influence. The firm also set high standards of pictorial and production excellence in low-cost, mass-merchandised books, especially children's books.

science fiction (SF)   Imaginative fiction describing life in the future or life on a world where reality is somewhat or greatly different from our own. Science fiction is a genre usually grounded to some extent on real scientific facts or on a prophetic exaggeration of them, as in interplanetary travel. Science fiction should be distinguished from *fantasy*, which is likewise highly imaginative fiction, but is based on nonrational phenomena that cannot be explained scientifically. The term *sci-fi* is considered a repugnant abbreviation of science fiction by many in the field.

Science Fiction Writers of America   A national association established in 1965 to further the professional goals of science fiction writers. To enhance the image of such works, the group initiated the annual Nebula award, which is presented to this kind of imaginative fiction in a number of categories.

scoring   Compressing the fiber of paper along a line either to facilitate folding or to facilitate tearing. Done on either a regular printing press, a special cutting and creasing press, or a folding machine by impressing a raised rule or disk against the paper. Scoring with a dull rule (also called *creasing*) actually increases the folding endurance. Scoring with a sharp rule partially breaks the paper fibers and is similar in its effect to perforating.

scout   (1) A person engaged by a publishing house or literary agency to look for new and promising writers or projects and to explore ideas for new books; or one hired by a motion picture company to find books, manuscripts, or other material suitable to be adapted into a film. (2) In the rare and secondhand book trade, a person who regularly visits bookstores and antique and thrift shops, buying items he or she believes are desired by book dealers, librarians, and collectors and that can be turned over at a profit.

screen   (1) A finely ruled glass or plastic sheet for converting continuous-tone images into halftones. (2) The dot pattern produced by photographing copy through a halftone screen. (3) The printing-image carrier in screen printing, traditionally made of woven silk but now made of woven plastics and metals. (4) In a computer system, the face of a cathode-ray tube on which images are displayed. *See also* cathode-ray tube.

screen printing   The major application (along with Mimeographing) of the stencil principle of printing in which ink is forced by a squeegie through the holes in a fine woven mesh in the printing areas. In nonprinting areas, the holes are filled in during the stencil-making process, preventing ink from passing through. The mesh or screen originally was made of silk (and the process was called *silk screen*), but woven plastic and metal wire screens have largely supplanted silk today. Although much screen printing is still done by hand, the development of automatic printing presses over the last two decades has made it possible for screen printing to become one of the fastest growing areas of the graphic arts industry.

Screen printing is much used for posters and book covers and for printing on glass, plastics, and textured surfaces. It cannot reproduce fine lines and halftones as well as other printing processes, but large improvements have been made in recent years. Screen printing is especially good for achieving heavy ink coverage needed for vivid colors.

script   A typeface having some characteristics of handwriting.

scroll   (1) A roll of papyrus or parchment and also, later, of paper. (2) A writing formed into a roll, such as the engrossed proceedings of a public body or a court.

seal   Leather made from the skin of the seal, with a coarse grain, soft to the touch. Pin seal is from the skin of the very young or baby seal, having a much finer grain and a lustrous finish.

search   In computer memory, the matching of coded data against specified criteria, also coded, to find desired information.

search service   A business that searches for out-of-print books wanted by customers. The service may be conducted by dealers in old and rare books, or by specialized searchers who advertise services and obtain orders by mail.

second printing before publication   *See* publication date.

second serial rights   The right to reproduce in a periodical either a portion or the entirety of a book in one or more parts after the book's official publication date (*q.v.*). *See also* first serial rights; rights.

secretary shift   The type of keyboard shift control that automatically reverts to the unshift condition when the shift button is released, eliminating the need for a separate unshift keystroke. Typically used on typewriters.

section   *See* signature.

see copy   In proof correction, a direction to the printer to compare the marked passage with the original copy, when there appears to be a discrepancy.

selection   (1) A book offered by a book club (*q.v.*) to its members. (2) The process of choosing books for a library.

self-publishing   The act of producing one's own book through writing, editing, printing, and distribution. Although this is sometimes the only way a book of little merit can be published, self-publishing is a worthy tradition that was pursued by Thomas Paine, Walt Whitman, Edgar Allan Poe, Mark Twain, and others.

self-wrapper   The printed or unprinted paper cover of a pamphlet or book. A self-wrapper, as opposed to *wrapper* or *wrappers* (*q.v.*), is an integral part of the sheet or sheets comprising the body of a publication so bound. For example, the self-wrapper of a sixteen-page pamphlet, printed in octavo, would be the first and last leaves printed as part of the body of the publication and not a binder's addition.

Senefelder, Alois (1771-1834)   The inventor of lithography (*q.v.*).

separation negatives   Individual negatives for each color to be printed in reproducing artwork. *See also* process color.

sequence   The order in which operations are to be performed in a computer.

sequential card system   A composing system in which cards containing copy to be photographed are placed in the order they are to appear in the publication. Then the camera unit photographs each card at high speed, forming columns of typeset copy or even pages in some cases. Later, cards are filed and held for the next edition and updated in the meantime.

sequential storage   Storage of data in a linear mode, such as a string of codes on tape, as opposed to random access storage (*q.v.*). Sequential storage often is less expensive than random access storage, but it also usually takes more time to find data.

serial   A publication issued in successive parts, usually at regular intervals, and intended to be continued indefinitely. Serials include periodicals, newspapers, annuals, proceedings and transactions of societies, and numbered monographic series.

serial rights   *See* first serial rights; rights; second serial rights.

series   Separate and successive publications usually on a given subject, having a collective series title and usually all issued in a uniform format by the same publisher.

serif   A finishing line or stroke crossing or projecting from the end of a main line or stroke in a letter, as at the top and bottom of the letter M. Gothic or sans serif letters (M) have no serifs. Cf. sans serif.

service basis   A method of pricing on a sliding scale, as determined by the library budget or by some other criteria.

set   (1) To assemble type into words, lines, paragraphs, and so on. (2) Width of type characters. *See also* set size.

set-off   In presswork, the unwanted transfer of incompletely dried ink from one sheet to the back of another. *See also* offset.

set size   The width of type across the character. Typefaces vary considerably in their set widths due to design differences. The width of a 10 point e in an old style face such as Garamond, for example, is less than that of a 10 point e in the more modern Century. A smaller set size, of course, permits more characters to be fitted into a given line length, but the smaller characters may not be as legible.

In Monotype and in virtually all photographic and electronic typesetting processes, the standard set sizes of characters can be altered by the compositor to set characters closer together or farther apart as desired, for special effects. Sometimes referred to as the *set* or *set width* of a type.

set solid   A direction to the printer to set the lines of type without leads between them.

set width   *See* set size.

sewing   The method of joining pages and signatures of a book together by means of thread. The terms *sewing* and *stitching* are sometimes used interchangeably, but the preference today among binders is to use *sewing* to indicate thread binding and *stitching* to indicate wire-staple binding.

Within these definitions, there are a number of forms of sewing. *Saddle sewing* fastens a set of folded sheets such as a signature together by sewing through the folded edges. *Smyth sewing* links side-by-side signatures by saddle sewing with a continuous thread through the folded edges of one signature after another, fastening each signature to the next. *Side sewing* passes thread through the side of the book along the binding edge. *Oversewing*, which is used in library rebinding, sews loose leaves together, in small groups, with an overlapping series of stitches across the spine of the book. *Cleat sewing*, a relatively new method, is a mechanized version of the basic hand-sewing method; cleats or notches are cut in the backbone of the book and adhesive-coated thread is passed around the projections and through the pages. *McCain and Singer sewing*, named after the machines used, actually are versions of the above processes. Singer sewing can be either side or saddle sewing, and McCain sewing is side sewing. All of these are machine processes; custom bound books are sometimes still sewed by hand. *See also* Smyth, David M.; stitching.

shaken In book dealers' catalogues, a term used to describe books in publisher's cloth, the inner hinges of which have become weak or torn.

shaved A book trimmed so closely that the top or bottom lines of type on the pages have been grazed. *See also* crop.

sheet-fed A printing press that takes paper previously cut into separate sheets, as opposed to paper in a continuous roll. *See also* web-fed.

sheets Printed pages of a book, either flat or folded, but unbound; individual cut pieces of paper, fabric, or other material.

sheetwise The process of printing the two sides of a sheet from two different forms, in contradistiction to work and turn (*q.v.*).

shelfback *See* backbone.

shift-unshift codes Special function codes that expand the capacity of a keyboard to produce other codes. In the shift mode, the same set of keys produces a different set of codes from those produced in the unshift mode. *See also* function code.

shingling (1) Any partial overlapping of items, such as sheets or signatures on feeding and delivery sections of printing and binding machines, to clearly separate items while maintaining their sequence. (2) In saddle-stitched binding, a technique used to compensate for paper thickness when many leaves printed on heavy paper must be bound. The inside, or binding, margins are reduced on pages closer to the center of the book in order to keep the printed pages aligned at the outside edges throughout the book.

short page   A shorter type page (*q.v.*) than has been specified.

short title   An abbreviated title of a book, in which only as much of the title is given as is needed to ensure identification in a bibliography.

Short-Title Catalogue   A *Short-Title Catalogue of Books Printed in England, Scotland, & Ireland, and of English Books Printed Abroad, 1475-1640*. Compiled by Alfred W. Pollard and G. R. Redgrave (with the help of others). London, the Bibliographical Society, 1926 (and facsimile reprint, 1948). Volume 2 of the second edition, revised and enlarged, was begun by William A. Jackson and F. S. Ferguson and completed by Katharine F. Pantzer in 1976. Volume 1 of the revision is in progress.

   Short-Title Catalogue of Books Printed in England, Scotland, Ireland, Wales, & British America, and of English Books Printed in Other Countries, 1641-1700. Compiled by Donald Wing of the Yale University Library, New York, printed for the Index Society, 1945-48-51. 3 volumes. Published as a continuation of Pollard & Redgrave's *STC ... 1475-1640*.

shorthand keyboarding   (1) A form of macro coding in which a single code is used to represent multiple codes. (2) Keyboard systems that use multiple keystrokes made simultaneously, as if playing a musical chord, to record data that would otherwise require a number of sequential keystrokes. *See also* macro code.

shorts   Items or quantities not in dealer's stock at the time an order is filled.

shoulder note   *See* marginalia.

side note   *See* marginalia.

side sewing   *See* sewing.

side sorts   Same as odd sorts (*q.v.*).

side stitching   *See* stitching.

side-wire stitching   *See* stitching.

sidehead   A heading set at the side of a page or column, either as a separate line set flush with the margin of the type page or run in with the paragraph to which it belongs.

signature   (1) A folded printed sheet forming one section of a book. A signature commonly has sixteen or thirty-two pages, although any multiple of four is possible. It is called a signature because originally signatures were folded by hand and the folders had to initial their own work so errors could be traced. *See also* book sizes. Sometimes called *gathering, quire,* or *section.* (2) The mark placed on the bottom of the first page, or on the outside fold of the signature, for the convenience of the binder in gathering.

silhouette   A halftone in which unwanted background has been eliminated to produce an outline effect.

silk screen   Old name for the modern screen process printing method. *See also* screen printing.

silked   *See* backed.

Singer sewing   *See* sewing.

Singer stitching   *See* sewing.

Single Title Order Plan (STOP)   A system devised and promoted by the American Booksellers' Association to maximize discount and minimize handling on special orders of one or more copies of a single title. Cooperating publishers will grant full trade discount, although some will offer less, to dealers using the prescribed single title order form available from the ABA. Formerly Single Copy Order Plan (SCOP).

sinkage   White space left at the top of a page, in addition to the regular top margins, as at the beginning of a new chapter; the location of headline, text, and illustration at a point below the top of a page—thus the sinkage from the top. Typically found on the opening page of an article, story, or chapter.

sixteenmo (16mo), sixtyfourmo (64mo)   *See* book sizes.

sized   Paper is said to be sized when its surface has been treated to make it less receptive to water. Blotting paper is unsized. Writing paper is hard-sized. Offset lithographers prefer to work with paper that has been sized for offset, to resist the moisture used in the process.

sizes of books *See* book sizes.

skid A quantity of sheet paper, usually about 3,000 pounds, varying with bulk and sheet size. The name comes from the movable wooden platforms (skids) on which the paper is delivered.

skiver (1) Leather split with a knife. (2) The grain or hair side of a split sheepskin.

slander Verbal (spoken) libel (*q.v.*).

slave A device totally dependent on another device in a computer system for all its input data and instructions required to operate it.

sleeper (1) In the trade book field, a book for which there is apparently little initial demand, but for which an unexpectedly steady, often wide, market develops over a period of several months or a year. (2) In the rare book field, any item on a dealer's shelves or in a catalogue marked at a very low price because the owner is unaware of its considerably higher monetary value.

slip-sheeting Placing pieces of paper between printed sheets as they come from the press so that the printing on one sheet will set-off (*q.v.*), if at all, on the slip-sheet, not on another printed sheet.

slipcase A protective boxlike container into which a book or books can be inserted. The simplest form of the slipcase is a cloth- or paper-covered box open at one end, into which the book is slipped with its spine exposed. More complicated slipcases have a cloth dust wrapper as additional protection, or an inner box is usually of chipboard covered with cloth and frequently lined with felt to protect the book against friction within the inner box. *See also* pull-case; solander.

slit-card A poster slit so as to fit into or around a book for display purposes.

slitting Cutting of paper into narrow ribbons or smaller sheets as it passes under special cutting wheels or disks on a printing press, a folder, or a special slitting machine.

slugs (1) Pieces of lead, about 3/4 inch high and 6 points or more thick, used as spacing material between lines of metal type. (2) Lines of type in the form of metal bars as produced on the Linotype, Intertype, or Ludlow machines.

slushpile   A collection of unsolicited manuscripts received by a publisher or agent without prior inquiry on the part of the authors. Many publishers and agents will no longer read these books because of the often fruitless time spent in doing so, hence the pejorative connotation to the word. *See also* over the transom; unsolicited manuscript.

small caps   *See* caps and small caps.

small press   A firm, sometimes one without an extensive national publishing program, that may have an interest in books suitable for a specialized, regional, or otherwise limited market. It may also be called an *alternative publisher* to distinguish it from a larger, more commercial publishing house.

smashing   Binding step that compresses folded signatures along the folds to render them more compact for binding.

Smyth, David M.   A pioneer in the manufacture of book-binding machinery. Smyth invented the first thread sewing machine for books in 1856, and sold it to the Appleton publishing house. In 1879 came the first wire stitching machine, and in 1880 the Smyth Manufacturing Co. was organized for the commercial production of such equipment. *See also* sewing.

Smyth sewing   *See* sewing.

soft copy   Images generated on the face of a cathode-ray tube, which will disappear when the data presented to the device for display change, as opposed to hard copy, which remains as a permanent record on paper.

softcover   Another term for paperback (*q.v.*) or paperbound.

software   Synonym for computer programs.

solander   A one-piece fold-over box for keeping books, paper parts, pamphlets, illustrative plates, etc. It is shaped like a book and made to open like one. A solander box is generally of a drop-back construction and is nearly dustproof and waterproof. The device was invented by Daniel Charles Solander, an eighteenth-century botanist, for his botanical specimens. A drop-front box, debatably called a solander box, is preferable for housing documents. *See also* pull-case; slipcase.

solid matter   Type set without leads between the lines. *See also* leads.

solid-state   A class of electronic components and devices made of semiconductor materials, as opposed to the earlier vacuum tube technology.

sort   To arrange data in a specific sequence by application of rules.

sorts   In metal typesetting, a supplementary supply of characters with which to replenish the main supply.

Sower, Christopher   *See* Sauer, Christopher.

spacebands   Wedge-shaped devices used on the Linotype and Intertype machines between words to expand word spaces to justify the line. In book work, narrow spacebands are often specified.

Spanish finish   *See* book cloth.

special interest publishing   The kind of publishing that addresses a particular and sometimes rather limited topic, one that would appeal only to those people who share a common interest in the matter. *See also* genre publishing; small press.

Special Libraries Association   International organization, founded in 1909, of professional librarians and information experts who serve all organizations, both public and private, requiring or providing specialized information. *See also* special library.

special library   A library maintained by a business firm, association, or other organization whose collections are limited in scope mainly to the subject areas of interest to the sponsoring organization. Special libraries serve manufacturing companies, banks, law firms, newspapers, advertising and insurance agencies, research organizations, museums, hospitals, and federal, state, and municipal government bureaus.

special order   To a bookseller, an order for a single copy of a book not in stock, handled at the customer's request. Because it requires special handling, and sometimes involves a short discount or no discount, the bookseller frequently adds a nominal service charge to the transaction to cover his cost. *See also* Single Title Order Plan.

special-purpose computer   A computer designed to accomplish one specific task or set of tasks, but not programmable for doing other kinds of work. *See also* general-purpose computer.

special sales   The book sales a publisher makes to nontraditional customers via nontraditional distribution. In addition to servicing the customary bookstores, a publisher may attempt to increase income derived from a book through bulk sales at a special rate to a company that will distribute the book to its employees or to its clients for its own purposes.

specification cover board　A paperboard used for book covers. Caliper for this product ranges between .060 and .120 inch. *See* also paperboard.

spin-off　Broadly, a by-product created from an earlier product, as in cases when one book can spawn another in reference book or data base publishing (*q.v.*). A publisher may also develop one or more books or periodicals of narrower scope by extracting material from a publication of broader scope.

spine　*See* backbone.

spiral wire binding　*See* binding.

sponsored book　*See* subsidy publishing.

sponsoring editor　An editor who works with the author to guide a book through publication. Cf. acquisitions editor.

sprinkled edges　Book edges that, after being trimmed smooth, are spattered with color by means of a brush. Usually done on all three edges.

square brackets　In a bookseller's catalogue, square brackets are used to enclose any detail of the description of a book—for example, the author or publisher, or the place or date of publication—derived from an external source rather than from the book itself.

stab marks　Punctures made in folded sheets of a book preparatory to sewing.

stabilization　A photographic development process in which the developing agents are embedded in the photographic paper.

stacks　Freestanding shelving, arranged in rows, usually double-faced, holding the main body of the book collection in the library.

stained edges, stained top　The edges (or top) of book leaves stained with color. Staining helps prevent dust smudges or finger marks from showing.

stamping　Pressing a design into a book cover using metal foil, colored foil, or ink, applied with brass or other dies. *See also* foil.

Standard Address Number (SAN) A unique identification code for each address of each organization in or served by the book industry. This includes book publishers, book wholesalers, book distributors, book retailers, college bookstores, libraries, library binders, and serial vendors. The Standard Address Number serves to facilitate such activities as purchasing, billing, shipping, receiving, paying, crediting, and refunding. In libraries, SAN serves the additional purpose of facilitating the interlibrary loan operation. Assignment of code numbers is centrally administered by the R. R. Bowker Company.

Standard Book Number *See* International Standard Book Number.

standing matter Type matter held in storage pending orders to print, reprint, or kill.

standing order An order to a publisher, wholesaler, or dealer to supply each succeeding issue of a publication, particularly of an annual or serial, as it is published, until notified otherwise. Also known as a *continuation order*.

state Minor textual variations in books from the same printing. Variant states are caused before publication, as distinct from *issues*, which are caused upon or after publication. Gaskell, *A New Introduction to Bibliography*, identifies five major classes of variant state: "(1) Alterations not affecting the make-up of the pages, made intentionally or unintentionally during printing, such as: stop-press corrections; resetting as the result of accidental damage to the type; resetting of distributed matter following a decision during printing to enlarge the edition quantity. (2) The addition, deletion, or substitution of matter, affecting the make-up of the pages, but carried out during printing. (3) Alterations made after some copies have been sold (not involving a new title page) such as the insertion or cancellation of preliminaries or text pages, or the addition of errata leaves, advertisements, etc. (4) Errors of imposition, or of machining (e.g., sheets perfected the wrong way round; but not errors of folding). (5) Special-paper copies not distinguished typographically from those on ordinary paper...."

Stationers' Company The company grew out of the fourteenth-century guild of university *stationarii* (scribes and dealers in manuscripts); chartered as a guild in London in 1403. The official charter of incorporation was granted by Queen Mary in 1556 and confirmed by Queen Elizabeth in 1559. It constituted an organization of the printing and publishing trade of London to represent the publishing interests of the country. The hall of the company, Stationer's Hall, in London, houses the register of copyright.

steel engraving　*See* engraving.

stencil　(1) The basic image-carrier device underlying Mimeographing and screen printing (*q.v.*). In stencil printing, the ink is applied to the back of the printing image carrier and reaches the front through the image areas, which are porous or open; nonimage areas are nonporous and block ink passage. (2) The wax-impregnated master used in Mimeographing or Elliott addressing.

stencil work　*See* pochoir; screen printing.

stereotype plates, stereos　Letterpress duplicate plates made by molding type pages in a suitable material, using a matrix. Molding the matrix from the original type form is followed by casting of duplicate relief plates in lead. Originally widely used for book printing, stereotypes have been replaced by offset lithography. Curved-cast stereotype plates are standard in many metropolitan newspapers. Some rubber and plastic plates for paperback books are made using similar principles; others are made using photographic processes.

stet　A proof mark meaning let stand as originally set. From the Latin verb "stare," to stand. When a word has been struck out in a proof and it is afterward decided it should remain, the word is marked underneath with dots and stet is written in the margin. *See also* Proofreader's Marks at end of book.

stipple engraving　A method of hand engraving in which the effects are produced by dots instead of lines. *See also* mezzotint.

stitching　The method of holding pages and signatures together by means of wire staples. The terms *stitching* and *sewing* are sometimes used interchangeably, but the preference today among binders is to use stitching to indicate wire-staple binding and sewing to indicate thread binding.

　　Within these definitions are two basic types of stitching. *Saddle stitching*, sometimes called *saddle-wire stitching*, staples folded pages together by means of staples through the folded edge. This method is widely used for booklets and magazines. *Side stitching*, sometimes called *side-wire stitching*, is used for thicker books and publications. Here the staples are placed through the side of the book along the binding edge. *See also* sewing.

storage   Section of a computer system in which data are stored until needed. Storage devices within a computer usually are magnetic in nature, including cores, tapes, disks, and drums. Data also can be stored externally to the system on magnetic tapes or disks, or in the form of perforated paper tape, punch cards, or optically readable images. *See also* core storage; disk; drum storage; perforated tape; punch card; tape.

stored-program computer   A computer in which program instructions are stored in a section of memory and can be changed at any time, as opposed to a hard-wired computer in which programmed operations are permanently wired into the machine. *See also* wired-program computer.

straight matter   Type composition that does not contain display lines, formulas, or tabular or other complicated matter.

Strawberry Hill Press   Founded in 1757 by Horace Walpole (1717-1797). The press was set up in a small cottage adjoining Walpole's villa at Twickenham. His first printer was William Robinson, who, following a dispute, was dismissed in 1759. Walpole had four separate printers in succession after Robinson. Finally in 1765 he engaged Thomas Kirgate, who remained in his service until Walpole's death in 1797.

Several of Walpole's own works were issued at Strawberry Hill, but not, strangely enough, his major literary work, *The Castle of Otranto*. The first work issued by the press was Thomas Gray's *Odes* ... (1757). The genuine first edition of this work is printed on thin paper, that is, the regular paper used by the press. The edition on thick Dutch paper is now accepted as a reprint made by Thomas Kirgate in about 1790. (*See* Allen T. Hazen's *Bibliography of the Strawberry Hill Press*, New Haven: Yale University Press, 1942.) Very little printing was done at Strawberry Hill after 1789.

streamer   A printed horizontal poster or display piece of the kind often used for window advertising.

strip in   To combine one photographic negative with others, preparatory to using all in making a printing plate. In lithography the operation of stripping is analogous to the operation of imposing in letterpress.

struck-image   Synonym for direct-impression (*q.v.*).

style sheet   (1) A guide to house style (*q.v.*). (2) A list of selected typefaces, sizes, arrangement of heads, etc., for a given publication.

subhead   A secondary heading or title, usually set in less prominent type than a main heading, to divide the entries under a subject.

subject heading   A word, or group of words, under which all material dealing with a given subject is entered in an index, catalogue, or bibliography.

subroutine   In a computer program, a small routine that is part of a larger routine. *See also* routine.

subscription agent   An organization that handles the entering and renewal of subscriptions for a library.

subscription books   Editions of single books or sets published for sale by subscription or by mail.

subscription library   A privately owned library operated by and for the members, who pay annual dues.

subsidiary rights   Rights to a literary property other than that of original publication. *See also* rights.

subsidy publishing   (1) The publishing of works of specialized interest to a small group (e.g., a corporation or local historians) or of scholarly works, generally not expected to be a commercial success, for which a grant or fund is provided by the author or by a foundation or other institution to cover costs wholly or in part. A work so published may also be called a *sponsored book*, especially if the sponsoring organization or person has guaranteed to purchase a significant quantity of the edition. (2) Another designation for vanity publishing, in which a book is produced with little or no regard to the merit of the work at the author's expense and at no risk to the publisher. *See also* vanity publishers.

subtitle   An additional, or second title of a book, usually an explanatory phrase. For example, *The Book: The Story of Printing and Bookmaking*.

super   (1) A gauze-like fabric (also called *crash*) glued to the backbone of a book during the lining stage of binding for added strength. (2) Short for supercalendered. *See also* lining.

super royal octavo   *See* book sizes.

supercalendered   The glossiest finish that can be given to paper, short of coating it. *See also* calendering.

superimposition   Upon the implementation of new library cataloging rules, the practice of retaining existing bibliographic entries as they are in the catalog, while cataloging newly acquired titles according to the new cataloging rules and interfiling the new entries with the old.

superior figures   Small superscript numerals, thus *footnote*[2], used to indicate footnotes or in formulas.

supplement   *See* appendix.

suppressed   Withdrawn from public sale or circulation, either by the act of the publisher or bookseller, by group pressure, or by a court decision. *See also* censor; censorship.

swash letters   Italic capitals having swirling flourishes.

Sweynheym, Conrad, and **Pannartz, Arnold**   The first printers in Italy (fl. 1465-1473). They had migrated from Mainz, Germany, and headed for Rome with the intention of starting a press there. While resting at the Benedictine monastery at Subiaco, some sixty miles from Rome, they were invited to set up a printing establishment in the monastery itself. Between 1465 and 1467 they printed four books at Subiaco and then moved to Rome and set up their plant at the Massimi Palace. In 1473 they dissolved their partnership. During their joint career they produced twenty-nine separate works.

The type used in the printing of the Subiaco books combined the better qualities of the gothic and of the roman. In 1900 Emery Walker and Sydney Cockerell designed a type for C. H. St. John Hornby based upon the semigothic type used by Sweynheym and Pannartz, and named their design the Subiaco type. It was first used by Hornby in the Ashendene Press edition of Dante's *Inferno* (1902).

symbolic language   Description by means of symbols. Symbolic language is used in the writing of computer programs to efficiently describe and specify arithmetic and logic functions.

syndication   The sale of all or a portion of an original work to a number of publications, often newspapers, that will usually print the material more or less simultaneously. A section of a book may be syndicated, as can a writer's regularly produced column. Radio and television programs can also be syndicated to broadcasters or cable television companies.

system   A collection of parts—people, machines, methods—organized to accept certain input and accomplish a specified objective. Although used most often in the narrower sense to indicate computer installations and operations, the term is properly applied to virtually any organized activity or endeavor.

systematic bibliography   *See* enumerative bibliography.

t.e.g.   Abbreviation for top edge gilt (*q.v.*).

TOP   Invoice symbol meaning temporarily out of print.

TOS   Invoice symbol meaning temporarily out of stock.

table of contents   A list of the divisions of a book, usually chapter headings or main subjects, arranged in the sequence in which they appear and constituting part of the front matter (*q.v.*) of the volume.

tail-piece   A small ornament or illustration at the end of a chapter.

talking book   A spoken rendition of a book, made available in recorded form, devised especially for the blind.

tall copy   A book that stands a bit higher than others printed at the same time by reason of having been trimmed more sparingly. Cf. large-paper edition.

tape   Paper or magnetically coated plastic ribbon used to carry computer-coded data to and from various machines in a system, or for storage of data in coded form.

tape merging   The process of merging data from two or more tapes into a single set of data. *See also* merging.

tape reader   A device for sensing data encoded on a tape and entering it in the computer. There are readers for magnetic tapes and readers for perforated paper tapes. *See also* magnetic storage; perforated tape; read; tape.

tapes   Strips of cloth or tape pasted or sewed to the back of a book block. The ends of tapes are glued or laced down to the cover to strengthen the binding.

tariff on books   Obsolete. *See* Florence Agreement.

tear sheet   Any page torn or cut from a book, magazine, or newspaper. When used in the plural, a clipped article.

teletext   A one-way transmission of data to a television screen passively receiving the picture, which is commonly text alone. Teletext is not interactive (*q.v.*) and requires some sort of cable connection or broadcast decoder. *See also* videotex.

television rights   The right to adapt a book or other property into a television program or series. *See also* rights.

temporary storage   An area of working storage not reserved for one use, but employed at different times during a computer run for various purposes.

terminal   A machine linked to a computer, usually by wire or cable, through which a data base (*q.v.*) or other automated memory bank can be reached, whether to retrieve information or to add further data. A terminal will ordinarily combine in some fashion a screen or cathode-ray tube (*q.v.*) and keyboard. *See also* video display terminal.

text   The main matter, as distinguished from the display matter, front matter, notes, appendix, and index.

text block   *See* book block.

text editing   Synonym for editing.

text edition   Some publishers provide both a trade edition and a text edition of certain books. The text edition carries both a lower list price and a lower discount, with the expectation that it will be purchased in quantity.

text-fiche   A term for the book format that combines a conventionally printed and bound text with pictorial microfiches that are housed in a pocket on the inside of the front or back cover. The concept was developed to give the reader a large number of images that can be viewed at their original size at a cost equal to or less than that of conventional illustrated books. *See also* microforms.

textbook   A book used for the study of a particular subject; a manual of instruction.

textile binding   An ornate fabric style of binding. There was a fad for binding of this sort during the Renaissance in France and England. In England this *textile* style, as it is now known to collectors, retained its popularity into the eighteenth century, many books being sumptuously bound in colored satin and velvet, often embellished with beautiful needlework in many-colored silks and with gold and silver threads.

thirtytwomo (32mo)   *See* book sizes.

Thomas, Isaiah (1749-1831)   American printer-publisher-bookseller. When very young he was apprenticed as a printer to Zechariah Fowle in Boston, and worked as an apprentice in various parts of the colonies. In 1770 he formed a partnership with Fowle and established *The Massachusetts Spy*, issued thrice-weekly; shortly afterward, under his sole ownership, issued semiweekly. In the spring of 1775 he moved his presses and types from Boston and set up in Worcester. Here he published and sold books, built a paper mill and bindery, and continued *The Spy*. He was the most noted printer of children's books of his time, and he reprinted, by arrangement, the charming juveniles of John Newbery of London and his descendents.

Isaiah Thomas printed some 400 works, including his own *History of Printing in America* ... (2 vols., 1810), a work described as important and thorough. In 1812 he founded the American Antiquarian Society, in Worcester; he endowed it with his fine library and served as its first president.

three-color   *See* process color.

three-decker   A term applied to the three-volume novels as published in England in the latter half of the nineteenth century. Most of these novels, in cloth bindings, were offered for sale at 31 shillings 6 pence, and they were sold at substantial discount largely to circulating libraries. The format was abandoned in the late 1890s after an attack was made on the method of publishing by Sir Hall Caine, whose novel, *The Manxman*, was published in one volume in 1894, after the big circulating libraries had refused to handle the book.

three-quarter binding   *See* binding.

throughput   The net amount of production that can be put through the complete computerized typesetting system, as opposed to individual processing speeds of various components in the system. Throughput usually is limited by the slowest device in the system.

thumb index   An alphabetical or subject index cut into the front edge of a book to facilitate quick reference.

tie In binding, narrow strips of leather, linen, or other material attached to the covers of a book to be tied across its fore-edges to prevent the curling of the binding. A feature especially of many vellum-bound books, old and new.

tie-in An auxiliary product—book, magazine, T-shirt, or any other object—that exists because of the movie, dramatic performance, or television program that inspired it. Frequently conceived as a means to cross-promote a product and one or more by-products, a book that is a tie-in is often a novelization (*q.v.*), but if a movie is based on a published work, that book may be reissued with a cover exploiting its appearance in a new medium.

tight-back A book in which the spine of the cover is glued directly to the backbone of the book, rather than the spine being loose to bow outward as in a hollow-back book.

'til forbid An instruction, usually in connection with a subscription, to treat as a standing order until notified to the contrary. *See also* standing order.

time-sharing Use of a computer or other device for multiple purposes during the same time period. A time-sharing computer system enables many people to use the computer at the same time.

tint block (1) A panel of color on which type or an illustration may be printed. (2) The plate used for printing the panel of color. A tint block may print the color solid or it may contain a screen or Benday so as to print a less-than-solid tint of the color.

tipping in The operation of pasting into a book a separate leaf, an illustration, or a signature. Known also as *pasting in*. *See also* inserts.

tissue In bookmaking, very thin papers, almost transparent, used to cover the face of an engraving or etched illustration to prevent set-off onto text pages.

title entry A catalog or index entry filed under the title of a work.

title page A page at the beginning of a book, usually on the right, giving the title, author (if acknowledged), and usually publisher, with place and often date of publication. *See also* front matter.

tooling Decoration on the binding of a book made by heated tools or stamps used to apply pigment or metal foil. *See also* blind tooling.

top edge gilt   A book in which only the top edges of the leaves have been gilt.

topping privileges   The right granted to a participant in an auction or other competitive sale, permitting the party to top all rival bids. The privilege is generally obtained by the prospective buyer who steps in first with a major bid.

torn-tape system   A system in which perforated paper tape is produced by each of the various machines in the system and torn off at each machine's output device, after which the tape is manually carried to the next unit and mounted on a reader for input.

Tory, Geoffroy or **Geofroy** (1480?-1533)   French artist, engraver, typographer, and designer of letters, borders, and devices. His decorative illustrations and borders introduced what was to become the characteristic style of French Renaissance book decoration, and he was mainly responsible for the abandonment of the black-letter type in favor of the modern roman letter. He also introduced into French printing the accent, the apostrophe, and the cedilla. The results of his research in the French language, his theories of geometrical letter design, etc., are set forth in his great work, *Champfleury*, published in 1529.

tracing   Information on a main entry catalog card, giving the other headings under which the work is listed.

track   (1) The portion of a moving storage medium that is accessible to a single reading device. (2) Synonym for channel.

trade binding   *See* binding.

trade books   Books intended for the general public, and marketed with trade discount through bookstores and to libraries, as distinct from textbooks, subscription books, etc. *See also* discount.

trade edition   An edition of a book intended for sale through bookstores to the general public or for general circulation in libraries, as distinct from an edition of the same book intended for some other use (e.g., textbook) or for sale through some other channel (e.g., subscription books).

trade list   Publisher's list of available titles, with list prices and discount categories.

trade paperback, quality paperback   A higher-priced paperbound book marketed through normal book trade channels. It can be an original title or a reprint published by either a hardcover house or a mass market house. Showing up in an extremely wide variety of sizes and shapes, trade paperbacks are generally made of materials superior to those used for mass market paperbacks. It is becoming common for a hardcover house to publish a title simultaneously as a hardcover book and a less expensive trade paperback. The former is thought, sometimes erroneously, to help the book maintain the traditional credibility of the hardcover and to appeal to the library market and to book reviewers. In these cases, the trade paperback edition, of which a significantly larger number are printed, receives the primary promotion and publicity. The hardcover house may sell rights for a mass market reprint edition to appear later. A mass market house will usually follow its trade paperback original with its own mass market edition at a later date. Established in 1953, Doubleday's Anchor Books is considered America's debut trade paperback line. *See also* mass market paperback.

trade publisher   A publisher of books intended primarily for sale through retail outlets or for general circulation by libraries.

translation   Conversion of one language into another, either manually or automatically.

transmission   The sending of material from one point to another. *See also* data transmission.

transpose   In printing to change or exchange the position of lines, words, or letters.

traveler   *See* publisher's representative.

tree calf   *See* mottled calf.

trimmed edges   One or more edges of a book trimmed by machinery, as opposed to uncut edges (*q.v.*).

tubular back   A book with a tubular piece of fabric glued to the backbone of the volume and to the spine of the cover. This produces a book with the cover fastened to the book as in a tight-back binding, but also with a flexible back that can curve outward when the book is opened, as in a hollow-back book. *See also* hollow-back; tight back.

turned letter   Metal type placed upside down in composed matter to show that type of the right letter is not available and is to be supplied later. It shows in the proof as two black marks, thus:
=

turnkey system   A computer program purchased and in place ready for the buyer to use. In a wider sense, a turnkey system is one supplied by a manufacturer of software (*q.v.*).

twelvemo (12mo)   *See* book sizes.

twentyfourmo (24mo)   *See* book sizes.

two up   (1) Printing two of the same subject side by side with one impression in any printing process. In letterpress, duplicate plates are used; in lithography, the plate holds two sets of printing images. For long runs of small items, time and cost are saved by printing multiples at the same time. Multiples are not limited to two; as many as will fit on the press sheet may be printed. (2) Binding two or more copies at the same time.

tympan   Hard paper used to cover the platen or cylinder of a printing press to provide the correct support for the sheet being printed.

type   The basis of modern Western printing, originally signifying small, individually cast metal units bearing a face in relief that will produce a letter, figure, or other character, capable of assembly into text and usable in a printing press. The growth of nonmetallic composition suggests redefinition of type with emphasis on its visual properties; e.g., as a standardized design of letter forms, numerals, etc., following a common style.

type-high   The height of metal type from the bed of a letterpress printing press to the paper being printed. Type in the United States is .918 of an inch high. Electros, engravings, and other plates that are to run with type must be blocked type-high. Unless there is type in the form, however, it is usual to make plates much thinner and fasten them to a patent base, which brings them up to type-high. Type-high has lost all importance in photographic and electronic composition.

type page   The part of a page that contains the type, exclusive of the margins.

typeface   (1) A basic artistic interpretation or design given to the letters of the alphabet, numerals, and other associated characters making up a font. (2) A particular version or variation of a basic type design.

Typefaces in the larger sense of a basic design are named after their designers (Garamond, Bodoni, etc.) or for some other attribute chosen at the time (Times Roman after the *Times* of London, the newspaper for which it was designed). In the more specific sense, typeface names are created by adding qualifiers to the basic design name (Bodoni bold, Helvetica extra bold condensed), which describe essential qualities of variations on the basic design.

All of the specific variations of a basic design, in form and weight, are called a *type family*. In a family, each specific variation is usually available in a range of sizes. Families, in turn, are classified loosely into more general groups—old style, modern, sans serif, gothic, cursive, etc.—which further describe their aesthetic and historic characteristics.

typescript   Typewritten material, as a manuscript.

typesetter   (1) Compositor; one who sets type. (2) Machines that set type.

typewriter composition   Synonym for direct-impression composition.

typographer   Originally, a printer thoroughly familiar with all aspects of type and typesetting. At present, a designer highly skilled in the selection and arrangement of type who often determines type and setting specifications to be used. Sometimes called *type director*.

typographical error (typo)   A mistake made by the typesetter. *See also* printer's errors.

typography   (1) The art of composing movable type. (2) The arrangement and appearance of type matter.

u & lc   Abbreviation for uppercase and lowercase. *See also* lowercase; uppercase; Proofreaders' Marks at end of book.

UTOPIA   Acronym for Universal Terminalized Online Printing and Investigative Aid. A data base that provides online access to auction prices of books. Established in 1980 by American Book Prices Current as a part of the Bookline family of data bases. *See also* auction prices.

unauthorized biography   *See* authorized.

unauthorized edition   An edition issued without the consent of the author or the original publisher.

uncial   Pertaining to or consisting of a form of letter found in early Latin and Greek manuscripts. The uncial characters are large and of nearly uniform size, resembling modern capitals but with greater roundness. *See also* majuscule; minuscule.

uncut edges   Edges of a book untrimmed by machinery. Not to be confused with *unopened* (*q.v.*).

underlay   In presswork, a piece of paper placed under a type form or press plate to bring it up to the proper height for printing. *See also* overlay.

underrun   Shortage in the number of copies printed.

union catalog   An author or a subject catalog listing the holdings of a group of libraries, generally established by a cooperative effort. The catalog may relate only to given subjects or to entire collections.

Universal Copyright Convention   An international treaty to which the United States is a party, the Universal Copyright Convention is, along with the Berne Convention, one of the two major international copyright agreements. The U.C.C. was drafted at Geneva in 1952 and revised in Paris in 1971. It has been ratified by ninety nations. Under it, each signatory country extends to foreign works covered by U.C.C. the same protection that such country extends to works of its own nationals published within its own borders. *See also* Berne Convention.

universal decimal classification (UDC)   A classification scheme issued under the auspices of the Federation Internationale de Documentation (FID). Originally based upon the Dewey Decimal Classification, but developed into a more detailed system to make it possible to class subjects very precisely. Not only books but also reports, patents, specifications, and articles in periodicals can be classed and indexed under the UDC scheme.

university press   A publishing house attached to a college or institution (or group of such institutions within a single state or a circumscribed geographical region) that is not primarily established for commercial purposes. It perpetuates the school's educational goals by specializing in the publication of scholarly books, and to do so, it relies on subsidies from the sponsoring institution and on grants.

unjustified tape   Encoded tape lacking any kind of coding to specify end-of-line breaks or hyphenations. *See also* idiot tape.

unopened   An unopened book is one whose untrimmed edges have not been opened by hand, as with a paper knife. Not to be confused with *uncut edges (q.v.)*.

unsolicited manuscript   An unpublished work submitted to a publisher or literary agent without inquiry, by an author hopeful of selling it. Since neither the publisher nor the agent asked to see the work, it is unsolicited. *See also* over the transom; slushpile.

until forbid   *See* 'til forbid.

Unwin, Sir Stanley (1884-1968)   British and international book industry leader; head of a distinguished house, George Allen & Unwin, Ltd.; twice president of the International Publishers' Association, and a fighter for the strengthening of international copyright.

Updike, Daniel Berkeley (1860-1941)   American printer and publisher. Founded the Merrymount Press, Boston (1893), for which Bertram G. Goodhue designed his Merrymount type. Updike was an anuthor and printing historian as well as a printer, and he had a strong influence on the development of typography in America. His *Printing Types: Their History, Forms and Use* (2 vols., 1922) is still a standard text. He was gifted in liturgical printing; the first work of his press was *The Altar Book ... Use of the American Church* (1896), and one of his finest works was the 1931 edition of the Book of Common Prayer.

uppercase   The capital letters in any font of type. So called because, in hand-set type, they were usually kept in the tray above the small or lowercase letters. *See also* case.

v.d.   Abbreviation for various dates.

VDT   Abbreviation for video display terminal *(q.v.)*.

VET   Abbreviation for video editing terminal *(q.v.)*.

VLT   Abbreviation for video layout terminal *(q.v.)*.

v.p.   Abbreviation for various places or various publishers.

v.y.   Abbreviation for various years.

Van Gelder paper   A brand of fine paper produced in Holland. Famous for a hundred years or more. Used principally for fine editions and also, in an antique finish, by artists for drawings, watercolors, and sketches.

vandyke   A type of blueprint (*q.v.*). *See also* proofs.

vanity publishers   A trade designation for publishing concerns that specialize in producing books not at their own risk, but at the authors' risk and expense. They often sign publishing contracts with inexperienced authors by appealing to their desire to see their writings in print at whatever cost. Sometimes called subsidy or cooperative publishers. *See also* subsidy publishing.

variant   A book that differs in one or more features from others of the same impression. Variations may occur in the sheets, binding, etc., or in two or more of these. There may be, and sometimes are, two or more variants within a single impression. These variations are of such nature that positive sequence of printing or stamping cannot be established. If sequence is known or discovered states and issues (*qq.v.*) are established.

variorum   Abbreviated from the Latin "cum notis variorum," with notes of various persons. Applied to a publication containing various versions of a text; e.g., a variorum edition of Shakespeare's works.

varnishing   Coating frequently applied to book jackets to give them a glossy appearance. Varnish in its liquid state is like printing ink, and is applied on a printing press. *See also* laminate.

vellum   The skin of a calf, unsplit and specially treated for use in writing or printing on or for the binding of books. It is a finer material than parchment (*q.v.*), although at one time the word *parchment* was used to mean both parchment and vellum. Most medieval manuscripts were written on vellum, and a few copies of various editions during the first seventy-five years of printing were also printed on vellum. The finest vellum, known as *uterine vellum*, was made in the thirteenth and fourteenth centuries from the skins of unborn or stillborn animals, and it was used only for the most expensive manuscripts. Vellum is extraordinarily durable, but tends to warp in dry air.

verbatim et literatim   Latin phrase meaning word for word, letter for letter; literally, a faithful translation or transcription.

verso   *See* recto.

vertical file   A collection of pamphlets, clippings, and other non-book materials, arranged vertically (upright) in filing drawers for ready reference.

video display terminal   A computer input-output device containing a cathode-ray tube for display and a typewriter-like keyboard. The material to be worked on is displayed on the tube face, and changes are made in this material via the keyboard. The displayed material changes as the changes are keyed in by the operator. *See also* video editing terminal; video layout terminal.

video display tube   Synonym for cathode-ray tube (*q.v.*).

video editing terminal   A video display terminal specifically designed for performing editing functions on text matter. *See also* editing; video display terminal.

video layout terminal   A video display terminal specifically designed for sizing and positioning type in a graphic arrangement, or a terminal that permits the operator to prepare a diagrammatic representation on the screen to guide placement of the actual type by the computer and phototypesetter. *See also* page map; video display terminal.

videocassette   The video counterpart of an audio tape cassette. The self-contained unit will, when played on the proper equipment or VCR (videocassette recorder), display moving pictures through a television screen as well as provide sound. Videocassettes may be prerecorded or they may be blank, ready to record on a VCR. Prerecorded videocassettes are easily copied and thus frequently raise questions of copyright control. *See also* electronic publishing.

videodisc   The video counterpart of a sound-producing record. The videodisc may be read by a needle or it may be read by a laser, both providing picture and sound through a television screen. The laser system allows an interactive (*q.v.*) program. Only prerecorded videodiscs are available, and they cannot be easily copied. *See also* electronic publishing.

videotex, videotext   The transmission of text and other data to a television screen by means of a cable, telephone line, or wire connection; a transmission that is probably interactive (*q.v.*).

vignette   (1) A small decorative design placed on a title page or at the head or tail of a chapter. (2) An illustration having a background that is shaded gradually away.

voice-grade service   A class of telephone-line service that can carry voice traffic or data at relatively slow speeds.

volume   (1) Printed sheets bound together; a book. (2) One of the books of a complete set, distinguished from other books or volumes of the same work by having its own title page and usually independent pagination.

Vulgate   The Latin Bible authorized by the Roman Catholic Church. Translated by St. Jerome in the fourth century.

W   Invoice symbol meaning will advise in a few days.

w.a.f.   *See* with all faults.

wf   In proof corrections, wf means that a letter (or letters) from a *wrong font* of type has been used.

Walker, Sir Emery (1851-1933)   Engraver and printer, a forceful spirit in the fine-printing movement of the late nineteenth century in England. After Walker's lecture on types and printing given at the Arts and Crafts Exhibition of 1888, William Morris suggested that they should design a new type together. Walker agreed, and this brought about the founding of the Kelmscott Press (*q.v.*) by Morris. In 1900 Walker formed a partnership with T. J. Cobden-Sanderson and founded the Doves Press. The partnership was dissolved by Cobden-Sanderson in 1908. For a brief summary of their association see Doves Press. Walker was knighted in 1930.

want list   *See* desiderata.

washed   Badly foxed or soiled leaves can, during rebinding, be washed in javelle water or other preparation and put under a warm iron or press, after which they must usually be resized. A book so treated is sometimes identifiable by the odor of javelle water.

watermark   A design faintly showing in paper when held up to the light. This is made by the dandy roll on a Fourdrinier machine, which presses down on the forming sheet just as the pulp is well drained and before the sheet begins to go through the series of drying rolls.

Paper for fine editions of books is frequently *watermarked* with a design to show that the paper was made specially for that edition.

waxing   The coating of photographic paper or reproduction proofs on the back side with a special wax that permits them to be adhered easily to a master sheet, yet also be removed and readhered readily. Used extensively in paste-up operations.

web-fed   A printing press or other machine that accepts paper in the form of a continuous web from a roll. Web-fed machines typically can run much faster than sheet-fed machines. *See also* sheet-fed.

web press   *See* rotary press.

Webster, Noah (1758-1843)   American lexicographer, author, teacher, lawyer, etc. He was president of the Amherst Academy (1820-1821) and helped found Amherst College. He was admitted to the bar at Hartford in 1781, and he did much work from 1782 to 1789 agitating for a uniform copyright law.

His first lexicographical publication, Part I of *Grammatical Institute of the English Language* (1782-1783), was a spelling book, later known as *Webster's Spelling Book* or *Blue-Backed Speller*. Parts II and III (1784-1785) were a grammar and reader. The speller was used in all schools, and in the course of a century sold some sixty million copies. Webster's first real dictionary was the *Compendious Dictionary of the English Language* (1806). His fame rests on his more important work, *An American Dictionary of the English Language* (2 vols., 1828).

weeding   Discarding books from a library collection.

Weems, Mason Locke (1759-1825)   American clergyman, book agent, and writer, known as "Parson Weems," was born in Anne Arundel County, Md. After 1794 he served as traveling book salesman for Mathew Carey (*q.v.*), Philadelphia publisher, and sold books throughout the southern and middle states.

He wrote books and tracts on morality and temperance, and "biographies" (fictionalized works) of notable Americans—Washington, General Francis Marion, Franklin, and others. His *Life and Memorable Actions of George Washington* (1800) was first issued anonymously. The third edition (called the second on the newly worded title) was the first to bear Weems's name as author. In the fifth edition (1806) the hatchet and cherry tree story (invented by Weems) first appeared in book form.

weldable paper   *See* welded binding.

welded binding   A new technology developed and patented by Mortimer S. and Bernard T. Sendor of Sendor Bindery, Inc., that combines a specially coated weldable paper and a high-energy source to produce a binding of superior strength that uses no glue, thread, or other fastening material. The high-energy source can be direct heat or high frequency, infrared, or ultra-sonic radiation. In the binding of a paperback or case-bound book, the gathered book block is gripped at the spine and a high-energy source is applied to the binding edge, penetrating all the sheets. This causes the resin on each sheet to flow and combine with the resin on adjacent sheets. On removal of the energy source, the resin returns to its original solid state and the radiated area becomes, in effect, a single piece of plastic, with the leaves of the book embedded in it. The weldable paper used is made with thermoplastic resin embedded in its surface. The area of the weld can be precisely controlled so the book can open easily and stay flat when open.

Western Writers of America   A professional organization formed in 1953 to gain greater acceptance of western novels and stories. An annual prize, the Spur Award, is bestowed by the group on the best work of the year in various categories.

whiteprint   *See* blueprint.

Whittingham, Charles   *See* Chiswick Press.

wholesaler   One who buys from publishers and sells to retail booksellers or libraries. Also called a *jobber*.

widow   A short single line at the top of a page or column, usually the last line of a paragraph. To be avoided in good typography.

window copy   Printed pages pasted up on sheets of paper with holes or windows cut in them so that both sides of each printed leaf are visible.

Wing, Donald Goddard   *See* Short-Title Catalogue.

wire-lines   In laid paper (*q.v.*), the closely spaced, narrower lines, as opposed to the heavier chain lines (*q.v.*).

wire marks   *See* wire-lines.

wire-program computer   A computer in which instructions and sequences for operations to be performed are permanently fixed by the interconnection of wires. *See also* stored-program computer.

wire stitching   *See* stitching.

Wise, Thomas James (1859-1937)   Book collector, bibliographer, editor, and forger. Born at Gravesend, near London; employed at the age of sixteen as office boy by a firm dealing in essential oils; became an expert in the field and by the 1920s he was rich and retired.

At the age of eighteen he founded the Ashley Library by purchasing some of the lesser first editions of Shelley at low prices; by 1884, when he was twenty-five, he paid £45 for the Pisa edition (1821) of Shelley's *Adonais*; he became an active member of the Browning Society, and later, in 1886, of the Shelley Society; instigated "type-facsimile" reprints by both societies, many of the publications being under his editorship.

Between 1888 and 1899 Wise was the creator and promoter of sixty-some bogus first editions of works by Matthew Arnold, Elizabeth Barrett Browning, Robert Browning, Dickens, George Eliot, Kipling, William Morris, D. G. Rossetti, Ruskin, Stevenson, Swinburne, Tennyson, Thackeray, and others. A number of these were suspect long before they were exposed by John Carter and Graham Pollard in *An Enquiry Into the Nature of Certain Nineteenth Century Pamphlets* (London: Constable, 1934).

The most spectacular of the Wise forgeries is Elizabeth Barrett Browning's *Sonnets*...bearing the imprint: "Reading: Not for Publication. 1847." It was produced in 1893. The rarest of the forgeries (only three copies known) is Matthew Arnold's *Alaric at Rome...*, which bears the imprint of the first edition, "Rugby: Combe and Crossley, 1840." This also was produced in 1893.

In addition to works edited by him, Wise produced many bibliographies, especially of Victorian authors. His magnum opus is the catalogue of his own great library of English literature: *The Ashley Library...Printed Books, Manuscripts, and Autograph Letters...*(11 vols., 1922-1936). The library was purchased after his death by the British Museum, for £66,000.

The checking of the Ashley Library books at the British Museum brought to light at least thirty thefts by Wise of leaves from copies of seventeenth-century English plays in the British Museum. Wise had stolen the leaves to "improve" or complete his own imperfect copies. The discovery was made by D. F. Foxon, a member of the museum's staff, and his discoveries were published in an article in the *Times Literary Supplement* on 19 October 1956. The total of Wise's depredations was raised in number during the next three years, and Foxon gives a more complete census in his monograph *Thomas J. Wise and the Pre-Restoration Drama*, published by the Bibliographical Society in 1959.

with all faults   An abbreviation used in antiquarian booksellers' catalogues to signify that the item described is or may be defective and is sold as is with no return privileges.

wood pulp   Paper pulp prepared from trees of various kinds. There are two distinct classes: (1) mechanical wood pulp or groundwood from which newsprint-type papers are made; (2) chemical pulp produced by various methods, as the sulfite, soda, and sulfate processes. *See also* chemical pulp.

woodcut, wood engraving   Illustrations or designs printed from inked wood blocks; or the blocks themselves. The design is drawn directly on the surface of the block and the parts that are not to print are cut away. The woodcut is cut with a knife along the grain of the plank; the wood engraving is engraved with a burin or graver across the grain on the cross section of the block.

The first dated woodcut (1418) is the *Brussels Virgin*; the earliest wood engraving was made by Thomas Bewick (1752-1828), who is generally considered to be its inventor. He also introduced the "white line," in which the design is in the white spaces rather than in the black lines. If many impressions from woodcut or wood engraving are needed, an electrotype is now usually made.

With the coming of photography, the design was transferred onto the wood block by photomechanics rather than by hand. This developed a craft of wood engraving rather distinct from the artist's. The camera, however, soon supplanted that process with the halftone (*q.v.*); woodcut and wood engraving are today used only in the making of artist's prints and, at times, in the illustration of limited edition books.

wooden boards   Prior to the time of Aldus of Venice in the fifteenth century and for some time afterward, the covers of bound books were made of thick wood over which the leather was stretched. Even small books had stiff covers a quarter of an inch thick and often beveled to a sharp edge to disguise this disproportionate thickness.

The use of pasteboard for bookbinding was not introduced until the end of the fifteenth century and at first was only employed upon books of small size.

word   A set of characters that occupies a single storage location in a computer memory and is handled as a unit in the machine.

word processor   A technologically advanced machine usually comprising a cathode-ray tube (*q.v.*) and a keyboard that permits the manipulation of words and larger blocks of text stored in computer memory. The final result may be electronically revised and edited on the screen and then printed in hard copy (*q.v.*) or the material may be transmitted elsewhere and composed or manipulated further.

Worde, Wynkyn de (d. 1535)   Native of Lorraine, served as an assistant at William Caxton's press at Bruges; followed him to England in 1476 and served as foreman at the Westminster Press. He succeeded to the press on Caxton's death in 1491. In 1500 he left Westminster and moved to Fleet Street in London; after 1509 he sold his books from his own shop in St. Paul's Churchyard. Between 1491 and 1535 he produced some 800 books, most of them undated.

work and turn   Use of a single form to print both sides of a sheet of paper. Normally, one side of a sheet is printed from one form of type, the other side from a second form. But if the type for both sides can be fitted on a single form, it may become economical to print by the work and turn method whereby all the type for both sides of the finished job is printed on one side of a double-size sheet. The sheets are then turned over, left for right, and backed up from the same form. The pile of double-size sheets is then cut down the center yielding two piles, each properly printed on both sides. Running work and turn saves half the impressions that would be required for running the same job sheetwise (*q.v.*).

work for hire   Under the U.S. Copyright Act (Section 101), a legal category under which the person who creates a work does not become the initial owner of copyright. Rather, his or her employer, or one who commissioned the work, becomes the initial copyright owner. Often, but not always, the creator of the work receives a salary or a flat fee rather than a royalty based on sales.

world rights   Publication rights to a particular work throughout the world, frequently restricted to a particular format. A publisher that has acquired world hardcover rights to a specific book will usually sell hardcover publication rights to houses in various countries, who may publish the work in its original language or, more likely, in translation.

wove paper   Paper that shows no pattern of the sort that distinguishes laid paper (*q.v.*).

woven materials   *See* book cloth; nonwoven materials.

wrappers   The printed or unprinted cover of a pamphlet or book bound in paper. Not to be confused with boards (*q.v.*), which, comtemporaneously, means paper-covered binder's boards, or with *dust wrapper*, the paper cover folded over a bound book. Specifically wrappers, while often of the same stock as the body of the publication, are not part of the printed sheets comprising the publication. Rather they are separately affixed to the body of the publication by the binder. Some authorities, notably Will Ransom, prefer the term *wrapper* to *wrappers*, the argument being that the object is singular and not plural. *See also* self-wrapper.

write   In a computer, to transcribe data onto an output medium or to transfer data into a section of memory.

writers' conference   A seminar, usually held at colleges in the summer, attended by both established writers and students of writing, featuring lectures, workshops, and discussions conducted by specialists in their fields.

wrong font   *See* wf.

wrong-reading   A film image that reads from right to left and top to bottom when the emulsion surface of the film is facing the viewer. *See* negative; right-reading.

XR   Abbreviation for no returns permitted.

xerographic paper   Photocopying paper for printing by the electrostatic process and used in the making of books on demand, where pages are photocopied xerographically and bound online.

xerography   An electrostatic printing process that uses dry resin powder and heat to fuse images onto any kind of paper, as opposed to other types of electrostatic printing that use toners in solution to create images on special papers. Xerography is widely used as a photocopying process marketed under the trade name Xerox. *See also* electrostatics.

x-height   The height of the main body of lowercase characters in a font, excluding ascenders and descenders. So named because the x has four points at its extremities that reach the maximum dimensions, thus providing good points for measuring this dimension. Also sometimes called *z-height* for the same reason. *See also* ascenders; descenders.

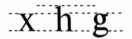

x-height, ascender, and descender. From *Printing Industry*, p. 56, col. 2.

xylography   Printing from blocks of wood, especially of an early or primitive kind. Such books, which usually contain more illustrations than text, are sometimes also called *xylographic books* or *xylographica. See also* block books.

yapp   *See* divinity circuit.

yearbook   An annual publication reviewing, with facts and statistics, the events of the previous year.

yellow-back   The name given to the cheap editions popular in railway book stalls in the mid-nineteenth century. They were usually works of fiction bound in yellow covers.

young adult book   Designation for a book intended for adult circulation, but deemed suitable reading for young people from ninth through twelfth grades. A decision customarily based on recommendations of library periodicals or library organizations.

Zamorano, Agustin Vicente (1798-1842)   Pioneer printer of California and executive secretary of California under the Mexican regime. Born at St. Augustine, Fla.; received his schooling and grew to manhood in Mexico. By establishing the "farthest west" printing press of the United States in 1834 at Monterey, he became best known to history as the first printer in California. Twenty-one of his imprints are known, in addition to letterheads and stamped paper headings. Eleven of his imprints were broadsides or folders on official matters; six were of a miscellaneous nature, and four were books. The private book club in Los Angeles, the Zamorano Clubs, is named for him.

zinc etching   *See* line cut.

A SELECTED READING LIST

THE ART AND HISTORY OF THE BOOK

Blumenthal, Joseph. *The Art of the Printed Book, 1455-1955.* David Godine, 1978. paper. $15.

Blumenthal, Joseph. *The Printed Book in America.* David Godine, 1977. $30.

Cave, Roderick. *The Private Press.* 2d ed. R. R. Bowker, 1983. $60.

Clair, Colin. *A Chronology of Printing.* Praeger, 1969. o.p.

Glaister, Geoffrey. *Glaister's Glossary of the Book.* University of California Press, 1979. $75.

Greenhood, David, and Helen Gentry. *Chronology of Books and Printing.* rev. ed. Macmillan, 1936. o.p.

Levarie, Norma. *The Art & History of Books.* Heineman, 1968. $25; Da Capo, 1982. paper. $18.95.

McMurtrie, Douglas C. *The Book: The Story of Printing and Bookmaking.* 3d rev. ed. Oxford University Press, 1943. $50.

Oswald, John Clyde. *A History of Printing: Its Development during Five Hundred Years.* Library Press, 1928. o.p.

Ransom, Will. *Private Presses and Their Books.* R. R. Bowker, 1929. o.p.

Steinberg, S. H. *Five Hundred Years of Printing.* 3d ed., revised by James Moran. Penguin, 1974. $3.25.

Vervliet, Hendrik D. L., ed. *The Book: Through Five Thousand Years.* Phaidon, 1972. o.p.

Wroth, Lawrence C., ed. *A History of the Printed Book;* being Number Three of *The Dolphin.* Limited Editions Club, 1938. o.p.

BIBLIOGRAPHY AND BOOK COLLECTING

Bowers, Fredson T. *Principles of Bibliographical Description.* Princeton University Press, 1949; reprinted, Russell & Russell, 1962. $21.

Bowers, Fredson T., ed. *Studies in Bibliography*; papers of the Bibliographical Society of the University of Virginia; vols. 1- . Charlottesville, Va.: The University Press of Virginia, 1948/49- . Issued annually with membership.

Carter, John. *ABC for Book Collectors.* 6th ed. With corrections and additions by Nicolas Barker. Granada, 1980. $15.

Carter, John. *Taste and Technique in Book Collecting.* Pinner, Middlesex, England. Private Libraries Association, 1970. £8.

Gaskell, Philip. *From Writer to Reader: Studies in Editorial Method.* Oxford University Press, 1978. $29.50.

Gaskell, Philip. *A New Introduction to Bibliography.* Oxford University Press, 1972. $16.95.

McKerrow, Ronald B. *An Introduction to Bibliography for Literary Students.* Oxford University Press, 1927. $24.95.

Peters, Jean, ed. *Book Collecting: A Modern Guide.* R. R. Bowker, 1977. $17.50.

Peters, Jean, ed. *Collectible Books: Some New Paths.* R. R. Bowker, 1979. $16.95.

Tanselle, G. Thomas. *Selected Studies in Bibliography.* The University Press of Virginia, 1979. $15.

COPYRIGHT

Bogsch, Arpad. *The Law of Copyright under the Universal Convention.* 3d ed. R. R. Bowker, 1969. o.p.

Johnston, Donald F. *Copyright Handbook.* 2d ed. R. R. Bowker, 1982. $24.95.

Wittenberg, Philip. *Protection of Literary Property.* The Writer, Inc., 1978. $12.95.

EDITORIAL

The Chicago Manual of Style. 13th ed. University of Chicago Press, 1982. $25.

Skillin, Marjorie E., and Robert M. Gay. *Words into Type.* Prentice-Hall, 1974. $18.95.

Strunk, William, Jr., and E. B. White. *Elements of Style.* 3d ed. Macmillan, 1978. $4.95. paper. $1.95.

PAPER, PRINTING, AND PRODUCTION

Bland, David. *A History of Book Illustration: The Illuminated Manuscript and the Printed Book.* 2d rev. ed. University of California Press, 1969. o.p.

The Dictionary of Paper: A Compendium of Terms Commonly Used in the U.S. Pulp, Paper, and Allied Industries. 4th ed. American Paper Institute, Inc., 1980. $22.

Diehl, Edith. *Bookbinding: Its Background and Technique.* Reprint of 1946 edition. Dover, 1980. paper. $12.

Field, Janet N., ed. *Graphic Arts Manual.* Arno Press/Musarts Pub. Corp., 1980. $65.

Grannis, Chandler, ed. *Heritage of the Graphic Arts.* R. R. Bowker, 1972. $24.95.

Hunter, Dard. *Papermaking: The History and Technique of an Ancient Craft.* 2d ed. Gannon, 1978. $14.50.

Lee, Marshall. *Bookmaking: The Illustrated Guide to Design/Production/Editing.* R. R. Bowker, 1979. $32.50.

Roberts, Matt T., and Don Etherington. *Bookbinding and the Conservation of Books: A Dictionary of Descriptive Terminology.* Library of Congress, 1982. $27.

Strauss, Victor. *Printing Industry: An Introduction to Its Many Branches, Processes and Products.* R. R. Bowker, 1967. o.p.

Updike, Daniel Berkeley. *Printing Types: Their History, Forms and Use.* 3d ed. Dover, 1980, 2 vols. $8.95 per vol.

PUBLISHING AND THE BOOK TRADE

Andersen & Co., Arthur. *Book Distribution in the United States: Issues and Perceptions.* R. R. Bowker, 1982. $60.

Bailey, Herbert S., Jr. *The Art and Science of Book Publishing.* University of Texas Press, 1980. paper. $7.95

The Bowker Annual of Library and Book Trade Information. R. R. Bowker, 1983. $45.

Cheney, O. H. *Economic Survey of the Book Industry.* R. R. Bowker, 1931. Reprinted 1960 with introduction by Robert Frase. o.p.

Dessauer, John P. *Book Publishing: What It Is, What It Does.* R. R. Bowker, 1981. $23.95. paper. $13.95.

Hackett, Alice Payne, and Henry James Burke. *Eighty Years of Best Sellers: 1895-1975.* R. R. Bowker, 1977. $18.95.

Manual on Bookselling: How to Open and Run Your Own Bookstore. 3d ed. American Booksellers Association, 1980. $15.95. paper. $8.95.

Mott, Frank Luther. *Golden Multitudes: A Study of Best Sellers, 1662-1945.* R. R. Bowker, 1960. o.p.

Nemeyer, Carol A. *Scholarly Reprint Publishing in the United States.* R. R. Bowker, 1972. o.p.

Norrie, Ian. *Mumby's Publishing and Bookselling in the 20th Century.* R. R. Bowker, 1982. $32.

Schick, Frank L. *The Paperbound Book in America: The History of Paperbacks and Their European Background.* R. R. Bowker, 1958. o.p.

Tebbel, John. *A History of Book Publishing in the United States.* 4 vols. Vol. I: *The Creation of an Industry 1630-1865.* Vol. II: *The Expansion of an Industry 1865-1919.* Vol. III: *The Golden Age Between Two Wars 1920-1940.* Vol. IV: *The Great Change 1940-1980.* R. R. Bowker, 1972, 1975, 1978, 1981. $37.50 per vol.

Whiteside, Thomas. *The Blockbuster Complex.* Wesleyan University Press. Distributed by Columbia University Press, 1981. $12.95.

PROOFREADER'S MARKS

Marginal Mark	Instruction	Mark in Text	Corrected Text
	Delete	Morison	Morison
	Delete and close up	bibliography	bibliography
	Insert additional material in margin	Nicolas	Nicholas
stet	Retain crossed out material	Edwin and Robert Grabhorn	Edwin and Robert Grabhorn
×	Broken type	bookseller	bookseller
	Straighten line	a foolish consistency is	a foolish consistency is
‖	Align vertically	Caslon Bodoni Janson	Caslon Bodoni Janson
¶	Start new paragraph	in 1474. / In the next few years	in 1474. In the next few years
no ¶	Run on. No new paragraph	engraver and printer. He was one of	engraver and printer. He was one of
tr	Transpose words or letters indicated	Let not me to the marriage	Let me not to the marriage
	Invert letter indicated*	editor	editor
	Close up. No space	horn book	hornbook
lig	Use ligature	an ever-fixed mark	an ever-fixed mark
#	Insert space	bookclub	book club
↓	Push down space to avoid printing*	A famous printer	A famous printer
	Insert en quad	1. The first item	1. The first item
	Indent one em	Hickory	Hickory
	Indent two ems	Dickory	Dickory
	Indent three ems	Dock	Dock
⅃⊏	Center	Tick-Tock	Tick-Tock
⅃	Move to the right	mountain peak,	mountain peak,
⊏	Move to the left	From the snow	From the snow
⊔	Lower to proper position	true minds	true minds
⊓	Raise to proper position	admit impediment	admit impediment
?	Is this correct?	not impossible	not possible
caps	Capitals	william shakespeare	William Shakespeare
lc	Lower case	Havre De Grace	Havre de Grace
sc	Small capitals	Berne Convention	BERNE CONVENTION
c & sc	Capitals and small capitals	Berne Convention	BERNE CONVENTION

Marginal Mark	Instruction	Mark in Text	Corrected Text
rom	Roman	_first_ printing	first printing
ital	Italic	in the Times	in the _Times_
bf	Bold face	Extra	**Extra**
bf ital	Bold face italic	Illustrations	**_Illustrations_**
∧	Insert comma	composition‿printing and binding	composition, printing and binding
;/	Insert semicolon	given‿it is also	given; it is also
:/	Insert colon	divided as follows∧	divided as follows:
⊙	Insert period	in all fields∧	in all fields.
?/	Insert question mark	to a summer's day∧	to a summer's day?
!/!	Insert exclamation point	Hark∧Hark∧the lark	Hark! Hark! the lark
/=/	Insert hyphen	book∧hunter	book-hunter
∨	Insert apostrophe	at Heavens gate	at Heaven's gate
⌄⌄ ⌄⌄	Insert quotation marks	∧Yes,∧quoth I.	"Yes," quoth I.
⌄2	Insert superior character	in his latest book∧	in his latest book^2
∧2	Insert inferior character	H$\not$O	H_2O
(/)	Insert parentheses	text∧see page 5∧	text (see page 5)
[/]	Insert brackets	n. d.∧1850∧	n. d. [1850]
1/N	Insert one en dash	1900∧1950	1900–1950
1/M	Insert one em dash	editor∧the person in charge of	editor—the person in charge of
wf	Wrong font*	upon me proved	upon me proved
eq #	Space evenly	nor⌵no⌵ever loved	nor no man ever loved
hr #	Hair space	ANNO DOMINI	ANNO DOMINI
sp	Spell out	4 score and 7 years	Four score and seven years
ld	Insert lead	If this be error and Then I never writ	If this be error and Then I never writ
(out-see copy)	There is an omission here. See copy	our fathers a new nation ∧	our fathers brought forth upon this continent a new nation
tr	Transfer to position shown by caret	(proposition)conceived in liberty and dedicated to the ⌐	conceived in liberty and dedicated to the proposition

⌄ *These three symbols (⌐ , ⌄ , wf) are unlikely to be needed in marking photocomposed text.